The Annual Garden

The Annual Garden

Jennifer Bennett and Turid Forsyth

FIREFLY BOOKS

A Firefly Book

Copyright © 1990, 1998
Jennifer Bennett and Turid Forsyth

First published in 1990 by Camden House
Publishing (a division of Telemedia
Communications Inc.)

Third printing 1998

Cataloguing-in-Publication Data

Bennett, Jennifer
   The annual garden

Previously published under title:
The Harrowsmith annual garden.
Includes index.
ISBN 1-55209-196-1

1. Annuals (Plants).   I. Forsyth, Turid.
II. Title.   III. Title: Harrowsmith annual
garden.

SB422.B45   1998   635.9'312   C97-932529-3

Front Cover: Alyssum and *Papaver* spp.
Photograph by Turid Forsyth.

Back Cover: Verbena, dwarf dahlias,
lobelia and dianthus.

Photograph by Turid Forsyth.

Illustrations by Turid Forsyth

Published by
Firefly Books Ltd.
3680 Victoria Park Avenue
Willowdale, Ontario
Canada M2H 3K1

Published in the U.S. by
Firefly Books (U.S.) Inc.
P.O. Box 1338, Ellicott Station
Buffalo, New York 14205

Color separations by
Mutual/Hadwen Imaging Technologies
Ottawa, Ontario

Printed and bound in Canada by
Friesens
Altona, Manitoba

Printed on acid-free paper

We would like to thank David Bell, Stella Wallace and Adrian Forsyth for their assistance and encouragement.

Many of our annuals grew in containers, and many of those were constructed at home by us or by friends—a good way to obtain just the right size and shape of pot. Friend David Bell prepares a cedar planter that was lined with sphagnum moss, filled with compost and planted with the collection of annuals illustrated on page 21.

Contents

Sunny oranges, yellows and reds are among the easiest colours to mix harmoniously in the annual garden. Daisies such as marigolds, dahlias and chrysanthemums usually bloom in these warm colours, which are complemented here by the green of parsley, the white of dusty miller and the cool blue accent of lobelia.

Introduction

Annuals offer a speed and versatility that perennials do not, and they often bloom ceaselessly from early summer until frost or beyond, sometimes self-sowing to reappear next year. Their temporary nature makes them excellent choices for gardeners who move frequently or who like to change their gardens at whim. Here, wax begonias and 'Cambridge Blue' lobelia provide pools of gentle colour in front of less profusely blooming perennials.

When we first planned this book, we had both grown annuals for many years but still harboured quiet prejudices against them. Somehow, the real garden was the one full of perennials. The annual garden was, well, annual – ephemeral and therefore not quite so important.

But after growing hundreds of different annuals in the process of writing this book – and new ones pop up in the seed catalogues every year – we found the flowers of a sea-son to be such variable and delightful things that they really deserved just as much respect as the perennials. Perhaps more.

They offered both a speed and a versatility that the perennials did not. Because we could draw upon not only frost-tolerant plants but also tropical ones, we were treated to a much larger artistic palette. Unlike the hardy perennials, many of these flowers bloomed ceaselessly from early summer until frost, sometimes even beyond. They were scented, they were good for cutting, they bounced back after rain and drought, they were short, they were tall – some as high as the eavestroughs. In a matter of weeks, they could hide unsightly walls or fences, give trellised shade for a growing season, colour pale walkways and fill difficult dry or shady spots. They are excellent, inexpensive choices for gardeners who move frequently, who have just arrived in a new place or

combinations are without number, and the effects you can get, by a study of height, colour and season of bloom, entirely satisfying."

What are annuals? Botanists define them as plants that go from seed through flowering to seed production in a single growing season. Annuals have, as Wright wrote, "a short life and a merry one." Like the northern summer itself, the true annual flowers appear slowly, burgeon with the heat, erupt into colour and scent and glorious windblown abandon, cast their seeds to the ground and are gone.

But our definition is looser. For one thing, some hybrid annuals never set seed; they are simply incapable of it, the reproductive parts having been bred right out of them. Also, many of the plants we grew as annuals are in fact tender perennials, which are capable of living longer than a year. Some we bring indoors to bloom all winter. With proper hardening off (described in chapter two), they may be able to go back out in next year's garden. The tender perennials impatiens and geranium are traditionally treated this way. We call them annuals only because they can be treated as annuals if the gardener wishes; they will bloom the first year from seed and may be grown for one season alone.

There are two types of annuals: hardy and half-hardy. Hardy annuals are those that can survive frost. Some, like calendula, larkspur and stocks, may bloom until the ground freezes. Their seeds can be sown outdoors in early spring, or even during the fall and winter, so that they soak into the ground to germinate as the weather warms. Many self-sow. Half-hardy annuals are not frost-hardy, and their seeds are generally sown indoors for later planting out, although the quick bloomers can be sown directly into the garden after the last frost in late spring.

Whatever they are called, annuals are generous flowers, well worth the purchase of the odd flat or peat pot or the time spent in sprinkling a few seeds on the earth in spring. We hope that you will come to enjoy these flowers of a season as much as we have.

— *Jennifer Bennett and Turid Forsyth*

who like to change their gardens every year.

Visitors who saw our gardens were amazed and converted. The time had come to grow annuals, a time predicted a couple of generations ago when Richardson Wright, editor of *House & Garden* magazine in the 1920s, wrote, "I wonder if, one of these days, we won't tire of perennial borders and return, in a sane degree at least, to a proper appreciation of annuals as border plants. The colour

Annuals—plants that go from seed through flowering to seed production in a single growing season—offer the gardener every possible floral attribute. Some are good for cutting, some are scented, some creep on the ground, and some are as tall as the eavestroughs. This bed, planted entirely with annuals, ascends from white alyssum at the edge through pink zinnias, yellow tulip poppies and orange venidium to the loftiness of snow-on-the-mountain and castor beans.

Bright Promise
Creating the annual garden

The annual garden can be simple or complex, large or small. What meets the observer's eye in summer is a result of site and climate combined with the gardener's design sense and horticultural skill. This section of author Turid Forsyth's Ontario garden, featuring annuals exclusively, is brightened by beds and pots of flowers backed by blooming vines.

An annual garden is the creation of its owner, an expression of his or her aesthetic sense and horticultural skill and knowledge. The garden can be simple or complicated, bright or quiet, as small as a window-box geranium or as large as a field sprinkled with fast-growing poppies, marigolds, alyssum and larkspur.

In a sense, too, the garden creates its owner. Once planted, its progress is unpredictable, dependent upon the weather, the quality of the seeds and plants and the height, colour and shape of flowers the gardener may have seen previously only in pictures or in other gardens. When visiting the garden, the gardener is refreshed and inspired, re-created by the creation. And the creation, like a play or a work of live music, happens just once in that particular way. It cannot be delayed or stopped or held, except in photographs—which can never duplicate the wind and the fragrance and the feel of the sun—or in the dried flower arrangements of winter, mere shadows of the former flowers.

This magic is easy to perform, whatever shape it takes. In our gardens, we had annuals in containers of all sizes, beds of both perennials and annuals, beds of transplanted annuals alone, beds of seeded annuals alone, beds of seeded annuals and transplants together. We had annual vines on our trellises and porches and annuals in pots by sunny windows indoors. The ways of planting annuals are truly limitless, and the choices you make will reflect your own personality. British garden designer William Robinson wrote in *The English Flower Garden*, "One might as well attempt to stereotype the clouds of heaven as get a stamped arrangement of the flower garden."

Planters

Growing annuals in pots and planters is a good way to begin to garden. It tends to keep the scale small, and the design elements are portable. In choosing the container, make sure it is at least 6 inches deep—a depth that will suit only the smallest flowers—preferably closer to a foot. In most cases, drainage will be needed (however, we have lined a window box in a hot, sunny place

with plastic to retain water, as the box would otherwise need watering twice daily). Most containers, then, should sit where drainage water will cause no damage, and they should be close enough to a water source that you will not come to resent watering, which may be required daily or even more frequently in hot weather.

Containers are generally plastic, terra-cotta or wood. Homemade ones, fashioned from any sort of recycled container or built from lumber, are a money-saving option. We made containers from a moistened mixture of three parts peat moss, three parts vermiculite or perlite and two parts Portland cement by volume. We pressed the mixture over chicken-wire foundations shaped over containers covered with plastic. Serviceable, stonelike containers resulted after about two weeks of slow curing under plastic and another two weeks off the mould and exposed to the air. The containers were rinsed thoroughly before use.

Beautiful hanging baskets can be made from wire or plastic forms available from good plant nurseries. Line the forms with sphagnum moss and fill with growing mix, as described in the next chapter. Insert seedlings through the sphagnum on the sides of the baskets and into the soil at the top. Plan to put about six plants in a 12-inch basket or twice that many in an 18-inch basket. Most baskets must be watered at least once a day and

fertilized monthly, so hang them in a handy place where they can drip without harming anything.

When choosing flowers for pots, be flexible. Too much is made of petunias and geraniums. For a sunny situation, consider any of the flowers listed in chapter seven and, for shade, any of those in chapter eight. Many of the plants in other chapters can be used too, especially if they are long-blooming and not too tall; leave the giants for only the largest containers. (We did, for instance, grow an ornamental tomato in a half-barrel, where it was eye-catching well into winter.) In almost all containers, taller plants should be underplanted with shorter ones. Trailers such as lobelia, nolana, black-eyed Susan vine, purple bell vine, portulaca, alyssum, 'Avalanche' begonias, trailing geraniums, nasturtiums, creeping zinnia and *Polygonum capitatum* are always useful because they cover the empty soil as well as the rim of the container. Hanging baskets always look best with some trailers. The colour scheme and design of any container can be very simple or lush and complex. (For a beautiful container of annuals, see the illustration on page 21.)

Some other container arrangements we found effective include:
• a wooden box overflowing with pale violet-pink 'Orchid Daddy' petunias, white portulaca, blue lobelia, pink and red 'Nicki' nicotiana, a varie-

gated geranium and a hanging geranium
• a hanging basket of pink viscaria, light blue nemesia, violet-blue browallia, deep blue verbena and dark red verbena
• a large basket on the ground, filled with pink and crimson dianthus, deep blue verbena, pink dahlias, blue browallia and red lobelia
• a window box of squat yellow marigolds, white portulaca and blue lobelia
• orchidlike butterfly flowers in mixed pastel tones underplanted with blue violas
• a half-barrel of purple heliotrope, golden ageratum, fire-red salvia and one 'Teddy Bear' sunflower as a highlight.

Not all containers need to be above the ground. A very effective way to increase the versatility of annuals in the garden design is to plant them in pots that can be set into the garden soil and moved from area to area as other more permanent flowers die. The same pots can also be brought indoors in fall, as most annuals will continue to bloom in a bright window. The best choices for indoor pots include browallia, Persian violet, wishbone flower, geranium, wax begonia, eustoma, African daisy, alyssum, coleus, polka-dot plant, bloodleaf, gazania, impatiens and petunia. The petunia, cut back twice over the winter months, was in full, glorious bloom again in February.

Annuals and Perennials

There are two closely related ways to design annual plantings. One involves planting annuals alone but using the same rules one would in planting a perennial bed: paying attention to height, flower colour, plant shape, foliage and even scent. The other involves planting annuals among perennials, the perfect solution to the empty spots that inevitably appear as certain perennials wax and wane during the season. We found this a very sensible way to garden, treating annuals and perennials like partners for a summer. According to Richardson Wright, "Perennials are like built-in furniture—you can't move them around; annuals are like tables and chairs—you can move

them around to suit your whims from year to year." Setting annuals in pots, as we mentioned above, means that the tables and chairs can move even during a single growing season.

In both of these styles—annuals with perennials or annuals alone—one's individual design sense has a lot of room for play. Since annuals last only a season, this year's mistakes can easily become next year's successes, a flexibility not so easy to achieve with perennials. Sometimes planting schemes that sound unlikely turn out to be spectacular, while supposedly safe combinations are boring and even dowdy. A few general pointers are worthy of note:
• Very bright colours are hot to handle. Be aware that they will pull the eye from everything else around, so handle the brilliant reds particularly —as in salvia and geraniums—with care. On the other hand, these brights can be beautiful, especially against a natural background such as unpainted wood or stone.
• White is useful almost everywhere and is not to be dismissed as monotonous. Remember that no plant is white alone; it is white and green or white and greyish. Whites are effective next to pastels and dark greens, they appear luminous in shady gardens and in the evening, and they provide rest for the eyes between brightly coloured flowers. Also, many white flowers are sweetly scented, making them good choices near windows or on patios.
• Complementary colours—green and red, yellow and purple, orange and blue—intensify one another.
• On the other hand, tones of the same colour can detract from one an-

Containers are versatile, movable and easy to tend—tiny gardens that are ideal for beginners. There is a pot for almost any annual that is not too big, such as a dwarf morning glory, FACING PAGE, *which shares a barrel with a polka-dot plant. Garden designs may incorporate pots or focus on plants in beds only, as in this all-white plot of cleome, impatiens, salvia, caladium and dusty miller,* ABOVE.

other. A light blue next to a brilliant one will seem washed out and uninteresting, whereas it will look beautiful next to yellow or orange. This is not a directive to steer away from using similar colours together. Provided the tints are right, some lovely combinations are possible. Many of the foremost garden designers have worked with only one or two colours to a bed. Oranges, from yellowish to reddish, are especially easy and gratifying to use this way.

• One safe and effective way to design is to choose either all cool colours for the same bed – blue, pink, white, purple, burgundy – or all warm ones – scarlet, orange, yellow, cream. An accent of blue in a warm bed or of orange in a cool one could make a spectacular show.

• Keep the colour of your house exterior, fence or any other garden backdrop in mind when choosing flower colours. If you are working with unpainted wood, stone or concrete, you are in luck – anything will match.

• Do not overlook the value of foliage for providing places where the eye can rest. Some annuals such as euphorbia, kochia and ornamental grasses are grown for their foliage alone, and perennials such as peonies and shrubs and trees also make good foliage backdrops and visual resting places. (See chapter six.)

• Consideration of flower height is critical. Three chapters of this book are organized to include only flowers of a certain height. Tall plants should be at the back or centre of a flower border, shorter ones nearer the front and ground covers and creepers at the edge of the bed. Vines, of course, must grow where they can be supported and will not screen sun-loving plants (although they may be used to shelter the shade lovers). Remember to take into account the height of perennials in the bed, as well as that of shrubs and trees.

• Avoid colour mixtures of a single species unless you really want them for a particular purpose. It is tempting, the first time around, to grow a mixture so that you can see which colours you like best, but too many mixtures in a garden make a higgledy-piggledy mess. The designer has much more control when work-

ing with single colours, and the garden will end up looking as though the gardener, rather than the seed house, is in control.

• Keep in mind the annuals that close their flowers during the day, such as four-o'clocks, evening-scented stocks, sun lovers and others. Couple these with busy day-bloomers such as poppies, nicotiana and marigolds.

From L.H. Bailey, 20th-century botanist and renowned American garden writer, comes another bit of sage advice: "Never fill a conspicuous place with a plant you have never grown." He also writes, "The staid perennials I want for the main and permanent effects in my garden, but I could no more do without annuals than I could do without the spices and condiments at the table. They are flowers of a season. I like flowers of a season."

Annuals Alone

One traditional manner of planting the flowers of a season on their own is called bedding out, a style begun in Victorian England and still commonly seen in public parks. In this style, an entire bed is devoted exclusively to annuals, usually only two to four kinds, with similar heights and often bright colours. The patches of individual varieties may have a geometric layout, and sometimes they may even spell a message or depict a

clock or the national flag. Bedding out has the advantages of being a sort of instant garden – the plants are usually already blooming or just about to when planted – and of requiring little maintenance. Low-care, drought-resistant, wind-tolerant, long-blooming flowers such as petunias, celosia, marigolds and impatiens are favourites for bedding out. The effect is one of high visual impact – these beds are the neon signs of horticulture. Some home gardeners, too, like the brightness, quickness and dependability of the bedding-out style.

A somewhat similar bed is the cutting garden. Any flower garden can be used to supply flowers for indoors, of course, but if you want to have large quantities for cutting, it is best to keep them to themselves so that the design of the garden is not spoiled when they are picked. One technique is to devote part of the vegetable garden to good cutting flowers such as zinnias and asters, which can be grown in beds or rows just like onions and carrots. (Cutting gardens are described more fully in chapter ten.) However, if you have a large garden relative to the quantity of flowers you like to pick, you will not need to set aside a separate plot for cutting flowers. We grew ours intermingled with other annuals and perennials and cut judiciously so as not to create gaps.

A very effective bed may be composed of just one type of annual, with generous groups of different colours and heights. We planted a bed of only zinnias that included the pink 'Rose Pinwheel,' red 'Crimson Monarch,' red-and-yellow 'Sombrero,' 'Green Envy,' deep lavender 'Dream,' light rose 'Exquisite' and the mixed 'Scabious Flowered.' Bordered with creeping zinnia, the bed was beautiful all summer and an excellent source of flowers for cutting. It had a serious shortcoming, however: zinnias are frost-tender, so the instant garden became an instant brown eyesore after one freezing night. Hardier annuals, such as alyssum, calendulas, stocks, cornflowers and snapdragons, will bloom far longer, and a mixture of both tender and hardy types will provide at least some colour into fall.

There are a few precious annuals that will self-sow. Left on their own, they will sprinkle little drifts of seeds downwind to produce a new crop of flowers next year. This process can be helped along by the gardener who wants the seeds in specific places. In late summer or fall, collect armfuls of the dried plants and heap them in empty prepared spots in the garden. The seeds will fall off, and the dry branches will act as a light mulch. This method works well for candytuft, cosmos, calendula, cornflower, evening-scented stock, alyssum, *Salvia horminum*, larkspur and all poppies.

All of the flowers mentioned above are good candidates for the direct-sown garden. Some direct-seeded annuals can be sown in the cool soil of early spring or even in fall or winter, while others will not germinate until the soil is warm. Some annuals cannot be treated this way, but where appropriate, direct seeding is the easiest, least costly way to make a flower garden. It can also be the most effective way, because the gardener can plant large drifts that would make setting out individual transplants a daunting prospect.

Making the Bed

Creating a new bed for annuals need not be a terribly difficult proposition. Out of what had been sod or weeds and rocks, we made several new beds in the process of growing the flowers for this book, and while a certain amount of muscle power was necessary, none of the beds was more work than a couple of reasonably vigorous adults — or perhaps a brawny teenager paid minimum wage — could finish in two or three days. A bed about 3 feet wide and 5 feet long can be made by one person in only an hour or two.

First, mark out the perimeter of the bed with a garden hose or rope or, if the edges are straight, a line of boards. All the vegetation, surface rocks and trash within the perimeter must be removed. This requires, at the least, a spade and a wheelbarrow. Leave large rocks in place and incorporate them into the design. But be sure to dig away any weeds tucked under the edges of the rocks. Cover-

ing the soil with weighted-down black plastic for a growing season is one effortless, nonchemical way to kill weeds.

With a sharp spade, divide the sod into sections that are about a foot square, lift the sod with a spade or pitchfork, and scrape off the loose soil clinging underneath. The sod that has been removed can be used for patching the lawn or creating a new grassy area, or it can be piled to compost slowly. When the sod is gone, remove any stones remaining in the bed, and dig down into the soil to loosen it. Now bring in enough topsoil, mixed half-and-half with compost or rotted manure, to make the bed slightly higher than the original soil level. The bed should be level on top and slope to a ditch all around the perimeter, except where it is bordered by a fence, wall or hard surface. The ditch can be dug away with a spade or edging tool once or twice during the growing season to keep surrounding sod or other ground covers from creeping in.

New annual beds can be quite ambitious, incorporating pathways and perhaps even a bench or an archway for vines. Remember, however, that the bigger the bed, the more work it will require, not just at the outset but all season long. Start small the first year to find out just how much garden work you can handle throughout the summer. A weed patch in July is a discouraging sight.

As we mentioned, the new annual bed is topped with a mixture of topsoil and compost or manure. The same is true of an existing bed, which should be built up with fertile soil every spring or fall. There is no

Annuals planted around perennials will extend the season of colour and camouflage fading foliage. Annuals alone, FACING PAGE, provide solid splashes of brilliance but must be carefully chosen so they do not die en masse with the first fall frost. Here, the marigolds and lobelia will be frost-killed, but the calendula and alyssum will continue to bloom. A bed dedicated to annuals can be prepared in fall or early spring, LEFT. The soil removed from pathways helps raise the beds.

point in setting expensive or lovingly raised little plants into dry sand, solid clay or a spot that will soon be overcome with quack grass or goutweed. Loving care for plants translates into good, weed-free soil, and that means soil dark and heavy with organic matter or humus.

Mark the planned borderlines of each patch of flowers with a stick or rake handle. These outlines can be brightened with a thin stripe of white flour, which will gradually disappear. Unless you really want a geometric effect, aim for gentle curves and slightly overlapping patterns that will give an artistic look to the garden when the different flowers are in bloom. Some areas of the bed can be direct-sown with an individual flower type, and others can be reserved for transplanting. If direct-sowing, make sure the soil is absolutely weed-free and raked smooth, water it, scatter the seeds thinly, and cover them with a fine layer of garden soil or peat moss to keep the seeds from drying out. Water with a fine mist. Do not let the seeds or seedlings dry out until they are well established. Check the soil daily.

Once the beds are created or improved and the plants are hardened off as described in the next chapter, the annuals can be planted almost anywhere, provided you keep in mind their height, colour, habits and desires and your own dream of your summer garden. That may seem a lot to keep track of and is the reason most gardens evolve over several years. The advice of Sen no Rikyu, the great Japanese tea-ceremony master of the 16th century, is still sensible—the proportions of a garden should be six of utility to four of beauty. Keep practicality a priority, if only a slight one: make sure beds can be easily weeded and watered, that everything is accessible and that the types of flowers you have chosen will not demand more time than you can give.

Wild Gardens

The wild garden is a departure from the more carefully planned direct-sown garden. In this case, seeds are simply scattered and left as they fall, one type mixed with an-

other. Again, choose types of flowers that will bloom no later than midsummer if they are sown directly into the garden in spring. This type of garden is best reserved for an out-of-the-way corner, a cottage or a rural plot where you really do not want things to look designed. The so-called wildflower mixtures or meadow mixes sold by many seed companies aim for this sort of effect, but you can do just as well yourself by combining the flower types and colours you want, often for a fraction of the cost. Do not overseed, however, or you will simply end up with straggly flowers or too much thinning to do; plan to use about 2½ ounces of seeds for 250 square feet.

For that amount of seed, put 1½ gallons of fine sand or peat moss into a large container. In a smaller bowl, mix various seeds selected for sun, shade or half-shade, depending upon the location of your bed. Do not mix shade lovers with sun lovers. Mix the seeds thoroughly into the peat or sand with your hands, and spread the mixture thinly over the entire plot in

small handfuls. Pass a garden rake over the area, then cover it with a light layer of peat moss or soil. Mist well, thin after sprouting, if necessary, and do not let the soil dry out until the plants are well established.

A very successful sunny mixture for us included tickseed, baby's breath, marigolds, cornflowers, love-in-a-mist, flowering flax, statice, poppies, catchfly, corn cockles, clarkia, godetia, California poppies, hawk's beard, ammobium, tassel flower and cosmos. All of these annuals resemble wildflowers in their simplicity, and all make good cut flowers. The meadow began to bloom in mid-June, flourished in the hot weather and continued until after the first frosts.

The wild garden is not really wild, of course. It is planted by the human hand and will need thinning and probably watering and weeding throughout the summer. But it comes closest of all the garden types to mimicking the way annuals grow in nature, the inspiration for all of the gardener's best designs.

When growing masses of flowers from seed, delineate the areas for each type with lines of white flour, FACING PAGE, and sow seeds within the borders. The lines will gradually disappear. The design elements for a basket, LEFT, are trailing, climbing and upright plants such as polka-dot plant, browallia, viscaria, thunbergia, nemesia and begonias.

19

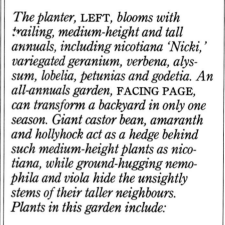

The planter, LEFT, blooms with trailing, medium-height and tall annuals, including nicotiana 'Nicki,' variegated geranium, verbena, alyssum, lobelia, petunias and godetia. An all-annuals garden, FACING PAGE, can transform a backyard in only one season. Giant castor bean, amaranth and hollyhock act as a hedge behind such medium-height plants as nicotiana, while ground-hugging nemophila and viola hide the unsightly stems of their taller neighbours. Plants in this garden include:

1. *Hollyhock*
2. *Castor bean*
3. *Wild foxglove*
4. *Spider flower*
5. *Amaranthus cruentus*
6. *Foxglove*
7. *Pennisetum*
8. Nicotiana sylvestris
9. *Ornamental cotton*
10. *Heliotrope*
11. *Nemophila*
12. *Gloriosa daisy*
13. *Tricolour sage*
14. *Mexican sunflower*
15. Impatiens balsamina
16. *Amaranthus tricolor*
17. *Lemon mint*
18. *Jewels of Opar*
19. *Blanket flower*
20. Rudbeckia amplexicaulis
21. *Nicotiana mixed*
22. *Blue lace flower*
23. *Snow-on-the-mountain*
24. *Monarch of the veldt*
25. *Dusty miller*
26. *Celosia*
27. *Mexican tulip poppy*
28. *Sun lovers*
29. *Viola*

A spectacular annual show appears only weeks after seeds are sown directly in the ground around the date of the last spring frost or a little later. Before seeding, mark the areas to be devoted to each cultivar, as shown in the photograph on page 18, and label each area or keep a diagram on hand. Water the beds and seedlings until they are well established. The plants here include:

1. Sunflower
2. Strawflower
3. Basket flower
4. Cosmos 'Sensation'
5. Snow-on-the-mountain
6. Dill
7. Shirley poppy
8. Zinnia mixed
9. Salvia
10. Coreopsis
11. Lavatera
12. Larkspur
13. Baby's breath
14. Zinnia 'Sombrero'
15. Candytuft 'Giant White Hyacinth'
16. Zinnia 'Rose Pinwheel'
17. Bells of Ireland
18. Cosmos 'Sunny Red'
19. Chinese forget-me-not
20. Swan River daisy
21. Calendula
22. Gazania
23. California poppy
24. Creeping zinnia
25. Marigold
26. Alyssum
27. Tahoka daisy

23

Planting Hope
Spring sowing and transplanting

Many annuals can be purchased as plants, but growing one's own supply lowers the price per plant while greatly expanding the gardener's design repertoire; many of the species and cultivars described in this book are available only to gardeners who grow them from seed. Also, plants that are slow to mature or have tiny seeds should be given a head start indoors, as should flowers that the gardener wants to bloom especially early, such as these homegrown marigolds.

In early spring, the annual garden is a potential thing, consisting of little more than seeds, seedlings, memories, plans and dreams. The real garden will not bloom until weeks or months later. Gardening is one of the slowest of arts, asking patience and foresight and some simple manual labour in exchange for its ephemeral beauties. What the gardener plants in spring is not so much seeds and seedlings as hope.

Whichever way one plants—seeds or seedlings—much of the gardening procedure is identical. Growing from seed simply means an additional step. Purchasing seedlings or transplants eliminates that first step and thus is easier, but it limits one's floral horizons. The six-packs of petunias, marigolds, impatiens, portulaca, alyssum and celosia sold each spring make up, for some gardeners, the whole of what the annual flower world has to offer. Yet there are literally hundreds more annuals that will grow in northern gardens, and many are prettier and more interesting than those appearing in commercial displays. Growing from seed offers the gardener flowers that are much more unusual and also far, far cheaper. One-sixty-fourth of an ounce of snapdragon seeds, for instance, will produce approximately 1,500 plants for a dollar or two. Few gardeners want 1,500 snapdragons, but even a dozen grown from seed will be less expensive than the snapdragons sold already growing. Seeds you do not use this year can be used the next, provided you store them in airtight containers in a cool place. Many seeds stay viable for several years—a bonus of free flowers the next year.

The catch—that gardeners who want these less common or less expensive annuals must grow them themselves—is a small one, because growing annuals from seed is a satisfying process and usually a surprisingly easy one. Given time, a sunny windowsill, containers, soil and water, anyone with a little gardening knowledge and the desire for adventure on a modest scale can grow charming wishbone flowers, towering cup-and-saucer vines, huge speckled thistles, breezy ornamental grasses, old-fashioned mignonette

and scores of other flowers that seldom see a commercial greenhouse. Many other beautiful annuals can be sown directly outdoors, an even easier process.

But all of this adventure depends, of course, upon a supply of seeds. Some you will find every spring on vertical racks in stores that may sell flats of young plants later on. While these seeds are often inexpensive and the displays are easy to find, the selection tends to be small. Unless you are blessed with a large local nursery that carries seeds from a well-stocked company, you will do best to order from mail-order catalogues. At the back of this book is a list of seed companies that will send out such a catalogue, sometimes for a small fee. Order it around Christmas or before in order to have time to browse through the pages, pictures and descriptions before placing an order in January or February.

The multitude of seeds offered in these catalogues is overwhelming, especially the selection from the biggest flower sellers such as Chiltern

Seeds, J.L. Hudson, Park Seed Co. and Thompson & Morgan. This book will help shed some light on the most appropriate plants for your skills and your garden so that you can make intelligent choices from among the hundreds of possibilities. In any case, order modestly, at least the first year. At the very most, 10 new annuals will provide a beginning gardener with entertainment and summer colour without too much work or frustration. As L.H. Bailey wrote, "The test of a good gardener is not how much he attempts to grow but how well he grows what he attempts."

To keep track of both what you grow and what you attempt, keep some sort of garden journal. Many gardeners create beautiful gardens without ever jotting down a word, but a notebook is handy for recording species and cultivar names, sowing dates, sprouting dates and transplanting dates.

Sowing dates, both indoors and out, are determined by one key date: the average last spring frost in your

area. In Canada, this date is available from the local office of the provincial department of agriculture (and dates for the entire country are printed in the Environment Canada book *Canadian Climate Normals*, Volume 6: *Frost*). In the United States, check with your state extension service.

The seed packet, seed catalogue and this book will tell you to plant seeds a certain number of weeks before the last frost. If the recommendation is to sow the seeds eight weeks before the last frost, for instance, they should be sown in late March where the average spring frost date is in late May, in late February if the last frost comes in late April, and so on. The sowing date is not critical, but if you are more than a week or two early, you'll likely end up with rootbound annuals whose growth is checked by planting time. Sow them more than a week or two late, and the flowers may not bloom much before the first fall frost—the other important date for northern gardeners, at least as far as frost-tender annuals are concerned. The hardy annuals, though, will continue to bloom despite frost.

Many gardeners have traditionally estimated that a safe date for frost-free outdoor planting is the last weekend in May—the Victoria Day holiday in Canada, Memorial Day in the United States. For anywhere within 100 miles north and south of the international border, this

is a reasonable reference point.

When your seeds arrive, separate them into those for sowing indoors and those for sowing outdoors. Most seed packets come with simple printed instructions, some seed catalogues give this information, and some seed companies offer a free handbook. Also, the flower descriptions in this book indicate whether seeds are best sown indoors or out.

Many annuals can be seeded directly in the garden. In fact, anything could theoretically be so treated, were it not for a few problems. The first is that some seeds are very slow to sprout, and some plants take several months to reach the flowering stage. If you have seeded them too late, you will not see flowers before frost. Second, some seeds are so tiny they are susceptible to drought, to weed competition and to falling into cracks in the garden soil. The resultant minute seedlings may be difficult to spot for weeks. Starting seeds indoors gives the gardener more control at this vulnerable stage.

The next few pages deal with seeds for indoor sowing. Once they sprout, all of the seedlings, like any indoor plants, have certain needs for light, soil, moisture, warmth and containers.

Light

Without exception, all seedlings need light, so before any seeds are

Light, one of the principal requirements of seedlings kept indoors, can be provided by a bright window or greenhouse, as it was for author Jennifer Bennett, FACING PAGE. *Young seedlings benefit from fluorescent lights suspended a few inches above the leaf tips. Once the seedlings are a few inches tall,* ABOVE, *they can be moved to a bright window.*

sown indoors, the gardener must think about this basic requirement. Seedlings fare best in natural light, of course. They need, at the very least, a south-facing window; better still is a greenhouse – light that comes from overhead is preferable to light from only one side. But if you do not have a bright window or greenhouse, seed starting at home is still quite possible. You may choose to use a cold frame, described below, or you can simulate natural light.

A variety of special plant lights is available, and these will do a fine job with seedlings. These lights are costlier than other fluorescents, however, because they emit light that is meant to make houseplants look attractive. A combination of warm and cool white fluorescents will do just as well. Ordinarily, household incandescent lights should not be used for seedlings, because they release a high percentage of their energy as heat and so can burn the leaves.

Some catalogues (see Sources) also sell plant propagation units, or a keen gardener can construct one. The fluorescent tubes should be about eight inches above the leaf tops and suspended from chains so that the lights can be raised as the plants grow. Or the plants can be lowered gradually under the tubes. Plants become leggy when they are not receiving enough light, which indicates that the tubes are too high or too old.

Most seedlings will do well with 14 to 16 hours of light a day. Do not make the mistake of leaving the lights on all night; plants do require darkness as part of the photosynthetic process. Some, in fact, such as globe amaranth, petunia, poppy, portulaca, painted tongue, starflower, snapdragon and verbena, flower best after short days of 12 hours or less.

There are, of course, gardeners who don't like to work with lights and who concur with Katharine S. White, longtime contributor to *The New Yorker* and author of *Onward and Upward in the Garden*, when she wrote, "I find that the chief pleasure of growing things indoors is that it can be a natural process – a simple way to bring nature into the house. Though I'm willing to be a floor nurse, I have no intention of becoming an electrician." Such gardeners

may want to consider a window greenhouse – an outdoor extension from a window – or perhaps even an outdoor or attached greenhouse. A greenhouse entirely separate from the house will, however, require heating, and that rekindles the problem of gardener-as-electrician.

Another place to put seedlings is in an outdoor glass case called a cold frame, a wooden frame with a glazed movable roof such as a recycled storm window. The frame, one or two feet high and oriented toward the south, is very effective for some purposes. It works very well by about March or April, when the daytime weather is warmer and, because of the greenhouse effect, the temperature under the glass soars on sunny days. One disadvantage of a cold frame is that it must be checked every day, sometimes every hour, so that the glazing can be opened or closed as needed to adjust the temperature. Unfortunately, most gardeners are not at home enough of the time. Another problem with a cold frame is that the greenhouse effect does not work on overcast days or at night, when the temperature under the glass may be as low as that outside the frame. Another traditional structure, the hot bed, was meant to remedy this shortcoming. Its heat came from fresh manure that composted inside the bed. A modern equivalent is an electric heating cable installed under a planting bed. Grow-

ing seedlings indoors in centrally heated houses makes more sense, as the plants are close by and warm.

Containers

A great variety of containers can be used to start seedlings. Two or three inches of soil depth is adequate for most; only if you intend to leave a plant in the same container from seed to outdoor transplanting should you consider something deeper. The container must drain from the bottom – poke holes in it, if necessary – it must be capable of holding together when wet and full of soil for at least a month, often two, and it should be scrubbable or disposable, because harmful fungi can live in uncleaned pots from year to year. If you are using terra-cotta containers previously filled with soil, either put them in hot water (160 degrees F or higher) for half an hour or soak them for the same length of time in a solution of one part bleach to nine parts water. Rinse well.

Then, whatever the container, remember to mark it with the name of the seed. Most seed houses sell plastic labels and special pens to use with them, though wax crayon will suffice. We have cut recycled foam coffee cups into strips to use as labels, and they can be marked with ballpoint pen. The same cups can be used as containers and marked directly. Remember that any pots will drip; put them where a little spilled or sprayed water will do no harm.

There is one more thing to keep in mind about containers. Some seedlings suffer when transplanted. They will sit for weeks in transplant shock without growing, or they will gradually fade and die. Such plants should be sown directly outdoors or started indoors in something that can itself be planted. Peat pots, peat pellets and newspaper pots are all satisfactory; roots grow right through them into the garden soil. Peat pots are available in various sizes. Peat pellets are hard little pancakes that, when submerged in warm water for a couple of hours, swell into cylinders of soggy peat held together in a mesh bag. Some seed companies sell special pot makers for newspaper pots. All of these plantable pots are suit-

able for one fairly small seedling each, and all should be kept in watertight trays while indoors. Pour water into the trays to keep the soil moist. Members of the families *Convolvulaceae, Papaveraceae, Umbelliferae, Cucurbitaceae* and *Malvaceae* almost always need peat pots, pellets or newspaper pots, but so do many other flowers, as noted in the individual plant descriptions in the following chapters.

Soils

Another seedling requirement is soil or some other growing medium.

Growing mixtures can be homemade or purchased. Compared with soil used on its own, they are lightweight, porous (roots require air to survive) and sterile and therefore free of weed seeds and pathogens.

Components of soil mixtures include:

• peat moss, pulverized mosses that have antifungal properties, are lightweight and hold moisture well if first saturated and thereafter not allowed to dry out completely

• perlite, a soil lightener composed of volcanic rock that has been heated to about 1,800 degrees F so that it expands and becomes porous

An assortment of different pots can be used to hold seedlings, FACING PAGE, *provided only that they are sufficiently large and easy to handle and allow water to drain from the bottom. In the pots, purchased soil mixes are handiest, as they are lightweight and sterile, but compost,* ABOVE, *one of the gardener's best allies for soil improvement outdoors, can be used indoors if it is first sterilized.*

• vermiculite, a mica compound that is also heated until it expands and becomes porous. Vermiculite holds water well and contributes some potassium and magnesium to the growing mix.

These three ingredients in varying proportions make up most professional planting mixes, which are sold in plastic bags from small to huge and are ready to use as soon as they are thoroughly soaked. Pour into a bucket enough of the mix for your immediate needs, add about half as much warm water by volume, and stir it with a trowel. Add more water, if necessary, so that the mixture is thoroughly moist, dark and doughy. Incidentally, inhaling these growing media can harm the lungs, so hold your breath or wear a mask while pouring out the dry mixtures, which tend to puff up, and when first adding water.

Garden soils and composts are acceptable for the last stage of transplanting. However, unless they are sterilized, they are risky for seedlings, which are very vulnerable to competition from weeds and fungi, especially fungi that cause the disease known as damping-off. This disease attacks seeds and seedlings either before or after emergence, particularly if the soil is constantly damp and seedlings are crowded. Asters, lobelia, marigolds, nemesia, wallflowers and stocks are most susceptible to damping-off, which can kill seedlings even before they emerge above the soil. More frequently, the disease causes seedling stems to strangle and topple at the soil surface. If you find damping-off in one part of a seed tray, transplant any remaining healthy seedlings into fresh sterilized mix in a clean tray, and water modestly from then on. Sowing in more than one container or in individual cells such as six-packs will minimize the damage from damping-off.

When using your own soil or compost for seedlings — a mixture of one-third compost or soil, one-third peat moss and one-third sand, vermiculite or perlite works well — pour boiling water over it so that it is thoroughly soaked, and let it cool before sowing.

Fill the containers to overflowing with the damp mix and press it down firmly. Add more soil and again firm it until the container is filled to within about a quarter of an inch of the rim.

Sowing

Seeds vary a great deal in size, colour and shape. Some are as fine as dust, others resemble common seeds such as sesame or pea, and still others may be winged, bristly or as solid as tiny lumps of coal. All carry within them the genetic information that will produce a plant which will, in turn, generally produce a crop of seeds just like the ones in the packet — a neat little summer miracle. Some of the new hybrid flowers cannot set seed, but if the flower is not a hybrid, you will be able to perpetuate your seed supply by picking the seed-pods when they are dry but still intact. Dry them thoroughly indoors, and store them in labelled envelopes in jars in a dry, cool place.

Variance in seed size, shape and

colour coincides with the plant's native habitat and its procreative strategies. Feathery seeds fly with the wind; bristled ones stick to skin, clothes and hair; smooth little ones are eaten by birds or animals that partially digest the seed coats and deposit the seeds within a glop of conveniently placed starting fertilizer. Some seeds need to experience the cold of winter in order to germinate; others sprout readily in warm soil.

After you divide the indoor seeders from those to be sown outdoors, sort out any that require special presowing treatment: stratification, scarification or presoaking. Stratification involves prechilling and exposure to moisture. The best temperature is just above freezing, from 35 to 45 degrees F – about the temperature inside a refrigerator. The easiest way to stratify seeds is to place the packets in the refrigerator for the prescribed time – about a week for pansies, for instance. Some gardeners sow the seeds first, then refrigerate the containers, while others combine seeds with moist soil mix and place them in a plastic bag in the refrigerator for the designated period, checking occasionally to see if sprouting has occurred. Sowing seeds outdoors in fall or in very early spring subjects them naturally to the period of cold that breaks their dormancy. After stratification, move the containers into a room-temperature environment with good light.

Scarification is the chipping or scraping of seeds with hard coats such as those of unicorn plants and sweet peas, and it speeds sprouting. Roll the seeds gently between two sheets of sandpaper for about 10 seconds, or scrape the seeds with a nail file or nick them with a sharp knife, being careful not to damage the tender embryonic plant within. Another presowing treatment is to soak the seeds in warm water for a day or two to soften the seed coat. Most very hard seeds, like those of morning glories, benefit from this treatment.

Now it is time to sow the seeds. The general recommendation is to bury seeds as deep as two or three times their diameter. If the seeds are not deep enough, they may be exposed to unwelcome light. If they are too deep, the shoots may not emerge

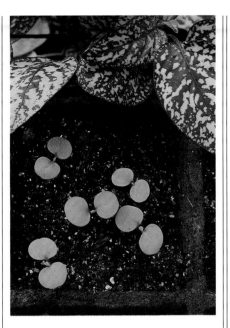

through the soil before the energy supply in the seeds is exhausted. Poke holes in the mix to bury the largest seeds, but spread smaller ones on the surface and cover them with a fine layer of soil, pressed lightly down and misted. Those that require light must be left on the moist soil surface.

There are several methods for sowing dust-fine seeds. One is to mix the seeds with a teaspoon of fine, sterilized sand and spread the mixture over the soil surface. Another is to cut a corner from the packet and shake out the seeds as evenly as possible, which is risky as you may end up with all the seeds in a tiny pile. You can also use a small paintbrush to pick up and deposit the seeds. The hands-on approach, which offers tactile awareness of where the seeds fall, is to pour the seeds into one (dry) palm, then dust them onto the soil with the forefinger of the other hand. Make sure any that stick to your skin are sown as well. Often these very fine seeds require light for germination; simply leave them on the already wet, firmed soil surface. If they need darkness, they can be pressed lightly into the soil surface and covered with black plastic or cardboard.

Care

Very fine seeds can be watered from the bottom of the pot – place the

Seeds that require covering are generally buried to a depth about twice their diameter, FACING PAGE. *Here, the large seeds of safflower are doubled up, and crowded seedlings will be removed later. The first leaves that sprout,* ABOVE, *like these of polka-dot plant, take their nutrients from the seed and look quite different from later leaves, which are nourished mostly by the roots.*

seeded containers inside a larger tray of water – but we have found that a plastic spray bottle set at the finest setting works better, as surface moulds are less likely to grow. Do not spray directly into the containers, as this can push seeds down into the cracks in the soil; instead, spray across the tops of the containers or upward into the air above them so that the mist drifts down onto the soil. Always use water that is approximately the same temperature as the soil mix – that is, about room temperature.

The amount of warmth seeds need depends on the species and on their stage of growth. Germination usually requires about 75 degrees F. Higher temperatures, in the range of 80 to 90 degrees, can be provided by bottom heat in the form of special heating cables, purchased propagating units or a warm spot in the house. Be sure not to bake the seeds, however; the temperature should not rise much above 90 degrees. Germination is slow or does not occur at all if temperatures are too low.

One system that works well for home gardeners who do not want to invest in new equipment is to turn a small room into a nursery. We simply posted a sign on the bathroom door: "Seedling Nursery. Please Keep Door Closed." On the counter beside the sink sat plastic flats of seeded foam cups and peat pots, while a small electric heater hummed on the floor. Containers of seeds that needed humid conditions were covered with a sheet of clear plastic. All containers were spray-misted at least once a day so that the soil surface never dried out. Seeds requiring light were closest to the window. The system did not look very elegant, but in combination with the kitchen table, where we left seeds that required room temperature, it germinated more than a hundred species of annuals in one spring.

Once seeds have sprouted, room temperature or a little cooler is fine for most plants. Too much heat at this stage encourages rapid but weak growth. Home gardeners need not worry about exact degrees; temperatures are not constant for long in nature, in any case. Just make sure the temperature does not drop below

about 50 degrees F or rise much above 90. Greenhouses can become excessively hot on sunny days, so do allow for ventilation or plan to move flats into a shady place outdoors when the temperature is high.

Fertilization of seedlings must begin as soon as the so-called second, or true, leaves appear. They develop after the first part of the plant, the cotyledons – the first, or seedling, leaves – appear above the soil surface. The first leaves survive on nutrients stored in the seed, and they are quite different from the characteristic leaves of the mature plant, most of whose nutrients come from the soil. Only if you have sown your seeds in a fertile mix such as sterilized compost can you delay fertilizing. We used a seaweed powder mixed at the rate recommended on the package and applied it with every second watering – about every two or three days – to keep the seedlings moving along nicely. Any soluble organic fertilizer with a slightly elevated phosphorus level (the second number in the three-number analysis written on the package) will be fine.

Watering should be done every morning. Make it part of your routine, perhaps after a first cup of coffee. Seedlings watered in the morning will have moist roots during the warm daytime but will be slightly drier by nighttime, when fungus could otherwise take hold.

Many seedlings will need to be

transplanted into larger containers indoors before they are ready for their final move into the garden. In some cases, transplanting is done several times. The alternative to transplanting when seedlings are crowded is thinning, most easily and safely done by pinching off unwanted plants at the base; pulling them out may disturb their neighbours. If you are growing a colour mixture, do not weed out only the smallest seedlings, as they may represent one colour of the mix. Instead, remove an assortment of sizes.

The transplanting of seedlings is known as pricking out, probably because the process is often carried out with the point of a knife. You must have ready the containers into which the seedlings will move – perhaps large wooden flats, plastic pots, six-packs or even foam cups, one plant per cup. This time, you will need soil at least 3 inches deep, and again, allow for drainage.

In pricking out a seedling, try to remove as much soil as possible with the roots. Using a small paring knife, dig down beside the seedling and pry it up gently, holding the plant by one of its first leaves. Grasping the stem is dangerous, as you may pinch and damage it. Lift the seedling, still supporting the roots with the knife, and insert the roots into a depression made in the soil in the new container. Add new, damp soil, as necessary, to fill in firmly around the roots so that the seedling is again growing at the same soil level. Once it is in place, firm the soil around the stem, water thoroughly, and put the container in a shaded place for a day before it moves back to its bright situation.

When transplanting, unless we are selectively removing just a few seedlings from the original containers, we find it easiest to tip out all of the seedlings with their rootballs and then pull them gently apart so that each retains as many roots as possible. You will have to pull at the soil and root mass and perhaps even cut it with scissors or a knife, but the seedlings themselves should still be handled only by their first leaves. Again, place each seedling in its prepared hole and proceed as described above for pricking out. Seedlings that transplant poorly should always

have individual pots from the start.

By late April or early May, you will have a container or two—perhaps five or six, dozens or even hundreds—of healthy little plants nearing the time when they can make the most traumatic move of their lives: to the outdoors. Frost-hardy annuals can go outdoors anytime after the soil can be worked; so-called half-hardy ones only after the last frost date for your area. The descriptions of individual flowers in the forthcoming chapters tell when to set transplants outdoors. On the other hand, some flowers suffer if they are transplanted, or they bloom easily and early from seed. Large quantities of flowers are better sown directly outdoors, as described earlier.

Transplanting

Whether you have bought your plants or started your own seedlings, before they can be planted in the garden, all have to go through a process of acclimatization called hardening off. The idea is to accustom the plants gradually to outdoor conditions before setting them into the garden. Plants that have been started indoors, where the air is still, temperatures are fairly constant and light exposures are usually lower than outdoors, will be set back and may die if planted immediately in the garden.

Ideally, for the first day of hardening off, which is about two weeks before your hoped-for planting date, place the flats of young plants outdoors for only an hour or so in a sheltered, shady place. The following day, they can stay out for a couple of hours and the next, half a day. Only toward the end of the week should they be exposed to some sun each day. By the second week, sun lovers can spend all day in the sun—but be sure to water them every morning, as they will dry out quickly in their containers—while shade lovers should see little or no full sun. Best for all plants is the amount of light they will receive in their permanent garden positions. By the second week, the plants will be outdoors around the clock and need be

Some annuals are easily damaged by transplanting and should be sown in peat pots or peat pellets, FACING PAGE, *which can be planted directly in the ground, minimizing root disturbance. Most species, however, are able to withstand a small amount of handling,* ABOVE, *although as much soil as possible should be moved with the roots. Here, seedlings sown in a six-pack have formed rootbound plugs that transplant easily.*

33

brought into shelter only if they are tender and frost threatens. A cold frame simplifies the process of hardening off.

The ideal day for transplanting is cool, overcast and humid, even with some light rain. These conditions place the least stress upon newly planted and sometimes damaged roots. The ideal is not always possible, however. If days are unremittingly sunny, do your transplanting in the evening so that the young plants will have a night of cooler, dark conditions for recovery. Water before and immediately after planting.

All transplants should be set as deeply in the soil as they grew formerly. If they are set into a slight depression, watering will be easier. Peat pots or peat pellets are planted directly in the soil. Ensure that the top rim of a peat pot is not above the soil surface, as it can act as a wick, allowing moisture in the pot to evaporate through the rim and the plant to dry out. It may be necessary to tear away the top edge of the pot.

With plants grown in other containers, try to retain as much soil around the roots as possible. In some cases, such as when plants have been grown in small individual cells or containers, the entire rootball will have become rootbound and will pop easily from the container in a solid lump. In other cases, individual plants may need to be gently torn or cut apart. These plants are the most susceptible to transplant failure, as they must get by, for a time, with a damaged root system. Water them as soon as they are planted and daily thereafter until they have begun to produce new growth.

If the sky is clear and especially if conditions are windy, protect all the young plants in the partial shade created by a canopy of evergreen boughs, fern fronds or long grasses, making sure that you do not weight the plants down in the process. The cover can be taken off in about a week or as soon as the plants show signs of new growth.

Space the plants according to their eventual width and height, listed in the descriptions in the following chapters. In general, you want the plants to just touch or slightly over-

lap when mature. Open areas of soil between plants are unattractive and will be invaded by weeds. On the other hand, too much crowding results in leggy plants.

Planting is, of course, just the beginning. Next come weeding, watering, dead-heading (the removal of faded flowers), staking and all the other incidentals that arise during the garden's quiet progress through the season.

Weeding is probably our least favourite garden task, but if it is done regularly, at least once a week, it never becomes a backbreaking chore, and it gives us a chance to inspect the garden and catch problems quickly. If unable to distinguish weed seedlings from those of unfamiliar flowers, we leave plants in peace until they bloom.

There are many ways to water. Sprinkling is the most popular and the easiest to set up, but a great deal of water is wasted through evaporation. One of us set up a system of pipes from a warm pond where a pump was installed—the best possible watering method. Trickle irrigation systems can be attached to any outdoor tap. Easiest, however, is starting out with plants that are suited to their environment—drought lovers for dry gardens and so on. Then, watering is necessary only until the annuals become established. Water seedlings deeply whenever the top inch of soil is dry.

British master garden designer and writer of the last century Gertrude Jekyll wrote, "It is a curious thing that many people, even those who profess to know something about gardening, when I show them something fairly successful—the crowning reward of much care and labour—refuse to believe that any pains have been taken about it. They will ascribe it to chance, to the goodness of my soil and even more commonly to some supposed occult influence of my own—to anything other than to the plain fact that I love it well enough to give it plenty of care and labour."

It is not enough to plant hope; one must also cultivate it.

Ongoing garden maintenance includes dead-heading, FACING PAGE, *the removal of spent flowers so that the plant continues to bloom rather than mature a crop of seeds. Regular dead-heading is also important to keep the garden looking attractive, as is weeding,* ABOVE, *done here by author Turid Forsyth.*

Small Pleasures
Low to knee-high plants

Low-growing flowers are indispensable in any well-designed annual garden, but they must take their proper place at border or container edges or on their own, where they will not be hidden behind taller neighbours. Here, annual phlox is planted in a mass to create a picture as showy as any mixed border. The planting is dense enough to cover the base of the trellis behind.

"Not until you have learned to enjoy flowers on your knees are you a really good gardener," wrote Richardson Wright. On your knees is where you will come to appreciate the smallest flowers, which are indispensable in any well-designed annual garden, even in one as modest as a single hanging basket or balcony pot. While zinnias, castor beans, sunflowers and other skyscrapers are the most impressive annuals in the garden, they would be less showy without the shorter foreground plants that cover the stems of the background beauties and bring the colours of their flowers down to earth. On their own, small flowers have unique roles to play, neatly occupying spaces between stones in a rock garden, spilling over the edges of an assortment of containers and colouring the ground between flagstones and along pathways. As cut flowers, they produce many tiny, perfect arrangements.

The most important thing to remember when situating low-growing plants is, of course, that they will be lost behind anything taller. Obvious advice, but gardeners tend to forget, when looking at an assortment of bedding plants which are all about the same size, that different types of flowers will reach very different heights at maturity. Often, despite your best efforts, you will learn from one year's mistakes what should edge the flowerbed next year. Remember, too, that even front-of-the-border choices need a bit of room to spread. They also tend to grow downhill from a raised garden bed into the lawn or onto the path below. Many low-growing plants have trailing stems that may extend a foot or longer; planting at least that distance back from the edge will, in most cases, leave sufficient room for them to grow.

Keep in mind, too, that many low-growing plants are naturally adapted to exposed, windy places such as mountain slopes, fields or semidesert plains. As such, they need no staking and can often tolerate open sites that would lay low taller flowers. They are, then, relatively easy-care flowers for certain difficult situations.

In a rock garden, they can imitate the blooms hikers find by happy acci-

dent on craggy mountain slopes. Although true alpine perennials are the traditional rock-garden plants, there is no reason the same type of garden cannot support a selection of small annuals. In designing a rock garden from scratch, always set the stones about two-thirds underground, the stripes (lines of stratification within the rocks) parallel, for a natural-looking outcrop.

As well as the small annuals in the following list, many other low-growing plants appear in other chapters. These include alyssum, mignonette, portulaca, California poppy, creeping zinnia, pinks, Livingstone dai-

sies, Swan River daisies, stocks, coleus, polka-dot plants, ursinia, Venus' looking glass and *Polygonum capitatum*.

Abelmoschus
(*Abelmoschus moschatus*)

New to North American gardens in the 1980s, this Indian native bears a huge crop of beautiful, 3-to-4-inch pink or red hibiscus flowers that last just a day but are replaced by new blooms each morning until frost. The plant is a stocky shrub of dense branches about a foot tall and twice that width. The deeply lobed foliage is dark green with a sheen of purple. This is an unusual and appealing edging plant combined with alyssum and also a good pot plant for a container outdoors or a sunny windowsill indoors.

Give abelmoschus an early start indoors, as the plants take at least three months to bloom from seed—longer if the weather is cool. Ten weeks before the last frost, lightly cover the dark brown, spherical seeds, covering pots with clear plastic or glass and setting them in a warm place. Seeds sprout in four days to two weeks. After all danger of frost is past, set plants a foot apart in good soil in full sun or partial shade. This native of hot places thrives in high heat and relatively dry soil and will self-sow in gardens in milder climates.

The genus and species names of *A. moschatus*, an Asian member of the mallow family *Malvaceae*, come from the Arabic *abu-el-mosk* (father of musk) because of the musk-scented seeds, which are used in the making of perfumes.

Ageratum
(Ageratum houstonianum, A. mexicanum)

These low-growing, bristly balls seem, at first glance, to have little in common with their cousins the sunflowers. Yet a close examination of the individual quarter-to-half-inch flower heads reveals that they are indeed daisies; they simply lack the usual ray flowers, or petals. Instead, ageratum has threadlike disc flowers distributed over a half-globe resting in a basket of bracts. The foliage is bristly and rough in texture.

Best known are hybrids and cultivars of *A. houstonianum* used for the front of a border, where the 5-to-8-inch plants provide dense clumps of pink, white or, most often, purplish blue flowers. The short varieties are available as bedding plants from nurseries in spring, but there are also taller, more open types—the best choices if you want cut flowers. The taller plants will likely have to be grown from seed and will not flower as persistently, but cutting them back in summer will encourage the growth of new flowers until frost.

Look in good seed catalogues for 'Blue Horizon,' over 2 feet tall, 'Blue Bouquet,' almost 2 feet, and 'Bavaria,' with bicoloured deep-blue-and-white flowers on 10-to-14-inch stems. The smaller blue cultivars show up best when grown with yellow, gold-orange or white neighbours such as 'Scarlet Sophia' or 'Lemon Gem' marigold, alyssum and low-growing calendulas.

Light helps ageratum seeds to germinate, which usually takes five days to two weeks. Six weeks before the last frost, press seeds into the soil surface and set pots, covered in clear plastic or glass, in a warm place indoors. After frost, set outdoors 6 to 12 inches apart, depending upon eventual height, in fertile soil in sun or partial shade. Alternatively, seeds can be sown directly outdoors around the last frost date. In trials at the Royal Botanical Gardens in Hamilton, Ontario, flowers that received some shade from taller plants did much better than those exposed to the sun in open beds.

The genus name of this Central American and Mexican member of the daisy family *Compositae* comes from the Greek words for "not" and "age" because of the long-lasting nature of the flowers. The species name honours William Houston, a Scottish physician who collected plants in Central America in the early 18th century. The native plant, which we saw growing in Costa Rica,

An exotic introduction to North American gardens is the Indian native abelmoschus, FACING PAGE, *which forms a stocky shrub covered with pink or red 3-to-4-inch-wide hibiscus flowers. Far better known and often available as a started plant in spring is the Central American native ageratum,* LEFT, *grown here with another member of the daisy family, marigold 'Scarlet Sophia.'*

bears its flowers on long, delicate stems. Unfortunately, it is not sold in any seed catalogues we could find.

Anchusa
(*Anchusa capensis*)

The flowers of anchusa were such a bright blue they virtually shone in our gardens. This annual forget-me-not bears its clusters of four-to-six-petalled, one-third-inch flowers on bushy, rough-textured plants with stiff stems. The star-shaped forget-me-nots burst from tightly packed buds. There are white selections and blue ones with white centres, the latter being the more attractive. 'Blue Bird' grows about 18 inches tall, 'Blue Angel' 8 to 10 inches.

Sow seeds, lightly covered, in a cool place indoors eight weeks before the last frost. Around the last frost date, set the transplants out 4 inches apart in good soil in sun or partial shade. Seeds can also be sown directly into the garden about two weeks before the last frost date. 'Blue Angel' bloomed three months

after a late-March indoor sowing for us, quit with the heat of summer and was in full bloom again by the first hard frost in late September. Anchusa is a good companion for candytuft and low-growing yellow or orange flowers such as California poppies and golden ageratum.

A member of the borage family *Boraginaceae*, the plant's Latin name is *anchusa*. The species name, *capensis*, signifies that the plant is native to the Cape of Good Hope.

Bird's-Eyes
(*Gilia* spp)

Bird's-eyes and blue thimble flowers are sold by few seed companies, yet they have many good qualities. They are unusual sources of what many gardeners consider the best flower colour, blue; they are adaptable to shade, an inescapable commodity for most gardeners; they are extremely frost-hardy and thus are among the last flowers still blooming in fall; and they make very good cut flowers. They are

also easy to grow from a direct seeding outdoors.

Bird's-eyes (*G. tricolor*) is a calming plant with a mass of fragile, greyish foliage that resembles asparagus fern and smells faintly of chocolate. The stem is 18 inches long and drapes nicely over the edge of a pot, curving upward at the tip—try five plants to a 12-inch container. In the garden, the stems can be held upright between stiffer flowers. The tricoloured flowers, in racemes at branch tips, are about half an inch wide with a dark purple centre surrounded by petals that are white at the base and fade to pale lilac at the tips.

Blue thimble flower (*G. capitata*) produces inch-wide clusters of lovely, quarter-inch, lilac-blue bells at the ends of 14-inch stems. The slender plant grows only about 5 inches wide and has airy, spiny-looking foliage. The stems feel as rough as sandpaper. This is a good companion for golden ageratum, which grows to about the same height, and is also excellent for cutting and for containers.

Sow the small, sand-coloured seeds, lightly covered, directly in the garden around the last frost date. Choose a place with average to dry soil in half-shade. Seeds sprout in about a week, and plants bloom about six weeks later. Thin to 8 inches apart.

Gilia is a North and South American member of the phlox family *Polemoniaceae*, named for Filippo Luigi Gilii, an 18th-century Italian astronomer. *Capitata* suggests that the flowers form in a head; *tricolor* means three-coloured.

California Bluebell
(*Phacelia campanularia*)

British gardener and writer Vita Sackville-West once wrote, "I never tire of recommending *P. campanularia* and never cease to be surprised when visitors to my garden ask me what it is. Try it. . . . Sheets of blue." The inch-wide, five-petalled flowers of this North American wildflower, loved by bees, are shimmering azure blue, the colour of anchusa or the dwarf delphinium 'Blue Butterfly.' In the centre of each bell, golden yellow pollen provides a small note of beautiful contrast. The reddish,

semireclining stems, 9 to 12 inches long, reach over rocks and weave through other plants. The emerald-green leaves are slightly fuzzy. California bluebell is attractive with alyssum and California poppy.

Lightly rake the small, tan-coloured seeds directly into the garden about two weeks before the last frost date. Choose a spot in sun or partial shade with sandy or otherwise well-drained soil. Seeds sprout in about 10 days, and plants bloom some five weeks later. Thin to 2 inches apart. California bluebell flowers best during cool weather. As it ceases blooming after several weeks, fresh sowings every two weeks will ensure constant colour. Cutting the plant back and watering it will encourage it to bloom again in fall. California bluebell is a favourite food of slugs, but setting it in containers or window boxes will raise it above these pests.

A member of the waterleaf family *Hydrophyllaceae, Phacelia* takes its name from the Greek word *phakelos* (a cluster), because one species bears its flowers in clusters. *P. campanularia*, a native of the western United States, derives its species name from the Latin *campana* (like a bell) because of the flower shape.

Chinese Forget-Me-Not
(*Cynoglossum amabile*)

A cloud of blue was our impression of Chinese forget-me-not in full,

glorious bloom. This is one of the most prolific blue flowers of mid- to late summer, growing as tall as 2 feet and branching from the base to about 18 inches wide. Typical five-petalled forget-me-not flowers, which buzz with bumblebees and honeybees, are three-eighths of an inch wide with lobed, pleated petals fused in the centre to form a curious raised collar surrounding the stigma and anthers. One flower stem emerges from each leaf axil on the upper part of the plant. The leaves and stems have a velvety coating that makes them feel very soft, although the deep magenta stems are tough and fleshy. The greyish green of the plant's own foliage is a good foil for the blue flowers. When the flowers have blown, they are replaced by sparkling, sticky little four-sectioned seedpods that resemble burrs. Chinese forget-me-

Welcome spots of intense blue come to the summer garden with both anchusa, or summer forget-me-not, FACING PAGE, *and the California bluebell,* ABOVE, *which was highly recommended by noted English gardener Vita Sackville-West. Like the California bluebell, the Chinese forget-me-not,* LEFT, *often resows itself in the garden, and both are best sown directly where they will grow rather than started indoors.*

not partners well with 'Giant White Hyacinth' candytuft, geraniums and asters. It is a good cut flower, one of the rare blues for indoors. Gather it with geraniums, candytuft, alyssum and calendula to create an old-fashioned country bouquet.

Scatter the bristly, greyish seeds thinly in large drifts in the garden in sun or partial shade about four weeks before the last frost or anytime until the end of June. Seeds sprout within two weeks, and plants bloom some two months later. Thin to 6 inches apart. Chinese forget-me-not self-sows and can become weedy, but seedlings are easy to pull out.

This member of the family *Boraginaceae* takes its name from the Greek *kyon* (dog) and *glossa* (tongue) because of the shape of the leaves.

Cup Flower
(*Nierembergia hippomanica,*
N. caerulea)

Little known but worth a search, this pretty, ground-hugging plant is perfect for a sunny border edge, container, window box or rock garden, where it resembles an alpine perennial with its dainty, cup-shaped flowers and inch-long, spoon-shaped green leaves. The slender, much-branched stems are covered all summer with inch-wide, five-lobed lavender blossoms with golden throats and stamens tipped with yellow pollen. The best-known cultivar, 'Purple Robe,' has dark purple flowers and an especially compact habit.

Cup flower is easy to grow from seeds sown, barely covered, in a warm place indoors. Start the small, brown seeds 12 weeks before the last

frost, however, as germination may take as long as a month and seedling growth is slow. After the last frost, set plants 6 inches apart in well-drained soil in sun where the weather is cool or, where summers are likely to be hot, in light shade. Transplant carefully or start in peat pots, as cup flower resents root disturbance.

This Argentinian wildflower must have caused problems for the first gauchos; the species name *hippomanica* suggests a plant that horses love to eat or that drives them mad. *Caerulea* simply means blue. The genus is named for Juan Eusebio Nieremberg, a 17th-century Spanish Jesuit. Cup flower is a member of the nightshade family *Solanaceae*.

Dwarf Morning Glory
(*Convolvulus tricolor*)

This nonclimbing version of the related morning glory has similar five-petalled trumpet flowers that bloom for just a day, but the sprawling, deep maroon stems of *C. tricolor* grow only about 2 feet long, making this compact plant an excellent choice for window boxes, tubs and flowerbed edges. 'Royal Ensign,' our favourite cultivar, has flowers that are deep purplish blue at the rim and taper to a white star surrounding a yellow throat, the typical tricoloured arrangement. Some flowers have a lilac, red, pink or white band in place of the purple. The spoon-shaped leaves are dark green with wavy edges and often maroon veins.

After the last frost, soak the big seeds overnight before planting directly outdoors one-quarter of an inch deep. For an earlier start, sow four weeks before the last frost in peat pots, three seeds per pot, thinning to the strongest seedling. Seeds sprout in about a week. Our plants, sown in peat pots on May 4, flowered by July 10. Set plants 8 inches apart in sun or half-shade. Two plants will fill and overflow a 16-by-18-inch container. The dwarf morning glory prefers deep, moisture-holding humus but should not be overwatered. Remove the faded flowers to encourage continued blooming.

The name of *Convolvulus*, a European member of the morning glory family *Convolvulaceae*, means "to twine around." *Tricolor* describes the three-coloured flowers.

Leptosiphon, Stardust
(*Linanthus androsaceus,*
Leptosiphon hybridus)

Few annual flowers illustrate the saying that there is strength in numbers as aptly as leptosiphon. This diminutive flower will disappear in the garden unless it is planted in masses in a place like a window box, a rock garden or the front of a bed where it will have no competition except, perhaps, from other tiny plants. Stems, segmented and deep purple, reach only 4 to 6 inches in height. The spiky foliage resembles pine needles but is as soft as moss. The quarter-inch, five-petalled, starlike flowers have a pronounced inner circle of deep yellow marks and bloom in various pastel shades. French hybrids include yellow, cream, lilac and rose. Edged in front by violet cress and fenced behind by Swan River daisies or *Chrysanthemum municaule*, French hybrids make a colourful rock-garden patchwork. Our reminder for the future is: "Grow lots!"

Lightly cover the small, beige seeds directly outdoors around the last frost date in partial shade. Seeds sprout in less than a week. Leave as is or thin to 2 inches apart. Our seeds, sown May 5, sprouted May 9, and plants were in full flower by July

15. Pinch the central stems early to encourage branching.

Leptosiphon is a western North American member of the phlox family *Polemoniaceae*. The genus name *Linanthus* comes from the Greek *linon* (flax) and *anthos* (flower) because of a resemblance to that plant. The species name *androsaceus* suggests that the plant resembles rock jasmine (androsace).

Mask Flower
(*Alonsoa* spp)

The mask flowers look like Quaker bonnets or smaller versions of their cousins the monkey flowers. *A. x meridionalis* 'Amber Glow' has inch-wide, light orange flowers, while *A. warscewiczii* is prettier, with scarlet flowers. The flowers of *A. linearis* are larger and darker orange.

The broad, toothed leaves are spiky and wild-looking. Flowers bloom from the bottom of the plant upward and are followed by seeds that develop rapidly in cone-shaped cups. Plants are sturdier and bushier than their garden relative Morocco toadflax (*Linaria maroccana*), a good companion for mask flowers along with ornamental grasses or dark foliage plants. Mask flowers are good for cutting.

Sow the seeds indoors, lightly covered, eight weeks early. Germination takes two or three weeks at about 60 degrees F. To encourage the side spikes to grow and flower, cut the middle stem when seedpods start to develop. Pot some plants in fall for indoor flowers.

Alonsoa is a Peruvian member of the figwort family *Scrophulariaceae*, named for Alonzo Zanoni, an 18th-century Colombian politician.

Meadow Foam
(*Limnanthes douglasii*)

This delightful North American native is also called poached-egg flower for its petal markings, egg-yolk yellow in the centre and white at the edge. (Vita Sackville-West, however, took exception to the description: "I should not have called it poached egg myself: I should have called it scrambled egg with chopped parsley; poached suggests something far more circular and cohesive.") Unlike eggs, either poached or scrambled, the inch-wide flowers have a sweet fragrance most noticeable on warm summer evenings, so limnanthes makes a good pot plant for a patio or balcony in sun. The flowers, which attract bees by day but close at night, are produced freely until well after the first frosts; ours were still blooming in November. Plants grow about 6 inches tall.

The hard, ash-brown seeds are the source of a unique oil used in lubricants, waxes, soaps and moisturizers. As soon as the soil can be worked in spring, sow the seeds directly out-

The small, delicate cup flower forms its inch-wide blooms on slender, rambling stems. The best-known cultivar, 'Purple Robe,' FACING PAGE, TOP, has an especially compact habit. Its seeds are best sown early indoors, as growth is slow, but those of the dwarf morning glory, FACING PAGE, BOTTOM, can be sown directly in the warm soil of the early-summer garden. The brilliantly coloured patterns on the petals of this cultivar, 'Royal Ensign,' are showy in pots or at the edges of sunny borders. Meadow foam, ABOVE, a pleasing, low-growing California wildflower, perfumes the air with its fragrance.

43

doors, lightly covered, in well-drained, sandy soil in sun or partial shade. Sprouting takes about two weeks. The celery-green seedlings resemble salad servers – the first leaves look like ladles, the second like forks. Thin the plants to 4 inches apart. Poached-egg flower does best in cool weather and often self-sows.

One of many plants named for Scotsman David Douglas, a botanist sent to North America to investigate the native flora of the Pacific region in 1823, *Limnanthes* receives its genus name from the Greek words for marsh and flower. It is a member of the family *Limnanthaceae* and is native to California and Oregon.

Morocco Toadflax
(*Linaria maroccana*)

These half-inch-wide "baby" snapdragons with yellow centres have five petals – two up like rabbit ears and three down like puffed cheeks. Another common name is bunny rabbits. The flowers also resemble upside-down acrobats wearing loose Chinese pyjamas or bring to mind little fish with splayed tails, their gills wide. The orange splotches inside the cheeks advertise an entrance to a narrow spur at the back of the flower, which holds a two-forked pistil and four anthers heavily laden with golden pollen. On warm days, toadflax buzzes with bumblebees that bend the tiny snapdragons down

as they dive in for nectar hidden in the long spurs. Small, grasslike leaves alternate on slender stems. 'Fairy Lights' blooms in shades of pure white, deep lilac, red, pink, copper-yellow and purple. The flowers of 'Northern Lights' are faintly violet-scented.

Chill the tiny seeds for three weeks in the refrigerator, then sow them outdoors, barely covered, around the last frost date. Alternatively, start them in a cool place indoors six weeks early, where the tiny seedlings will be easier to monitor. Toadflax is best transplanted in clumps when seedlings are about an inch high. Plant them in groups in sun or partial shade behind other mass-effect plants such as alyssum. They stop flowering in hot weather.

Linaria is a member of the figwort family *Scrophulariaceae* and takes its name from the Greek *linon* (flax) because of the similar foliage. The species name *maroccana* indicates the plant's origin in the Mediterranean region of Africa.

Nemesia
(*Nemesia strumosa*)

Intricate floral designs in jewel-like colours are the gifts of nemesia, a mound of yellow, orange, light blue, purple, brilliant pinkish red or white flowers over soft, slightly toothed, lettucelike leaves. The blooms, which grow in clusters at the tips of

10-inch or longer stems, have an upper petal divided at the edge into four sections and a lower lip that acts as a landing pad for pollinators. The throat is marked with dark speckles as a nectar guide. Stems are lush, ribbed and well branched, but they will not support the mounded plants unless plants are set close together among stronger-stemmed neighbours or staked with slender twigs. Plant nemesia at the border edge or in a pot or hanging basket (see page 19) partnered with viscaria, browallia and bird's-eyes. Nemesia will also thrive in a cool, bright window, where the shortest cultivars, such as 'Carnival,' are most satisfactory.

Cover the fine, black seeds lightly, and set pots in a cool place indoors six weeks before the last frost. They should sprout in about a week, and plants will bloom two months later. After frost danger, space 8 to 10 inches apart in a group in well-drained, rich soil in partial shade. Nemesia does best in cool weather and moist soil and may stop flowering in intense heat; plant it where a more heat-tolerant annual can fill in the spaces if flowering does flag.

A member of the figwort family *Scrophulariaceae*, nemesia, a native of southern Africa, takes its name from *nemesion*, the Greek name for a similar plant. *Strumosa* describes the plant's cushionlike swellings.

Nolana
(*Nolana paradoxa, N. atriplicifolia*)

Because this beautiful flower is a gentle trailer, it is an excellent candidate for window boxes, rock gardens, hanging baskets, containers and the tops of walls. There, the succulent foot-long stems can best display their crop of elegant flowers. The 2-inch flower's five fused, periwinkle-blue petals lead to a deep, lime-green throat tucked into two finely haired leaves that meet at the base. The short-lived flowers stay open in rain but close at night and on overcast days. Side branches bear three to seven buds that open in succession to be replaced by domes of hard, closely packed seeds. These seed balls, enclosed by sepals, look like Bavarian church towers.

Six weeks before the last frost,

sow the hard, beige, chunky seeds one-eighth of an inch deep in peat pots, since nolana develops a long taproot and does not transplant easily. Sow three seeds per pot, and thin to the strongest seedling. Seeds sprout in about 10 days, and plants bloom some three months later. Set plants 4 inches apart in fertile, well-drained soil in sun or partial shade.

Both the genus *Nolana* and the family *Nolanaceae* take their names from the Greek *nola* (a small bell) because of the shape of the flower. *Paradoxa* means paradoxical or strange; *atriplicifolia* suggests that the leaves resemble those of the plant atriplex.

Pansy, Viola
(*Viola* spp)

There are many garden violas, from the smallest Johnny-jump-ups to the biggest hybrid pansies. All are flowers of distinction. Frost-hardy and easy to grow, they are among the most elegant and versatile of all the common bedding flowers. The colour

range is wide, from white to almost black, including purples, reds, yellows, oranges, blues and pinks. Many flowers have centres bicoloured or blotched with a contrasting colour, while others resemble faces decorated with tiny black lines like cat whiskers. Most grow 6 to 8 inches tall, one flower per square stem held above soft clumps of green, oval leaves. Violas used to be highly regarded as medicinal flowers, and all family members are still valued as edible decoration for summer salads.

Pansies, violas and violets are all members of the genus *Viola*, but violets and violas are the smaller-flowered of the group and may be sold under species names.

The wild Johnny-jump-up (*V. tricolor*) fits the first category. This eager volunteer with three-quarter-inch bicoloured yellow-and-deep-violet flowers with dark nectar lines tends to spread by seed but can be pulled up if it appears where it is not wanted. In half-shade, it grows about a foot tall. We found the 1989 All-

Like tiny snapdragons, the complex flowers of Morocco toadflax, FACING PAGE, *display the usual characteristics of the plant family* Scrophulariaceae. *After a brief chilling in the refrigerator, the seeds can be sown directly in the garden around the last frost date. Also appreciative of a chilling are the seeds of violas, such as the little Johnny-jump-up,* ABOVE, *and its larger-flowered cousin, the pansy, which often survives mild winters.*

America Selections (AAS) pansy 'Jolly Joker' a pleasantly large version. Its happy, deep-purple-and-orange faces suit containers and the edges of beds. All pansies, violas and violets, in fact, are ideal container flowers either on their own or partnered with small companions such as forget-me-nots and alyssum. They are also lovely in a herb garden.

Sow the small, glossy, orange seeds one-eighth of an inch deep eight weeks early, setting pots in the refrigerator for a week to stratify the seeds (they need at least 24 hours at 35 to 40 degrees F), then move pots to a warm place, where seeds should sprout in about two weeks. Around the last frost date, set the young plants into fertile soil in sun or partial shade. Started early in March, our small violas blossomed by mid-May in the cold frame before they were transplanted to their permanent spots. Even by the end of August, with some dead-heading in the meantime, they showed no sign of exhaustion.

We often have violas and pansies resow in the garden. Actually perennials too tender to overwinter in most of the north, they do best in cool weather, although much breeding work has gone into developing more heat-tolerant cultivars such as 'Jolly Joker' and the 1991 AAS pansy 'Maxim Marina.' Do not let the soil dry out completely. If the weather is not too hot, the flowers will bloom all summer, provided ageing flowers and seedpods are removed.

The genus *Viola* belongs to the violet family *Violaceae*. Both genus and family take their names from the Latin word for several scented flowers. Most family members are native to the northern temperate zone and the Andes.

Phlox
(*Phlox drummondii*)

In northern gardens, the perennial types of phlox are best known, but annual phlox is worth investigating. It is smaller, producing the typical clusters of open, five-petalled flowers on stiff stems only 6 to 15 inches tall. The blooming period is far longer than that of the perennial, from early summer till well after the first frost. Each plant, about 8 inches wide, is a self-supporting bouquet of half-to-one-inch flowers shaded pink, crimson, violet, white, salmon and bicoloured. The cultivar 'Beauty Mixed' ('Dwarf Mixed') includes a pale yellow. 'Twinkle,' another cultivar, has tiny, starlike flowers. Annual phlox makes an excellent cut flower, and the smallest cultivars are good for rock gardens, window boxes and containers.

Sow the large seeds directly in the garden, an eighth of an inch deep, around the last frost date, choosing a spot with rich soil in full sun. Seeds can also be started indoors four weeks early and will sprout in a week or two. Around the last frost date, carefully transplant 6 inches apart. Give the plants plenty of water. Flowering may slow if the plant is allowed to go to seed. If this happens, cut the plant back to a couple of inches high and it may bloom again before frost.

Phlox, a member of the phlox family *Polemoniaceae*, takes its name from the Greek word for a flame. The species is named for Thomas Drummond, a botanist who introduced the species to Britain in the 19th century. *P. drummondii* is a native of Texas and is also called pride of Texas.

Pimpernel
(*Anagallis linifolia, A. monellii* [*A. arvensis*])

The Scarlet Pimpernel, hero of a turn-of-the-century novel, lived a double life. Sometimes he was a dashing rescuer of distressed aristocrats of the French Revolution; otherwise, he was the foppish Percy Blakeney, an upper-class British version of Clark Kent. Similarly, the flower of the same name is not exactly what it seems. A weed in Britain, *A. arvensis* supposedly has magical powers. It can also be a pretty garden plant, even though its brilliant orange quarter-inch flowers close in overcast and wet weather, hence the common name poor man's weatherglass. This is a trailing plant that acts as an airy ground cover.

More ornamental is the spreading, foot-tall bush of flaxleaf pimpernel (*A. linifolia*), a tender perennial well worth choosing as an edging alternative to the usual ageratum. It produces five-petalled, three-quarter-inch flowers whose petals curl inward during midday heat and close at night and in overcast weather. The flower is usually an intense ultramarine blue with a purple crown of pistil and stamens topped by deep yellow pollen. When the plants are covered with flowers, they glow deep blue in the afternoon shade. There are also pink and lilac selections.

We sowed the seeds one-eighth of an inch deep directly into balcony boxes after the last spring frost, and the plants were in bloom by July 23.

Seeds can also be sown indoors six weeks early. Germination may take as long as a month. Space or thin to 4 inches apart. The plants withstand heat but are best with a little afternoon shade. Both types of anagallis are excellent for rock gardens and edgings; they also make attractive indoor plants. In the garden, they will often self-sow.

A member of the primrose family *Primulaceae*, *Anagallis* is named for a Greek plant. The species name for *A. linifolia*, a native of the Mediterranean region, suggests that the leaves resemble those of flax. The species name *arvensis* describes the plant's growth in cultivated fields.

Tidy Tips
(Layia elegans, L. platyglossa)

"Keep California green and golden," say billboards on the highways leading into that state. Three of California's native plants seem to be doing their best to colour the state appropriately. California poppy, described in chapter seven, meadow foam, described in this chapter, and tidy tips are all green and golden, although the latter two add accents of white to the colour scheme.

The daisy flowers of tidy tips, better known as a garden annual in England than in North America, have overlapping, three-lobed ray petals of lemon-yellow bordered with white, hence the common name. The flowers are about 1½ inches wide with a half-inch, dark yellow disc, and they bloom from midsummer until after the first light frosts in fall. The shrubby, branching plants are as tall as 18 inches and have hairy, feathery, grey-green foliage that resembles summer savory and smells of wild mint.

Branches require staking unless plants are set among sturdier neighbours. Tidy tips partners well with Swan River daisies and Tahoka daisies, either in the garden or in a window box or pot. On its own, it will decorate walkways and rock gardens as well as vases indoors.

Sow seeds one-eighth of an inch deep directly outdoors in spring as soon as the soil can be worked, since the seedlings do not transplant well. Choose a fertile, well-drained spot in sun. Seeds will germinate in a week to a month in warm soil, and plants bloom about three months later. Thin to 8 inches apart.

Layia is a Californian member of the daisy family *Compositae*. The genus name honours 19th-century British botanist G. Tradescant Lay. *Elegans* means elegant, *platyglossa* broad-tongued.

Verbena, Vervain
(Verbena spp)

Verbena is a somewhat stiff plant, in the manner of annual phlox, but this quality can be an advantage

Pimpernel, whose name is best known because of its association with a dashing hero of English fiction, is most attractively represented in the garden by the species Anagallis linifolia, *the flaxleaf pimpernel,* FACING PAGE, *which produces blue, pink or lilac flowers on a small, airy shrub. The easiest way to grow both pimpernel and annual phlox,* ABOVE, *is to sow seeds directly in the garden around the last spring frost date. Phlox will produce its bouquets of showy flowers through fall's frosty weather.*

where the gardener wants something small and self-supporting. Plants branch at the base and throughout, growing about 10 inches tall and wide. On its strong stems, verbena produces 2-inch clusters of 10 to 20 small flowers that resemble miniature bouquets in several striking colours, including blue, blood red, mixed pinks and deep purple, any of which may have white centres or eyes. The petals of each individual quarter-to-half-inch flower join into a half-inch tube. The stems and toothed leaves are rough-looking and feel like sandpaper. Plant verbena with dianthus and sweet alyssum at the edge of a border for a delightful garden in miniature. Brought indoors in fall, verbena makes a good pot plant.

Sow and lightly cover the elongated beige seeds 8 to 10 weeks early in a warm place indoors. Blanket pots with black plastic or cardboard, as seeds require darkness for germination. They sprout in about two weeks, and plants bloom 10 to 12 weeks later. After frost danger,

set seedlings 8 inches apart in good soil in sun. Water until well established. Soil that is too fertile will encourage the growth of foliage at the expense of flowers. Verbena will flower profusely all summer until frost, if dead-headed often.

Verbena, the genus name of these members of the vervain family *Verbenaceae*, comes from the Latin name for vervain (*V. officinalis*), a herb once thought to have magical properties. The usual garden type is a tender perennial hybrid of several South American species.

Violet Cress
(*Ionopsidium acaule*)

This is such a modest flower that one scarcely notices it unless it is grown in a large drift at the front of a border or between the stones of a rock garden. The four-petalled flowers, white to lilac-blue, are just a quarter of an inch wide. The floppy 6-inch stems reach only a few inches above ground, forming soft, cresslike clumps. The tiny, green, spoon-

shaped leaves taste like watercress. This is a companion for leptosiphon, which is almost as small and a bit more colourful.

Sow the tiny, rust-brown seeds directly in the garden around the last frost date, sprinkling them thinly in a moist, fertile spot in sun or partial shade. Seeds sprout in about a week and bloom a month or so later.

A Portuguese member of the mustard family *Cruciferae*, *Ionopsidium* takes its name from the Greek *ion* (violet), *opsis* (like) and *eidos* (form). The genus consists of only one species, *acaule*, which means stemless.

Virginia Stock
(*Malcolmia maritima*)

Virginia stock is well known as an edging plant in England, where it is considered as indispensable in the garden as sweet alyssum and is just as floriferous and frost-hardy. The flower deserves to be better known in North America, but few seed companies sell it. Sow the seeds around the last frost date or anytime until the end of June—wherever there are empty spaces near the fronts of borders—for a profusion of pink, lilac, purple and white flowers that start to bloom in about a month and continue long after the first hard frost. At the end of September, Virginia stock still buzzes with bees.

Trailing stems grow about 8 inches long; the leaves are small, green and pointed; and the slightly scented, four-petalled flowers are about half an inch wide. Virginia stock can be mixed with evening-scented stock (*Matthiola bicornis*) for evening scent and daytime colour.

Virginia stock can grow too leggy in rich soil. It does best in well-drained, slightly poor soil in sun or partial shade. Sprinkle the seeds thinly on the soil, rake them in lightly, and thin seedlings to 2 or 3 inches apart. Cool, sunny weather keeps it blooming.

No Virginian at all, but a Mediterranean member of the mustard family *Cruciferae*, Virginia stock is named for William Malcolm and his son, English horticulturists of the 18th and 19th centuries. The species name suggests the plant's native habitat near the sea.

Somewhat stiff but well suited to pots is verbena, which grows in company with dwarf dahlias, lobelia and dianthus, FACING PAGE. *Individual flowers, which often have a white centre, or eye, are only about a quarter of an inch wide but grow in comely miniature bouquets. Also excellent in pots or at border edges are Virginia stocks,* LEFT, *which can be directly sown in large drifts in the spring garden to produce masses of small flowers that will often self-sow.*

Reach for the Top
Middle-sized to tall plants

Tall annuals, many of which grow to lofty heights with amazing speed, form eye-catching focal points and backdrops in the garden. They are generally the flowers visitors notice first and gardeners remember most vividly. Many require staking, but these supports can be hidden by foliage or by lower-growing foreground plants. Here, spider flower is a graceful accent to a slightly shorter perennial neighbour, Monarda didyma.

The corn in the musical *Oklahoma* grew "as high as an elephant's eye," yet the much prettier sunflowers and a few other ornamental annuals soar to heights of 4, 6, 8 or even 10 feet in a single northern summer. These fast-growing plants, which seem as dedicated as the gardener to taking as much as they can from two or three months of hot weather, have long had their attractions for gardeners limited by a short season. A description of Canadian gardens in an 1833 magazine mentions spiring hollyhocks and bachelor's buttons, as well as large perennials such as roses and peonies. Sheer size is simply an indisputable sign of horticultural success.

There are many uses for tall plants besides cheering the gardener. They provide shade and shelter for smaller plants. They create good visual transitions from lower plants to background trees, walls or high fences. And planted in groups or rows, they can create a private secret garden. They are the obvious choices for the back of the border but are also so eye-catching that they can create highlights almost anywhere in the garden when planted on their own.

Urged skyward to attract high-flying pollinators and escape competition closer to the ground, tall plants have either soft stems that blow with the wind or stiff ones that remain rigid in breezes but may topple in storms. In the latter category was our splendid collection of 9-foot castor beans, which provided a beautiful focal point for the garden all summer until it was flattened into a pathetic heap of branches by a September gale. While nothing short of embracing them all night could have been done to save those big, heavy plants, this toppling problem, called lodging, can be avoided in more slender-stemmed annuals.

Staking is a term that includes not only tying plants to stakes but also enclosing them in cages or propping them on Y-shaped twigs. Begin staking plants as soon as they look top-heavy, as stems may snap if they become accustomed to sprawling. Press the stakes or sticks firmly into the soil close to the plant stem, and loosely bind stem to stake with twist

ties or slender strips of soft cloth. If you are supporting an entire clump of stems or a shrubby plant, you may need several stakes strung together or a cylinder of chicken wire narrow enough that the foliage will stick out through the holes and conceal the cage. Watch that you do not bunch the plant but rather allow it to spread naturally. As Gertrude Jekyll says, "The rule, as I venture to lay it down, is that sticks and stakes must never show."

Anyone who wants to avoid staking should keep in mind that most plants will be taller, weaker and more likely to lodge if grown in rich,

moist soil. And of course, stems will more likely fall over in open, gusty places than in protected city backyards. Plant the towering flowers on the leeward side of the house or garage. A wall, a hedge or nearby trees will help shelter the entire garden from wind. Most tall plants have dwarf selections too, so if modest height will suit, choose a shorter version, which is sure to be more self-supporting. Sowing or planting tall plants densely will enable them to hold one another up.

Besides the plants listed below, many tall annuals are described in other chapters. They include foxgloves, wild foxgloves, four-o'clocks, cosmos, some dahlias, salvias, zinnias, marigolds and ornamental grasses.

Amaranth
(*Amaranthus* spp)

The best-known garden amaranths are the small, feathery types described in chapter seven. They can be somewhat unkempt-looking, but Joseph's coat (*A. tricolor, A. gangeticus*) is something else entirely, a beautiful, tall (to 5 feet), self-supporting amaranth with not a hint of déclassé behaviour. The entire plant is a spire of colour, sometimes green and burgundy from top to bottom and at other times displaying that combination at the base and bright pink and yellow variegated foliage at the top. The cultivar 'Molten Fire' has copper or crimson leaves. Tucked into each leaf axil is a tiny hedgehog of amaranth flower. Start this plant indoors about two weeks before the last frost, and transplant 3 feet apart.

We preferred Joseph's coat to another tall foliage plant, the unrelated *Atriplex hortensis*, mountain spinach, or orach, a 4-to-5-foot plant whose edibility is its chief attribute; both the green- and red-leaved types look decidedly weedy, like tall versions of their relative, lamb's quarters. Orach is definitely a background plant. Sow the seeds six weeks early indoors, lightly covered with fine soil. Sprouting occurs in a week or two. Space the plants a foot apart in sun after the last spring frost.

Amaranthus caudatus, love-lies-bleeding, or tassel flower, is an old-fashioned favourite whose catkinlike flower spikes, instead of standing upright, are as pendant as the branches of a weeping willow, hence the species name, which means "tailed." Love-lies-bleeding is photoperiod-sensitive—flowers begin to grow when days are about 12 hours long. As with other amaranths, the young leaves are edible. This one grows 2 to 3 feet tall with flowering tails as long as 16 inches that are suitable in dried flower arrangements. Set plants a foot apart.

Grain amaranth (*A. cruentus*—the

species name means bloody), whose seeds are valued as a high-protein crop, is the tallest of the group, reaching up to 7 feet. Like Joseph's coat, it has a rigid central stalk with few side branches, lending a strong vertical element to the garden. Again, the young leaves are edible. When it is fully in flower, it looks like a tall, slender Christmas tree glowing deep maroon. Green selections are also available, but they are used as grain plants rather than as ornamentals. Each plant requires about a foot of space all around in full sun. For a stunning display, grow grain amaranth in the company of *Nicotiana sylvestris* or ornamental grasses. For grain, after the first frost, cut, thresh, screen and winnow the mature seed heads.

All amaranths are as eager to sprout as pigweed. Lightly buried in warm soil, the seeds germinate almost immediately, appearing in about three days. The seedlings grow so quickly that, indoors, they should not be given too much warmth or they will become leggy; keep them at a cool room temperature in a bright place. Start them two or three weeks before the last frost, and move them outdoors when the nights are warm, or sow them directly outdoors in warm soil. The amaranths do well in full sun and will tolerate some shade.

All are members of the family *Amaranthaceae*, whose name comes

An essential aspect of garden design is a consideration of plant height. Tall species must be planted behind shorter ones, or some flowers will be hidden. A gradual ascent from front to back, FACING PAGE, makes the most effective display. Standing regally near the back of the bed is the showy 5-foot amaranth known as Joseph's coat, ABOVE, which forms a spire of coloured foliage that hides tiny flowers in the leaf axils.

Solanaceae, the apple of Peru takes its genus name from Nikander of Colophon, a Greek poet of the second century B.C. who wrote about the medicinal uses of plants. *Physalodes*, the only species in the genus, has a name that suggests it resembles physalis, Chinese lantern. The plant is a native of Peru.

Bishop's Flower
(*Ammi majus*)

Bishop's flower has gained great popularity with floral artists in Europe because its large, lacy, white flower heads play the same lofty role as baby's breath in cut-flower bouquets. The hollow stems, about 2½ feet tall, support long-lasting, round flower heads as wide as 6 inches that are made up of tiny, five-petalled snowflakes. The greyish green leaves resemble the celerylike potherb lovage. Grow bishop's flower against a wall, let it lend softness to any tall, rigid-looking character like cleome, or mass it in a border. In a container, bishop's flower, heliotrope and pink poppies create a gentle trio set in front of a cloud of four-o'clocks.

Sow the thin, greyish seeds indoors, lightly covered, eight weeks before the last frost. Seeds sprout in a week or two, and plants bloom some 10 weeks later. Seeds can also be sown directly in the garden about two weeks before the last spring frost to create large drifts of white. Seedlings, which look like little celery or parsley plants, should be thinned to stand 8 inches apart. Plant in sun or partial shade.

Bishop's flower is a North African member of the carrot family *Umbel-*

from the Greek *amarantos* (unfading) because of the long-lasting nature of the flowers.

Apple of Peru
(*Nicandra physalodes*)

Surprisingly little known for such a big plant with pretty flowers and somewhat weedy ways, the apple of Peru is a conversation piece in any garden that features it. Even during a northern season, provided it is given reasonably fertile, moist, warm soil, it will grow at least 5 feet tall, resembling a frost-tender tree with strong horizontal branches and a woody, purplish stem 1½ inches wide at the base. In every leaf axil is a flower stem. Within a five-sided, papery calyx blooms the solitary 2-inch flower, delicate but scentless, consisting of five fused lilac-blue petals that fade to creamy white toward a centre decorated with yellow stigma and anthers. By early September, the plant is mostly covered with brown seedpods and looks a bit forlorn, although branches

of seedpods make attractive additions to everlasting arrangements.

Once in the garden, the apple of Peru will often self-sow modestly, and the seedlings need only be transplanted to desired places. But the first time around, sow the small brown seeds, lightly covered, in a warm place indoors about four weeks early. Sow three seeds in a small container or peat pot, thinning to the strongest seedling. The seedlings grow vigorously and will begin to bloom in about 10 weeks, indoors or out. Indoors, set three plants in a 10-inch container for a decorative houseplant, but beware of pests; another common name is shoo-fly, but the plant does not live up to its reputation for repelling aphids and whiteflies. If you are growing it outdoors, where it will assume its full height, set it into the garden around the last frost date, providing full sun or light shade and moist, fertile soil. Give plants 3 feet of space all around, and position them at the back of the border or grow them as specimens.

A member of the nightshade family

liferae. Ammi is an ancient Greek name for the plant; *majus* means big.

Castor Bean
(*Ricinus communis*)

The queen of tall annuals is the castor bean, an evergreen tropical tree that grows with incredible speed to unusual heights when treated to its preferred conditions of heat, moisture and full sun. With its bamboo-like, notched stem and fanning, deeply lobed leaves, some more than 2 feet wide, this majestic plant, often 9 feet tall and 6 feet wide even in a northern garden, is an attention-grabber wherever it grows — on its own, at the back of a bed or against a house wall. The 18-inch taproot seems impossibly small to support so much aboveground greenery, and indeed, the castor plant may topple if it grows in an exposed place without a sturdy stake.

There is a dark side, however, to all this generosity. The brown seeds within the spiny, reddish fruits produce not only the medicinal purgative castor oil, bane of generations of children, but also a poison, ricin (which is not present in the oil). Some seed companies do not even sell the seeds because of their toxicity. Castor bean should never be grown where children play, although we have seen the plants unashamedly dominating a corner of a city park near the swings and slides. Also,

some people develop an allergic rash from contact with the leaves or seedpods, so wear gloves when working with the plants.

There are several cultivars, such as 'Zanzibarensis,' with huge green leaves; 'Combodgensis' or 'Black Beauty,' with dark purple leaves; 'Gibsonii,' a smaller (to 5 feet) plant with red foliage; 'Impala,' with showy yellow flowers and reddish purple leaves; and 'Carmencita,' with bright red flowers and dark brown foliage. Good companions include ornamental grasses, celosia, coleus, tithonia, hollyhocks, cleome and sunflowers. The castor bean can also be positioned to produce welcome shade for such flowers as foxgloves and woodruff. English gardener Graham Rice recommends planting the vine *Eccremocarpus scaber* at the base of a castor bean so that the orange flowers show through the leaves.

Soak the brown, bean-sized seeds for a day before sowing them. We have had success sowing seeds three-quarters of an inch deep directly into garden beds and along a house wall. Seeds sprouted in a week or two, and plants had their first set of true leaves in five weeks, when they could be transplanted elsewhere in the garden. For an earlier start, sow the seeds indoors in a warm place about six weeks before the last frost. Harden them off according to the directions in chapter two, and when nights are warm, plant them out-

The apple of Peru, FACING PAGE, TOP, *will attain a height of 5 feet or more in a season, producing beautiful light blue flowers that later yield decorative seedpods which are excellent in dried arrangements. Bishop's flower, about 2 feet tall,* FACING PAGE, BOTTOM, *is a wonderful cut flower much like Queen Anne's lace, while the castor bean,* ABOVE, *is the most massive plant in the annual garden, capable of growing 9 feet tall and 6 feet wide in a northern summer.*

species name suggests the plant's use as a dye.

Corn Cockle
(*Agrostemma githago*)

Like its lovely relatives, the campions and the catchflies, corn cockle has slender, breezy stems 2 to 3 feet tall topped all summer with deep rose, 1½-inch flowers. Before they open, the five flower petals are rolled like umbrellas into long sepal sockets. Upon opening, the paddle-shaped petals reveal a white flower centre. The long, fine, white hairs on the calyx, stem and undersides of the leaves create a silver-green effect. Corn cockle is best sown densely in a semiwild-looking bed with other soft-stemmed annuals such as cornflowers, larkspurs and poppies. We also liked it intersown with the aster 'California Giant.' It makes a good cut flower, and it has interesting seedpods for dried arrangements.

About two weeks before the last frost, sow the hard, charcoal-coloured seeds, just covered, outdoors in well-drained soil in sun. Seeds sprout in about 10 days, and flowers bloom less than two months later.

Corn cockle is a member of the pink family *Caryophyllaceae*. The genus name of this Mediterranean native comes from the Greek *agros* (a field) and *stemma* (a crown or garland). *Githago* is the Latin name of the plant.

Cornflower
(*Centaurea* spp)

Cornflowers (*C. cyanus*) are the best-known blues of the annual garden, and justly so. They are easy to grow, very frost-tolerant and given to generously self-sowing. These curious little daisies – curious because cornflowers lack the ray flowers that distinguish most daisies – vary from the usual blue to pink, rose, lilac and white. The plant has a sweetly herbal scent, like that of bedstraw or woodruff, and the leaves and slender windblown stems 1 to 3 feet tall are covered with silver cottonlike spikes and threads which give them a greyish cast.

Our 'Emperor William' plants

doors in rich soil with good drainage in full sun, allowing each plant about 3 feet of space all around. Fertilize once a month with manure tea – a shovelful of well-rotted manure in a pail of water. After a heavy frost, castor bean quickly collapses.

The castor bean is a tropical African member of the spurge family *Euphorbiaceae*. The only member of its genus, its name comes from the Latin *ricinus* (a tick) because of the shape and colour of the seeds. The common name derives from the Spanish *agno casto*, literally, pure oil. *Communis* means common.

Coreopsis, Calliopsis
(*Coreopsis tinctoria*)

Much more pleasant than their common name, tickseed, suggests, these cheerful 2-inch sunflowers display warm shades of rusty red, bright yellow and mahogany around dark centres bearing orange pollen. The flowers are grouped like an open fan, the plants bearing showers of gold and red when in full bloom in mid-

summer. The foliage is slender, soft and grasslike. Most plants grow 1½ to 2½ feet tall, branching like candelabra, although there are also dwarf versions.

This is a very easy flower for direct sowing in sun and ordinary soil. Sprouting occurs in about a week, and flowers grow quickly. Thin to 8 to 12 inches apart, and provide twiggy branches or small stakes for support. In an informal annual garden, mix coreopsis with baby's breath, poppies, flax, statice, strawflowers and winged everlasting. Blanket flowers, which have a similar colour scheme, are also good companions. Stems of cup-shaped seedpods can be collected for dried flower arrangements.

The genus name and unpleasant common name of this North American member of the daisy family *Compositae* come from the resemblance of the seeds, which have two small "feelers" at one end, to ticks (Greek *koris*). At one time, mattresses were stuffed with tickseeds in the hope that they would repel pests. The

reached a stately 3 feet. Similar to both the wild plant and the perennial *C. montana*, its dark marine-blue flowers 1½ inches wide were singles—unusual, as most cultivars are doubles, with fluffy flowers that droop easily when wet. The 15-inch 'Polka Dot Mixed,' in the full range of cornflower colours, made a nice show between grey boulders as a rock-garden edging. Good companions for cornflowers include baby's breath, *Chrysanthemum segetum* and calendula (which can also be fall-sown).

In Europe, *C. cyanus* was once one of the most common weeds in grain-fields (hence the common name cornflower), where it grew in pretty abandon with corn poppies, larkspurs and chamomile. To use *C. cyanus* as an everlasting, cut the newly opened flower when the weather is dry and immediately hang it head down in a cool, dark, dry place.

C. americana, basket flower, is difficult to find in North American seed catalogues, yet it was one of the most appealing lesser-known flowers in our garden. It has strong, 3-to-5-foot stems supporting buds enclosed by bracts resembling woven baskets that open into glorious, 4-inch, rose-lilac flowers. The flowers, which

The slender, breezy, 2-to-3-foot stems of corn cockle, FACING PAGE, *support open flowers more than an inch wide, which are good for cutting. Seeds can be sown directly in a sunny spot in the garden in spring. The impressive basket flower,* ABOVE, *is a lesser-known relative of the cornflower whose huge 4-inch flowers bloom atop stems as tall as 5 feet. Cut in full bloom, the flowers make excellent everlastings.*

americana of America and *moschata* musk-scented.

Hollyhock
(*Alcea rosea, Althaea rosea*)

Most hollyhocks are biennial, producing rosettes of ground-hugging leaves the first year and flowers the next, but a few new cultivars such as 'Summer Carnival' and 'Pinafore' form towers of big, velvety flowers the first year from seed. The annual hollyhocks are less vulnerable than the biennials to rust, a fungus that produces ugly yellow spots and causes leaf drop. Now, we simply start new annual hollyhocks every year and avoid the disease.

Onc or two round, fat buds develop in each leaf axil and open into 5-inch single or double flowers—the former have five petals, while the latter resemble double poppies. The double flowers of 'Summer Carnival' are scarlet, rose, pink, yellow or white on narrow, pyramid-shaped plants 4 to 6 feet tall and about 2 feet wide. The wrinkled, rough-textured leaves are 10 inches wide on 8-inch petioles.

Sow the large, flat seeds directly outdoors, an eighth of an inch deep, about two weeks before the last spring frost. Seeds sprout in 10 days to two weeks. Seeds can also be sown in peat pots or peat pellets eight weeks early and planted outdoors around the last frost date—like all mallows, they do not transplant easily. Set plants 18 inches apart in rich, moist soil in sun or partial shade, and water frequently. Stake the hairy, silver stems when they are tall but before the flowers become massive and heavy. Remove the dead flower heads. Hollyhocks are good for the back of any border or in front of castor beans.

The names *alcea* and *althaea* come from the Greek *althaia* (to cure), because some species are medicinal. Hollyhocks belong to the mallow family *Malvaceae*. The name of the Chinese species *rosea* describes the rose colour of the flowers.

Larkspur
(*Consolida* spp, *Delphinium* spp)

Smaller versions of the towering perennial delphiniums that dominate

close at noon to resemble the flat tips of paintbrushes, are loved by bumblebees. When cut in full bloom, basket flowers make good everlastings.

C. moschata, sweet sultan, is another excellent cut flower that grows up to 2½ feet tall with double, sweetly scented, white, yellow, pink or purple flowers.

Scatter the seeds, and cover them with a quarter of an inch of soil as soon as the ground can be worked in spring. Centaureas do best in sun or partial shade, in good, well-drained, relatively dry soil. Thin to 8 to 12 inches apart, depending upon even-

tual height. The taller types may need staking; a loosely woven fence of sticks provides an attractive support. The downy covering on the flower stems and leaves of these plants is a perfect shelter for aphids, especially in the crevices of leaf joints, but the pests do not affect flowering for us. Insecticidal soap can be used for severe infestations. Dead-head regularly to encourage continued flowering.

The name *centaurea* commemorates the centaur, the Greek half-man, half-horse of mythology, who allegedly used the plant medicinally. *Cyanus* means blue, temperate gardens in June, larkspurs provide spikes or bushes of jay-blue, pink, lilac, purple or white flowers, whose upward-curving spur at the back of the corolla gives them their common name. Botanically, larkspurs are somewhat confusing, as they are listed under several different species names of *Consolida* (depending upon seed catalogue) as well as the genus *Delphinium*. In any case, the height of the bushy plants varies from 1 or 2 feet for the dwarf types to 3 feet for the standards. The bright green foliage is deeply cut. All are very hardy – their seeds are among those that self-sow abundantly or can be sown in fall or winter – and all are excellent long-lasting cut flowers.

In general, northerners wanting flowers the first year will do well to look among flower-seed packets for anything called a larkspur or any of the smaller delphiniums. Some perennial delphiniums – the dwarf 'Blue Butterfly,' for instance – will bloom profusely the first year from seed and may not survive the winter. We have had great success growing this cloud of brilliant blue flowers as a hardy annual, sown indoors in early March. It flowers by the end of June, continuing for several weeks on a dense bush about 18 inches tall. 'Connecticut Yankees' also blooms the first year from seed, with lavender, blue, purple or white single flowers on 3-foot spikes. In November, we sowed two larkspurs, 'Rocket' and 'Blue Cloud,' directly in the garden with corn poppies and calendula, for a beautiful blue, red and gold combination the following summer.

Sow the small, dark seeds, lightly

covered, about eight weeks early. They will sprout in about three weeks. Seeds can also be sown directly outdoors as soon as the soil can be worked in spring. They require cool weather to get started and must be transplanted carefully, as they form a slender taproot. Choose a spot in fertile, well-drained soil in full sun or partial shade. Space 8 to 12 inches apart, depending upon eventual height. The taller types may need staking.

Consolida, a member of the buttercup family *Ranunculaceae*, is a Latin word meaning to make whole, either because of past medicinal use of the larkspurs, which are poisonous plants native to southern Europe, or because the petals are consolidated. *Delphinium* comes from the Greek *delphis* (a dolphin) because of some species' flower shape.

Lavatera, Rose Mallow
(*Lavatera trimestris*)

Lavatera, an elegant, easy flower, should be known and grown by more short-season gardeners. On a self-supporting shrub 2 to 4 feet high and almost as wide grow a profusion of cupped, hibiscuslike flowers 2½ to 3 inches wide with five silky, overlapping petals. There are white varieties – our favourites – as well as deep roses and light pinks, which

Although most species of hollyhock, FACING PAGE, are biennials, blooming the second year from seed, annual types such as 'Summer Carnival' and 'Pinafore' can bloom on stems as tall as 6 feet from an outdoor seeding in late spring. Sown in the same manner are larkspurs, LEFT, smaller versions of the towering delphiniums that grace perennial gardens. The seeds of lavatera, including those of the cultivar 'Mont Blanc,' ABOVE, are best sown in the warm soil of early summer.

59

have darker veins and change in colour as they age. (Despite its name, 'Silver Cup' is pink; for white, look for 'Mont Blanc.') The leathery leaves are smaller versions of hollyhock leaves, and the stems are hairy. Lavatera makes a beautiful cut flower; snip entire branches covered with blooms. In the garden, the pink and white cultivars are good companions and can be nicely combined with snow-on-the-mountain and planted in front of cosmos and hollyhocks.

There are several additional tall mallows, usually listed under hibiscus by better seed catalogues. For instance, the sunset hibiscus (*Abelmoschus manihot*) produces 6-inch, maroon-eyed, yellow flowers on 5-foot stems. Another mallow, anoda, is a 3-to-4-foot shrubby plant with lavender or white blooms.

It is easiest to sow the large seeds of all mallows directly outdoors after the last spring frost, one-eighth of an inch deep and 4 inches apart. Seeds will sprout in a week or two. When the weather warms, plants grow quickly, provided the soil is rich and watered frequently. Thin to stand 18 inches apart. Sown outdoors on May 15, our lavatera was in flower by August 4. For earlier flowers, sow the seeds in peat pots four to six weeks before the last frost in a warm place indoors, setting the frost-tender annuals outdoors after danger of frost is past. Our anoda seeds sown March 25 sprouted March 30, and plants bloomed June 11.

Both lavatera and anoda are members of the mallow family *Malvaceae*. Lavatera is named for J.R. Lavater, a doctor and naturalist of 16th-century Switzerland. The name of the species *trimestris*, which is native to Portugal and the Mediterranean, refers to a three-month flowering period. The name anoda comes from the Greek *a* (without) and *noda* (a node) because the plant lacks stem nodes.

Malope
(*Malope trifida*)

All of the mallows are fast-growing in warm soil and attractive in bloom, but malope is one of the nicest, with a late-summer crop of intricately constructed, royal purple, 2½-inch flowers on long, individual stems.

Each of the five petals narrows at the base to leave spaces through which one can see a star of the green calyx, resembling a cathedral rose window. Red-, pink- and white-flowering types are also available. The central stem, about 3 feet tall, has alternating branches and a slender growth habit like the related hollyhock and lavatera. The toothed leaves are deep green and heart-shaped. Accompany malope with lavatera 'Mont Blanc' and ornamental cotton at the front of a border. Malope also makes an excellent cut flower and a good pot plant for the cool greenhouse if the gardener can control the aphids that inevitably appear.

Eight weeks before the last frost, chill the seeds in their packets in the refrigerator for a few days before sowing them, barely covered, in peat pots. Leave pots in a warm place. After the last frost, transplant malope outdoors, a foot apart, in a sunny spot with good soil. The seedlings will grow slowly until the weather warms, but then they make up for lost time. Seeds can also be sown directly in the garden about two weeks before the last frost.

Malope, a member of the mallow family *Malvaceae*, takes its name from the Greek word for a similar plant. *Trifida* is a species from Spain and North Africa named for its three-lobed leaves.

Mexican Sunflower
(*Tithonia rotundifolia*)

These neon-orange daisies emulate the appearance and suggest the sound of trumpets. As an accent bush 5 to 7 feet tall, the Mexican sunflower is not easily surpassed except, perhaps, by mammoth sunflowers or castor beans. The individual, single, dahlialike flowers are as wide as 3½ inches, with a yellow half-globe disc at the centre. The intense colour of the petals is enhanced by their velvety, nonreflective texture. They attract hummingbirds, moths, wasps, bumblebees and butterflies, especially monarchs. The flaring, hollow stems are velvety, the leaves long and hairy.

We were captivated by Mexican sunflower grown both on its own as a tall accent—it is decorative from its tip to the ground—and in masses at the back of the border, planted just a foot apart to form a shrubby hedge. Unlike the brash red of celosia, the bright orange of Mexican sunflower harmonizes beautifully with dark green foliage and orange-red, yellow or blue flowers. There are smaller versions and also yellows. Tithonia makes a nice cut flower and should be dead-headed to keep flowers coming until frost. The seed heads, too, are attractive and spiky like globe thistles.

Sow three seeds per peat pot, and thin to the strongest seedling. Start indoors about six weeks before the last frost. Sprouting takes a week or two, and flowers appear as soon as 10 weeks after sowing. After frost, plant 2 feet apart in deep, rich soil in sun. Provide manure tea occasionally. In exposed places, staking is important, as the wind will twist it; the rootball seems far too small to support such a heavy plant.

Mexican sunflower, a native of Mexico and Central America, is a member of the daisy family *Composi-*

Lavatera 'Silver Cup,' which blooms clear pink despite its name, produces a shrubby plant as tall as 4 feet, ABOVE. *The big, bushy Mexican sunflower grows 5 to 7 feet tall in good soil in sun and dominates its part of the garden with wide leaves, velvety stems and trumpet flowers of yellow or the more common brilliant orange, as in the cultivar 'Torch,'* FACING PAGE.

tae and takes its genus name from the legendary Tithonus, whom the goddess Aurora turned into a grasshopper. *Rotundifolia* means round-leaved.

Nicotiana
(*Nicotiana* spp)

The common garden types of nicotiana, or flowering tobacco, are described in chapter nine, but some taller types deserve separate mention. *N. sylvestris* can grow 5½ feet tall. Its typical nicotiana flowers are borne in ghostly white sprays, each flower extending 4 inches and culminating in an inch-wide, five-petalled star. Hundreds of aphids are trapped on the sticky surface of the leaves and fleshy stems. *N. sylvestris* is an arresting plant for the back of a border, where it will create a dense wall if planted 12 to 18 inches apart. The sprigs of brown seedpods are decorative additions to everlasting bouquets. Our *N. sylvestris* seeds were sown on March 25. They sprouted April 1, and plants bloomed July 26, when they were 5 feet tall.

Also tall and scentless is *N. alata* 'Lime Green,' which grows about 3 feet tall and 18 inches wide, with very pale, greenish yellow flowers that provide a beautiful transition between such brightly coloured flowers as poppies, larkspur and amaranth. Of all the nicotianas, this is the only one we have found to be bothered by Colorado potato beetles, which can be hand-picked. Our 'Lime Green' plants started indoors on May 4 were in flower by July 5.

Sprinkle the black, dustlike seeds on the soil surface of individual peat pots or six-packs about eight weeks early indoors. Seeds sprout in about a week. When seedlings show their second leaves, thin to the strongest per pot. Harden off before planting in sun or partial shade after the last spring frost.

Nicotiana, a member of the nightshade family *Solanaceae*, honours Jean Nicot, who introduced tobacco to France. The species name of *N. sylvestris*, a native of Argentina, means "of the woods." *Alata*, referring to the petioles, means winged.

Poppy
(*Papaver* spp)

With their clear, almost translucent colours and big, fragile petals on gently windblown stems, poppies are the perfect symbol for the ephemeral northern summer. Each flower lasts only a day or two, but if poppies are dead-headed, new flowers will continue to appear for weeks, making them some of the best of all hardy annuals. There are many annual types, but all bear fat, nodding buds, one per stem, that open into four-petalled, bowl-shaped flowers in all warm shades from orange, yellow and cream to pink, rose, purple and red; some are bicoloured, and some are blotched with black or white marks. At the centre of the single or double flowers is a circular fringe of stamens surrounding a barrel-like pistil that becomes a decorative seedpod when dry. The slender stalks contain milky sap. Leaves, formed in a rosette at the plant base and sparingly up the stems, vary from plate- to spoon-shaped to deeply indented. Gardeners are not alone in enjoying these elegant flowers: "Bee and bumblebee playgrounds," say our notes.

Corn poppies (*P. rhoeas*), native to Europe and Asia, have 2-to-3-foot hairy stems bearing bright red, 2-inch flowers with a black patch on the base of each petal. Shirley poppies are a strain of *P. rhoeas* that appear in many solid shades of white, pink and rose as well as bicolours, both single and double. The petal margins are often picotee. The cultivar 'Mother of Pearl' has unusual greyish-toned flowers. The Flanders poppy, among the smallest of the annuals, is considered a corn poppy or a member of the species *P. commutatum*. Its 18-inch stems support single, crimson flowers up to 2 inches wide, whose inner wheel of black splashes surrounds a tuft of greenish black stamens. The hairy, deeply lobed leaves are dark green with a bluish tint. Our corn poppies, sown in spring, finished blooming in early August.

Opium poppies (*P. somniferum*), native to Europe and western Asia, are wonderful, stately ornamentals as tall as 4 feet. They volunteer in rural gardens in our area, sending forth their 4-inch, pink, rose, purple and white flowers with no human inter-

Nicotiana sylvestris, FACING PAGE, TOP, *bears its ghostly white sprays of scented flowers atop self-supporting stems that are sometimes taller than 5 feet. Less enduring are the flowers of Shirley poppies,* FACING PAGE, BOTTOM, *which have fernlike leaves, and opium, or peony, poppies,* LEFT, *which have broad, greyish leaves. Both types of poppies lose their petals in only a day or two, but new flowers will appear for weeks if spent ones are removed.*

ference except for ruthless thinning. The blue-grey, clasping leaves resemble those of cabbage. The cultivar 'Danebrog' has curiously fringed petals. The peony poppy, which is the double type, is sometimes given the variety name *paeoniaeflorum*. The seeds of all types of *P. somniferum* are excellent for use in cooking, and the large seedpods left after the flowers are blown are good material for dried flower arrangements.

As poppies do not transplant well, they do best when the seeds are scattered directly in the garden. They can be sown in fall, perhaps with another hardy annual such as larkspur; they can be sprinkled on the last snow, in which case they will settle into the soil as the snow melts; or you can sow them in spring as soon as the soil can be worked. Lightly rake the soil in a sunny spot, scatter the seed, and top it with a fine layer of soil or peat moss so that the tiny seeds do not dry out. If you sow the seeds among tulips, the fading tulip leaves will be hidden among bushy poppy seedlings. By the end of June, the early-summer garden shines with the reds of corn poppies, the oranges of California poppies (which are described in chapter seven) and the pastels of Shirley poppies. Continue dead-heading, but let some seedpods ripen for use in dried flower arrangements and for seeds to plant in the next year's garden.

Poppies are members of the poppy family *Papaveraceae*. The genus name is the Latin word for poppy.

Spider Flower
(*Cleome hasslerana, C. spinosa*)

Botanical allegiances may be noticed by only the most scientifically minded gardener, yet some plants are so different from everything else that it is obvious they are unrelated to their bedding companions. The spider flower, the only member of the caper family to appear in the annual garden, is such a plant. Some people can't get enough of it, while others find even one is too many. In any case, the spider flower is certainly eye-catching, with woody stems as tall as 4 feet, stiff, erect branches, decorative divided foliage and big white, pink, purple or rose flowers. The buds are a darker shade than the open flowers, which are composed of three or four paddle-shaped petals, a curiously stalked ovary like a hotdog on a stick and five or six threadlike 3-inch stamens, all of which create an airy, spidery appearance. Stems and shoots terminate in flat rosettes of three to eight leaves, a little like the fingers of a spread hand. There are also small leaves growing directly from the central stem. The slightly sticky, thorny plant, which forms a shrub if well grown, is unpleasant to the touch. As the spiny leaves are similar in shape to those of castor beans, spider

flower is a good foreground companion for the taller plant. Spider flower is also an attractive cut flower.

Sow the seeds directly in the garden on the soil surface after the last frost, or for earlier flowers, sow eight weeks ahead indoors. Germination may improve if seeds are first chilled in the refrigerator for a week. Sprouting takes a week or two. After the last frost, plant in good soil in a sheltered, sunny place 2 to 3 feet apart – 18 inches for a dense hedge. In a windy position, the plant will need staking. Spider flower will often self-sow.

Spider flower is a member of the caper family *Capparidaceae*. *Cleome* was the name used by Greek philosopher Theophrastus for a different plant and adopted by Linnaeus for this genus. The species, *hasslerana*, a Caribbean native, is named for Emile Hassler.

Sunflower
(*Helianthus annuus*)

A delightful story has it that sunflowers were introduced into Nebraska by an advance party of Mormons, who scattered the big seeds as they crossed the plains on their way from persecution in Missouri. When the wagon trains of women and children followed the next summer, they had a sunflower trail to follow. One can easily imagine how welcome those big,

golden faces must have looked to the weary pioneers.

Even in a small garden, sunflowers are friendly and inviting. Children love them because they grow so big so quickly. At the edge of a vegetable garden or at the back of a flower border, sunflowers can provide a taller focal point than any other annual – 'Giant Mammoth,' the type usually grown for seeds, grows as tall as 10 feet, its huge, foot-wide discs surrounded by 3-inch rays. Unfortunately, sunflowers are also inviting to squirrels, chipmunks and birds, who may pick out the seeds before the gardener has a chance. Cover the flower heads with paper bags or cheesecloth to protect them, but grow a hedge of sunflowers unveiled if you wish to attract and treat the local wildlife.

Not all sunflowers are skyscrapers. Many, such as 'Zebulon,' 'Sunspot' and 'Teddy Bear,' grow only 2 feet or a little taller, but they provide better material for cut-flower arrangements. Grow the smaller sunflowers in masses with calendula, salvia and heliotrope. Middle-sized sunflowers include 'Ultra,' 6 feet tall, which has no main stem but forms a bush of 2-to-4-inch flowers. It makes a good summer hedge in the manner of the annual sunflower's perennial relative, Jerusalem artichoke. 'Colour Fashion' is 5½ feet tall and 3 or 4 feet wide. It branches like a tree and produces bouquets of 5-inch, yellow, bronze,

red, purple or bicoloured flowers that are excellent companions for Mexican sunflower.

Sow the big seeds directly outdoors half an inch deep and 3 inches apart in spring, thinning to 1 or 2 feet apart, depending upon plant height. The seedlings transplant quite well. Choose a place with fertile, well-drained soil in sun. Our 'Sunspot' seeds sown on May 30 sprouted June 4, and plants bloomed August 10. Sunflowers tolerate high heat and drought, but they will die after the first fall frost.

If you want to eat the seeds, harvest the head when the back of the flower is brown and no traces of green remain. Hang the seed head in a warm, airy place to cure. When the back is papery, brush off the seeds and store them in airtight containers to eat raw or roasted. (While you do this, the sunflower head is a good place to observe phyllotaxis, also seen on pineapples and pinecones, in which opposing spirals are arranged with mathematical precision.) Sunflower seeds are very high in protein and calories – they are now the world's second largest oil crop.

The genus name of this member of the daisy family *Compositae* comes from the Greek *helios* (sun) and *anthos* (flower). In western North America, sunflowers have been found in archaeological remains from as early as 3000 B.C. The species name *annuus* designates an annual.

Some types of sunflowers grown for their edible seeds may attain a height of 10 feet or more, making them the tallest annuals in the garden aside from vines. Sunflowers are cultivated as a field crop, FACING PAGE, *but they also make good focal points at the back of flower or vegetable beds. Some smaller-flowered types, such as 'Colour Fashion,'* ABOVE, *are better for cutting.*

Above All
Climbers, trailers and other vines

Most vines, such as bottle gourds,
FACING PAGE, *are tropical plants
whose remarkable stems transport
water and nutrients to great heights,
twining around their supports or
holding on securely by various other
means such as tendrils or hooks.
Annual vines accomplish enormous
growth in one season, provided they are
protected from wind, heavy traffic and
full days of hot sun.*

The tallest elements in the annual garden, the vines are almost all exotic southerners, lovers of heat and humidity that are content to stay a brief summer in a northern garden but no longer. Adrian Forsyth, a biologist who specializes in rainforest ecology, points out that vines are truly tropical plants—there are very few species native to temperate places such as Canada or the northern United States. For vines, then, one must turn almost exclusively to annuals or to tender perennials treated as annuals.

In part, vines are tropical because freezing and thawing will distort the circulation of fluids in them just as it will destroy pipes full of water. In fact, the plumbing of vines is little short of miraculous. Some species are able to pump water hundreds of feet from the forest floor to the treetops. As any gardener knows, the problem of kinks and knots impeding the flow of water is formidable even in a 20-foot garden hose.

An equally remarkable achievement of vines is their ability to climb in the first place. Charles Darwin showed that some vines climb by coiling; there is a neat mathematical relationship between the width of the stem and the diameter of the support it ascends. He also found that many plants climb with the aid of sucker-like thickenings that lodge in cracks like a mountain climber's pitons. Other vines have tendrils that develop into hooks like cat claws. Most, like sweet peas, have tendrils that wrap round and round, producing a springy yet strong attachment that can give and take as the plant is buffeted by the wind. Other vines are not able climbers but flourish when allowed to spread out across the top of some supporting structure.

Wooden lattices, sold in lumber stores, are attractive supports for most climbing vines. Alternatively, some vines are suited to strings strung from the gutter to the railing of a porch or to a tepee or lean-to arrangement fashioned from strings or slender stakes. Vines can also climb trees, just as they do in the Tropics, but the gardener should avoid a heavy overhead canopy. If there is a long section of unbranched trunk, tie around it a piece of netting

that the first tendrils can grasp. Hedges can support vines too. All vines except trailers have this in common: they shoot up with a remarkable spurt of growth when given something to hold onto. Contact with an ascending structure seems to stimulate the hormones that control growth and elongation.

Keep the Tropics in mind when planting and caring for the tender vines. In order to give them an early and uninterrupted start, sow the seeds indoors in peat pots, thinning to one seedling per 3-inch pot. When the fine roots penetrate the peat pot, set it into a larger one filled with rich soil. In the larger pot, insert a small stake for the plant to climb. When the weather is warm, either carefully remove the larger pot or set the whole thing directly into the ground. Most tropical vines are tender perennials, so they can be cut back in fall before frost and the pot can be brought indoors. Cut off roots that extend out from the pot bottom.

Because vines are rapid growers, they need good soil and a fairly

constant supply of water. Their love of growing in the dappled light of the rainforest makes them best suited to a position that offers some shade during the day. They suffer, too, in strong winds. Also, do not plant a vine in the rain shadow at the base of a wall or high fence. Plant it at least a foot from the wall unless you are prepared to water even after a rain.

Balloon Vine
(*Cardiospermum halicacabum*)

Too little known and thus a wonderful horticultural curiosity is the balloon vine, so named because of buoyant green seedpods, up to 1½ inches across, that bob up and down in the wind. These spritely three-sided balloons swell giddily from white, wasp-pollinated flowers that are tiny by contrast—only about a quarter of an inch wide. Because the balloons are light green, they stand out like misplaced children's toys against the dark green, deeply notched, semigloss leaves, which look like airier versions of those of the unrelated cherry tomatoes. The plant's fine tendrils will hook onto any support, forming a fine screen, but the square stems are rather stiff and occasionally need to be tied to the trellis. The plant reaches about 10 feet tall by summer's end.

About three weeks before the last frost, file the hard seeds lightly, soak them overnight, then sow them half an inch deep in individual peat pots kept at a fairly cool 50 to 60 degrees F. Germination usually takes a little longer than a week. Plant outdoors after the last frost. Give this vine deep, rich soil and some shade, and perhaps place it in company with Chilean glory flower and cardinal climber. A tender perennial, the balloon vine will overwinter in frost-free gardens or greenhouses.

The genus name of this tropical American member of the soapberry family *Sapindaceae* comes from a distinctive heart-shaped (Greek *kardia*) white spot on the seed (*spermum*). The species name is the Latin term for bladderwort.

Black-Eyed Susan Vine
(*Thunbergia alata*)

From a distance, this appealing flower looks like a daisy too neatly fashioned to be true. But a closer look reveals that the centre is not a cluster of tiny flowers (like that of the true black-eyed Susan and other daisies) but rather the entrance to a trumpet; in fact, this inch-wide mimic is a member of the acanthus family. The most commonly grown type is orange with a deep-purple-to-black centre, although there are white and yellow varieties as well, and some lack the dark centre entirely. Most thunbergias have no scent, but the cultivar 'Angel Wings' has lightly fragrant, snow-white blooms. All flower best during cool summers and in fall. The soft, hairy leaves are arrowhead-shaped, slightly toothed and borne in opposite pairs along the slender stem. Two green sepals, which make a tent over the developing buds, later hold the mature flowers and then enclose the ripening fruit. Only when the four hard seeds are ripe do the sepals wither.

About eight weeks before the last frost, sow the rough seeds a quarter

Vines are most valued in the garden for their ability to cover screens and trellises. This porch, FACING PAGE, is sheltered by Japanese hop, best known for its wide leaves. On the other hand, the black-eyed Susan vine, LEFT, appreciated for its bright flowers, makes a colourful trailing plant over a wall or from a hanging basket. The balloon vine, ABOVE, is an unusual but easily grown vine whose small, white flowers yield seedpods more than an inch across.

of an inch deep in a warm place indoors. Alternatively, wait until after the last spring frost to sow the seeds directly outdoors in a partly shaded place in fertile, well-drained soil by a trellis, strings or wires. Germination is often slow and can take as long as three weeks. Allow about a foot between plants. Do not let the soil dry out.

Because the black-eyed Susan vine seldom exceeds 6 feet in length, it has become a popular trailer in window boxes and containers, although it can also be allowed to twine its stems up a trellis or over rocks or tree stumps, as it does lavishly in the Tropics. As it is a tender perennial, a black-eyed Susan vine growing in a container can be brought indoors before the first fall frost and moved back out the following summer. Pay attention, in both moves, to hardening off, described in chapter two.

Carl Peter Thunberg, who introduced many plants to Europe, is honoured in the genus name of this African native. The species name,

which means winged, suggests the shape of the leafstalks, or petioles.

Bottle Gourd
(*Lagenaria* spp)

This is one of the few annual vines whose fruit is useful. The beige gourds, borne in all shapes and sizes, depending upon the cultivar chosen, can be used for everything from bowls and birdhouses to flasks (*lagenos* in Greek). Traditionally, bottle gourds have been used as containers by aboriginal people throughout the Old World Tropics. Some varieties have thin necks more than a yard long and have been used by Amazonian Indians for flutes or dipping spoons. The round types have served as bodies for such Eastern stringed instruments as the sitar.

The fruits may be harvested when young and then dried indoors, or they can be dried directly on the plant and brought indoors before they are damaged by frost. Wash them in a solution of household bleach, then carve or cut as you like. We often

drill a single hole into the swollen part of a gourd for an excellent birdhouse. If the hole is enlarged in fall, the container does double duty as a winter bird feeder. Bottle gourds are extremely durable if they are properly dried at the outset.

To grow gourds for eating, allow flowering to continue unimpaired and pick the gourds when they are hand-sized. These young, tender gourds are a common vegetable in India and China, and one can buy them in late summer in the Chinese markets of many large cities. The flesh is white, firm and bland—ideal for stir-frying and sautéing in Asian cooking.

Bottle gourds bear white flowers that open in the evening and emit a light perfume. The velvety leaves smell unpleasant when rubbed.

Sow the seeds indoors four weeks before the last frost, half an inch deep in 3-inch peat pots, thinning to one seedling per pot. When nights are warm, transplant carefully because, like all members of the cucumber family, lagenaria gourds have roots that are easily damaged. For flowers but not gourds, sow the seeds directly outdoors, 2 feet apart, in early June or well after the last frost. With steady warmth and moisture and a little shade in the hottest weather, the vines will create a dense, green curtain of foliage within a couple of weeks. We have seen bottle gourds planted as late as June literally surge over a trellis, growing 6 inches a day and finally reaching a length of 34 feet, completely covering the trellis and reaching up another storey to the peak of the house by August.

Lagenaria gourds, members of the gourd family *Cucurbitaceae*, are native to the Old World Tropics.

Canary Creeper
(*Tropaeolum peregrinum, T. canariense*)

Canary describes the colour of this flower, and some gardeners have likened the appearance of the two upper petals—frayed on the edges and held upright—to birds' wings. The flowers also resemble little orchids, but they are, in fact, nasturtiums and, like other nasturtiums, are among the best cut flowers in the

annual garden. Take lengths of the side shoots with plenty of buds, and enjoy them for weeks in a vase. From buds that resemble unicorn heads, the inch-long flowers develop in rows, each on the end of its own slender stalk.

Even without flowers, however, this South American vine would be decorative, with its distinctive five-fingered, muted green leaves with pronounced veins. The plant produces a mass effect, reaching about 8 feet tall and entirely filling in the spaces between strings suspended a few inches apart. The fleshy leaf-stalks are touch-sensitive (thigmo-tropic is the botanical term), and so will curl around any object they touch. Unfortunately, the cabbage butterfly loves this plant more than any other in the annual garden. Hand-pick the caterpillars or spray them with *Bacillus thuringiensis* or rotenone.

The canary creeper has large seeds that germinate in one or two weeks in warm, moist soil. Plant them indoors half an inch deep in individual peat pots four to six weeks before the last frost date or directly outdoors when the nights are warm, in a lightly shaded place next to a fence or trellis. Thin to a foot apart.

The attractive white flowers of the bottle gourd vine, FACING PAGE, *will produce useful gourds if the season is sufficiently long and hot. The canary creeper,* ABOVE, *is a nasturtium relative whose intricate flowers are excellent for cutting.*

heit degrees of frost finally killed it. Cuttings taken early in the season should root in moist sand or vermiculite in a warm place.

The name of this South American native comes from the Greek *ekkremes* (hanging) and *karpos* (fruit), referring to the pods produced after the flowers. *Scaber* means rough.

Creeping Gloxinia
(*Asarina* spp, *Maurandya* spp)

Overhead gloxinias are the apparent reward of this lovely vine — apparent because this is not a gloxinia at all but a member of the same family as snapdragons (*asarina* means snapdragon in Spanish). In its native Mexico, the vine can reach incredible heights, spreading over shrubs, trees and, of course, haciendas. In the north, it is more modest, its twisting leaf stems taking it to about 6 to 8 feet before frost. The dense screen of soft green leaves is brightened by 2-to-3-inch bells: rose-pink in the case of *A. erubescens* (*M. erubescens*) — the species name means blushing — deep indigo for the more elegant *A. scandens* (*M. lophospermum*). *A. barclaiana* (*M. barclaiana*) has rose or purple flowers.

Sow the small, winged seeds indoors on the soil surface three or four months before the last spring frost. Germination takes two weeks or more, given constant moisture and room temperature, and growth proceeds slowly at first — the plants seem to just sit there, waiting for conditions to improve. Transplant the seedlings carefully into individual peat pots when small. Plants can grow indoors on stakes or on a trellis in a warm greenhouse — the species is actually a tender perennial that will survive winter indoors as a beautiful trailing houseplant. Or as soon as all danger of frost is past, plants can be grown along a lattice or arbour. Asarina begins flowering in about 18 weeks from seed and continues profusely until fall, provided dead flowers and seedpods are removed. The flowers are favoured by hummingbirds, giving it its Central American name, hummingbird vine.

These are Mexican members of the figwort family *Scrophulariaceae*. *Maurandya* takes its name from

Avoid too-rich soil, or you will get only leaves and no flowers. Cascading from a windowsill in partnership with the common nasturtium, described below, or with the related *T. speciosum*, the flame flower, which produces small nasturtiums of brilliant scarlet, the canary creeper creates an arresting picture.

The vine can be multiplied from cuttings taken during the summer and rooted in wet vermiculite. Even cuttings made just before the first fall frost will become nice trailing plants for hanging pots indoors.

Chilean Glory Flower
(*Eccremocarpus scaber*)

Like inch-long goldfish with their mouths open, the fascinating little flowers of *E. scaber* grow in orange clusters — schools, as it were — of as many as 15 at the stem tips. There are also pink-, scarlet-, crimson- and yellow-flowering forms. All make excellent, long-lasting cut flowers, but they are elegant outdoors as well. The soft green, slightly hairy, deeply

notched leaves, which create a light screen, resemble those of cherry tomatoes, although this is not a tomato relative but a member of the family *Bignoniaceae*, which is composed entirely of New World evergreen tendril climbers. The vines hold on to their trellis with tendrils bearing tiny hooks at the ends.

Like the seeds of the purple bell vine, those of eccremocarpus resemble fried eggs, with raised black centres surrounded by a papery rim. Sown on the soil surface of individual peat pots two to three months early and kept warm and moist under plastic and out of bright light, they will sprout in 11 days to three weeks. Thin to the strongest seedling. Plants set outdoors into well-manured soil after the last frost will be about 6 feet high by early August. They need strong trellis support in partial shade or full sun and should be protected from wind and traffic. Actually a fairly tender perennial that will survive mild winters, an eccremocarpus vine grew and flowered for us until November 4, when 5 Fahren-

Catherine Maurandy, wife of
Professor A.J. Maurandy.

Cup-and-Saucer Vine
(Cobaea scandens)

The flowers of the cup-and-saucer
vine are remarkable for their
transformations – fit subjects for
time-lapse photography. Five-
cornered, inch-wide, papery buds
hanging from purple stems open to
become green saucers that release
green, 2-inch-long cups within. Then
comes an even more interesting
development: within about two days,
the colour of the entire tea set
changes from pale green to striped
lilac to deep violet. While the flower
is pale lilac, five curved, pollen-
rimmed croquet mallets hide an
undeveloped pistil within the flower
trumpet. When the pollen has gone,
the stamens shrivel and a stigma is
exposed for pollination within the
flower, which is now purple. Holes
that may appear at the end of the
corolla during this process are the
traces of piercing insect tongues that
have stolen the nectar without pollinating this changeable flower. The
fruit left in the wake of all this
activity is a dark green melon similar
to passion fruit.

So determined and capable is this
lovely climber that it needs no trellis
or strings – only a textured wall. Its
strong tendrils can creep between
boards, hold onto shingles and grasp
rough concrete. In fact, the beautiful
network the plant forms naturally on
a wall is more attractive without the
distraction of string or trellis.

Cobaea needs a long season of
almost four months from seed to
flower, and germination may take
longer than two weeks, so it is best
started indoors around early March.
Plant the flat seeds edgewise (to shed
excess moisture), two or three seeds
to a 3-inch peat pot, thinning to one
seedling per pot. After the last spring
frost, transplant outdoors a foot or
two apart. The plant can reach more
than 20 feet in a summer and will
become woody and survive for years
where winters are frost-free. In fact,
even in cold places, if the vines are
planted by the house, as ours were,
they will survive light frosts and
continue blooming well into fall.

This member of the phlox family
Polemoniaceae is named for Bernard
Cobo, a Spanish Jesuit missionary in
Mexico, where cobaea grows wild.
Scandens means climbing.

Cypress Vine
(Quamoclit spp, Ipomoea quamoclit)

Many of the less well known vines
have smaller, more delicate flowers
than the more popular choices. The
quamoclits, for instance, are finely
textured vines that produce small
morning glories of rare beauty – tiny
flowers whose long funnels widen
into flaring hoop skirts. The throat is

The cup-and-saucer vine, FACING
PAGE, *is a determined climber whose
2-inch flowers change colour from
green to purple as they age. The lovely
creeping gloxinia,* ABOVE, *is a
snapdragon relative whose tender vines
are brightened by 2-to-3-inch bells that
attract hummingbirds. This vine can
make a lovely houseplant.*

pale, the anthers within tipped with white pollen. Like all the morning glories, the flowers last only a day, though they are borne in such profusion that no day goes by without blooms. The leaves of the cardinal climber (*Q. x sloteri*) are finely lobed and fernlike, while those of the cypress vine (*Q. pennata*) are needle-like, suggesting the common name. Visitors remarked more than once that the green cypress vines with their bright red flowers resembled Christmas decorations.

Soak the hard, black seeds in warm water overnight before sowing directly outdoors in a sunny, sheltered spot after all frost danger. Or for an early start, sow the seeds four weeks before the last frost, three to a peat pot, thinning to the strongest seedling. Seeds should sprout in about a week. Plant or thin to 8 to 12 inches apart in rich soil high in organic matter. Feed the vines with manure tea every week throughout the summer.

Given good conditions and a trellis or strings – both species twine around their supports – the quamoclits can reach 3 feet tall within six weeks and 25 feet by the end of the summer. Early flower buds should be removed to allow the vines to strengthen. The plants form an airy screen, clinging very close to the support. They are attractive on twine on a porch or balcony or climbing the wires of a hanging basket. If they are

planted in partnership, the mix of white and red together looks beautiful on a trellis against the blue sky or against a white wall, where the filigree of the fine leaves can be best appreciated. Also, quamoclits fit well into window boxes, especially when paired with other vines such as thunbergia, and they will cascade over a wall or spread over the ground, low shrubs and rocks. They are killed by the slightest frost.

The quamoclits are members of the morning glory family *Convolvulaceae* and are native to tropical South America. *Quamoclit* is the Mexican name. There are many additional species, including *Q. coccinea*, which has very finely cut foliage, *Q. pennata alba* with white flowers and *I. lobata* or *Q. lobata*, which produces sprays of red-and-gold flowers.

Hyacinth Bean
(*Dolichos lablab*)

Like the nasturtium, this vine is entirely edible – seeds, young leaves and flowers – though it is an acquired taste in the north. The J.L. Hudson catalogue comments that the seeds contain 20 to 28 percent protein and that in the Old World Tropics, the vines are "eagerly grazed by cattle, sheep, pigs and goats." For human consumption, the mature beans can be either sprouted like mung beans or boiled and the water discarded. The immature pods can be served

like snap beans, and the young leaves and flowers can be steamed or boiled like spinach.

More important for annual flower gardeners, however, are the spikes of fragrant, wisterialike, three-quarter-inch flowers, which may be white or, more interesting, purple. The vine, a tender perennial, is very decorative when covered with both flowers and flat, papery pods that resemble snow peas left too long on the stem. The light green, broadly oval, 3-to-6-inch leaves are soft on the upper surface and roughly veined underneath. Nonclimbing forms of hyacinth bean are also available.

Soak the seeds overnight before planting them a foot apart in a warm, sunny, sheltered place in any garden soil. Plant them directly where they will grow, as they do not transplant well. The vines may grow to 10 or 20 feet tall in a season, twining on a trellis, strings or a tepee of slender poles. They form a dense screen and can even act as a garden windbreak.

A tropical, probably Old World member of the pea family *Leguminosae*, *D. lablab* takes its genus name from an ancient Greek word for bean. *Lablab* is an Indian name for the plant.

Japanese Hop
(*Humulus japonicus, H. scandens*)

Like the hardy perennial hop *H. lupulus*, which bears green fruits that impart their characteristic flavour to beer, the tender Oriental version is also a rapidly growing vine with male and female flowers on separate plants. *H. japonicus* provides a good screen for sunny porches, walls and trellises: "ideal for camouflaging eyesores quickly," says the Thompson & Morgan catalogue. The vine is best known, then, not for its inconsequential flowers but for the deeply indented May-green, maplelike leaves as wide as 6 to 8 inches. They are soft in appearance but disconcertingly rough to the touch because their surfaces bear tiny hooks that cling to any surface. If you don't want scratched hands, provide supports for Japanese hops before the plants are large.

Nick the seeds and soak them overnight before sowing in groups of three, 18 inches apart, directly in the garden after the last spring frost. Sow along a fence or trellis or in front of vertical strings. Or sow seeds in individual peat pots indoors four to six weeks early in a warm place, as germination may take as long as a month. Given warm weather, sun and plenty of water, the plant grows 15 feet or more during the summer by twining itself around slender vertical supports. There is a variegated form marbled with white. Sweet peas planted with hops will give the latter a touch of colour – and scent as well, if you choose the right sweet peas.

As members of the hemp family *Cannabaceae*, all hops received some attention during the 1970s as potential grafting partners for marijuana, with the aim of using the hop to disguise the distinctive appearance of its more notorious cousin. The genus name *Humulus* is derived from the Old German name of the plant. *Japonicus* means of Japan, *scandens* climbing.

Moonflower
(Ipomoea alba, Calonyction aculeatum)

In apparent imitation of the moon itself, the white (*alba*), 6-inch platters of the moonflower unfold rapidly just before sunset. They then yield a

Small morning glories of rare beauty decorate the cardinal climber, FACING PAGE, *which twines about slender supports to heights of 25 feet or more in a summer but which is also well suited to hanging baskets and trailing over walls. The hyacinth bean, another twiner, is best known for its edible pods,* LEFT, *although its young leaves and flowers are palatable too.*

75

sweet scent meant to attract moths, whose amazingly long unfurling tongues can reach the nectar at the base of the 4-inch trumpets. By noon the next day, last night's blooms have wilted, a reminder of things past.

The large seeds have a hard coating, so they benefit from soaking overnight in lukewarm water or from scraping with a file or sharp knife. Sow the seeds an inch deep indoors in peat pots three or four months before the last frost date. Thin to a foot apart. Moonflowers do best in spare soil that is a little on the dry side, and they should be given some shade and a trellis or strings to support the heavy twining plants. Like the morning glory, this South American native forms a dense screen of heart-shaped foliage about 15 feet high.

The morning glory family *Convolvulaceae* includes several beautiful annual climbers, including cypress vine and cardinal climber, listed above, moonflower and its day-blooming counterpart, the morning glory itself, below. All are tender natives of tropical America. *Calonyction* is a Greek term that refers to the beauty of the flower and its night-blooming habit.

Morning Glory
(*Ipomoea* spp)

Morning glories are the most popular tender vines among northerners – and justifiably so. When grown from seeds sown directly in the garden, their growth is fast and dependable – as long as the weather stays frost-free – and they yield showy flowers as wide as 5 inches in clear shades of white through pink, red, violet, purple and blue. Gertrude Jekyll wrote that "there is no lovelier or purer blue" than that of newly opened 'Heavenly Blue.' The five-petalled trumpet flowers open in the early morning and bloom for only a day, an ephemerality typical of the genus – this is the diurnal version of the moonflower – but they continue to open for most of the summer. We have had old trellises so covered in heavy morning glory vines, with their big, heart-shaped leaves, that the entire contraption has fallen over in midsummer; the flowers, however, continued to bloom as the vines trailed out over the lawn. The gorgeous cultivar 'Blue Star' looks best planted where it can ramble over a stump or rocks.

After the last frost, soak the big seeds overnight, or file them lightly to penetrate the seed coat, then sow them directly outdoors half an inch deep and 2 inches apart, the easiest method. For earlier flowers, sow the seeds indoors a month early, half an inch deep, two seeds to a peat pot. Keep the pots in a warm place until the seeds germinate in about a week, and thin to the better plant by pinching the other off at soil level. A week or two after the last spring frost, plant the peat pots 8 to 12 inches apart in full sun near stakes or strings. Planted in peat pots and transplanted outdoors, ours did not look well for weeks, but by mid-July, lush, green leaves and climbing stems pushed through the eavestroughs, buds swelling.

Give the vines a feeding of manure tea about every two weeks.

While standard morning glories will reach 8 to 10 feet, there are dwarf cultivars suitable for hanging baskets and window boxes. There is also a wide variety of species, such as the purple-flowered *I. purpurea* and the pink *I. brasiliensis*. New ones will continue to show up in the seed catalogues.

Ipomoea is a member of the family *Convolvulaceae*, which takes its name from the Latin *convolva* (to twine around). *Ipomoea* takes its name from the Greek *ips* (a tendril) and *homoios* (similar) because of the shape of the tendrils.

Nasturtium
(*Tropaeolum majus*)

The nasturtium has become a bit of a *cause célèbre* in the past few years because it is edible. Most diners would want only a few of its peppery, lily-padlike leaves in salads or stir-fry dishes, but the seedpods can be pickled like capers, and the bright, five-petalled flowers, which bloom in shades from white through soft peach and yellow to deep reds and oranges, are lovely accents on summer foods. Nasturtiums are also excellent cut flowers. A few in a vase, a few in the salad.

Most of the nasturtiums offered by seed catalogues have stems only a

foot or two long. The shorter ones grow into shrubby border plants, while the slightly longer ones can spread over the top of a wall or cascade from a hanging planter. The foot-long 'Alaska Mixed' has variegated green-and-white foliage.

Only a few nasturtiums are climbers, and they grow about 6 feet tall, held up by long, twining petioles that grow from fleshy stems. Although these nasturtiums will fill the spaces between vertical wires or strings a foot apart to form a solid screen of foliage, they are weak climbers that twist and clamber about their supports, so some training and tying and

Their fragile blooms appear for only a day apiece, but morning glories, FACING PAGE, *are such fast-growing, floriferous climbers that they are the most popular annual vines in northern gardens. Also well known, nasturtiums,* ABOVE, *are available in two versions: compact plants that do not climb at all and somewhat weak climbers,* LEFT, *that can be coaxed to climb along strings beautifully.*

vidual containers about three weeks later. Set plants outdoors a foot apart near a trellis in half-shade after the last spring frost. Blooming begins about four months after sowing.

Beth Chatto, who owns a famous garden and nursery in England, calls this native of southern Mexico "the most exciting" of the tender climbers she has recently discovered. "It would be the loveliest idea to train this plant up and around a pillar in a conservatory, since once started, it flowers under cover long into the winter months."

Rhodochiton is a Mexican member of the figwort family *Scrophulariaceae*. The species name *atrosanguineum* means dark blood-red, referring to the flower colour. *Volubile* means twining.

horizontal wires may be necessary. On all nasturtiums, the almost round leaves, which feel like rubber, are up to 5 inches wide and have spiderweb-like veins of lighter green. The 2½-inch-long, sweetly scented flowers end in a spur. Their two upper petals are often strikingly marked with darker colour.

Sow the seeds a quarter of an inch deep indoors in March or, better, outdoors about two weeks before the last frost. This is an easy plant to grow directly from seed in a warm, sunny part of the garden in soil that is not too rich. Water during dry weather. A native of the Andes, it blooms best in cool weather.

To enjoy the plant's flowing shape indoors for weeks, take good-sized stems a foot or longer, with plenty of buds that will open one by one. Roots will also likely grow underwater. Plant the cuttings, shortened to 4 to 6 inches, for winter plants on a sunny windowsill.

Tropaeolum is the only genus in the family *Tropaeolaceae*. The common name nasturtium derives from the Latin *nasus tortus*, a twisted nose, because of the scent of the foliage of the true *Nasturtium*, watercress.

Purple Bell Vine
(*Rhodochiton atrosanguineum*, *R. volubile*)

Like the cup-and-saucer vine, the purple bell vine is full of surprises.

One might think that the little purple lampshades—inspiration for the genus name from the Greek *rhodon* (red) and *chiton* (cloak)—are the flowers of this plant, but after a week or two, a dark, slightly hairy horse's nose descends from the centre and opens to become a bell within a bell, somewhat in the manner of a fuchsia. Each of these lovely double bells hangs on its own thread from the main stem, waving in even the slightest breeze. The small leaves are heart-shaped with a slightly serrated edge and form a light screen as the plant climbs by twining around slender supports such as vertical lengths of twine.

In March or early April, cover the seeds lightly, and keep the containers warm and moist under plastic. The seeds should sprout in two weeks and can be transplanted into indi-

Sweet Pea
(*Lathyrus odoratus*)

The cool, wet weather of England so favours the growth of sweet peas that British seed companies sell 30 or 40 different cultivars of this sentimental favourite, the equivalent of petunias in the United States. What makes sweet peas so beloved is not only their delicious fragrance, which can perfume an entire garden or living room, but also their subtle blooms, as beautiful outdoors as in a vase, and their tolerance of cool soil and light frost. These are among the few cultivated vines that are not tropical but hail from the Mediterranean area. In fact, the first sweet peas were sent to Britain from Italy in 1699. A great deal of selection has been done since then to develop cultivars of this tendril climber that have larger blooms and longer stems for cutting, though many of the breeders' creations have lost their scent entirely. (Other dubious achievements are dwarf cultivars that lack tendrils and thus trail on the ground.) Appropriately, the sweet pea was the subject of Gregor Mendel's 19th-century experiments with plant genetics.

Because of the enthusiasm for sweet peas among some of the world's most opinionated (and expert) gardeners, a mystique has developed about the right way to grow prize flowers. Some gardeners keep their

secrets; others admit that they soak seeds overnight before sowing, they sow them three weeks early indoors in individual peat pots, or they go out the previous fall to prepare a special bed for them, a trench of well-rotted manure 2 feet deep and 2 feet wide.

For the rest of us, however, sweet peas will yield perfectly good flowers in any deep, moist, fertile soil. They can be directly sown half an inch deep and 2 inches apart as soon as the soil can be worked in spring, close to a fence, a trellis or strings about 6 feet long. Germination takes approximately a week. Thin them to stand 4 inches apart. Pinching the plants back when they are about 6 inches tall will encourage branching, and mulching will keep the roots cool and prolong flowering, as the plants suffer in hot weather. Particularly heat-resistant is the 'Old Spice Mixture,' a scented, older variety whose flowers bloom in shades of white, cream, pink, rose, scarlet, lavender and purple. Cutting flowers for bouquets encourages continued flowering.

Sweet peas are members of the pea family *Leguminosae. Lathyrus* derives from the Greek word for pea. *Odoratus* means scented.

Little lampshades are produced in profusion on the purple bell vine, here trailing from a hanging basket, FACING PAGE, TOP, *although it will also twine about slender supports such as string. Sweet peas, such as 'Old Spice Mixture,'* FACING PAGE, BOTTOM, *are unusually cold-hardy annual vines that thrive in the moist soil of early spring and produce some of the most sweetly perfumed bouquets in the garden,* ABOVE.

Supporting Players
Decorative leaves and grasses

Some annuals are best known not for their flowers but for their leaves. If variegated and brightly coloured, as is this carpet of coleus, foliage plants assume centre stage, while in other cases, they may become quiet understudies to the more flamboyant flowers, both in the garden and in the vase.

Compared with the vibrant annual flowers, foliage is modest and common and likely to be overlooked. But this quiet understudy to the more flamboyant flowers is as essential to the plant as to the garden as a whole. For the plant, leaves perform the near miracle of using sunlight to turn water and soil nutrients into carbohydrates, the biochemical process known as photosynthesis. For the garden, leaves provide a constant bass line to the floral treble. They fill in and flesh out, offering places of rest for the eye.

If that eye is observant, it will notice that leaves are as varied from plant to plant as the individual players in a Shakespearean crowd scene. Foliage may assume centre stage when it becomes particularly showy or large, but any leaves, however modest, have a role to play. They may be all manner of shades of green, from greyish to blue and emerald. Some leaves are yellow, white, pink, orange or reddish, the result of a lack of chlorophyll, the green pigment, or of the presence of other substances such as the red anthocyanins or the orange carotenes. Leaves may be reedlike or flat, tiny and stiff or big and floppy. In the sensitive hand, they reveal themselves as soft, bristled, hairy, smooth, leathery or papery.

Some of the most eye-catching leaves are patterned. This phenomenon, called variegation, which embraces all the speckling, splashing, striping and blotching one is likely to see on plants, arises from variable amounts of pigment in different layers of plant tissue. Variegation occurs naturally—in polka-dot plants and coleus, for instance—but it is more common in domesticated plants; a splotchy sport, relatively lacking in chlorophyll, is a poor competitor in the sun, which limits its ability to survive in the wild. But gardeners willing to cosset it and perhaps take cuttings can keep it thriving for generations. Variegated plants tend to be smaller and slower-growing than their all-green relatives, and they may be more difficult to propagate. (Some splotching can also occur as a result of disease or nutrient deficiencies. In this case, it is usually progressive and the plant may die.)

Besides the plants listed in the following pages, a few are mentioned elsewhere in the book that are at least as well known for their foliage as their flowers. Among vines are the Japanese hop (*Humulus japonicus variegatus*) and the morning glory 'Roman Candy.' New Guinea impatiens has flashy leaves in a bright yellow-green colour scheme, while the leaves of variegated geraniums bear zoned circles of yellow, white and green, sometimes with splashes of pink. The variegated nasturtium 'Alaska Mixed' has white-and-green variegated foliage, as do prickly poppies. The bluish green leaves of cardoon have an eye-calming effect. Joseph's coat is a tall, beautifully coloured amaranth, and the castor bean produces some of the biggest leaves in the garden. Some marigolds, such as *Tagetes filifolia*, are best known for their foliage. The feathery cladanthus is similar in effect. A plant that resembles dusty miller, although it is quite unrelated, is pheasant's eye (*Adonis aestivalis*), whose lacy foliage is its most impressive feature. Another dusty miller look-alike is the desert marigold (*Baileya multiradiata*), which bears white, woolly foliage and solitary, bright yellow daisies on 18-inch stems. The Tahoka daisy, too, has beautiful greyish leaves.

Foliage plants can be used in many ways. Some can act as spacers between showier flowers, some, such as castor beans, are sufficiently interesting to be used on their own as specimen plants, and some, like kochia and basil, can become temporary hedges. Foliage plants can find their way into pots and hanging baskets and may, when cut, complement vases of cut flowers. Snow-on-the-mountain and tricolour sage are particularly lovely for cutting. A bonus is that all this refreshing colour and texture comes with relatively little work; no dead-heading is necessary, as it is with flowers.

The garden that includes foliage plants is evidence of a gardener who looks for subtlety, texture and tone, not just high drama. As Philip Miller wrote centuries ago in *The Art of Gardening*, "What can be more pleasant than to have Groves or Walks (when the Flowers that are but for a Day are retired) apparalled with Gilded party-colour Garments, some with yellow and Green, others with white and Green, emulating the two royal Metals that by the Gilders hand adorn the Palaces of Princes?"

Basil
(Ocimum basilicum)

Among the annual herbs comely enough for the flower garden is basil, a foliage plant with a savoury fragrance that wafts forth whenever the plant is touched or watered. There are many cultivars, from the tall 'Let-

tuce Leaf' to the spicy sacred basil to burgundy, wavy-edged 'Purple Ruffles.' But none is more ornamental than 'Spicy Globe,' which forms a ball of tight little leaves so neat it might have been fashioned by a topiarist. At 6 to 8 inches high and about a foot across, 'Spicy Globe' is suitable for the front of a bed, where it alternates nicely with small marigolds or mounds of purple-flowered exacum. Other varieties may reach as tall as 2 feet. Plant them between bright flowers of a similar height for beauty in the garden and a supply of leaves for pesto and tomato salad all summer.

Sow the small, ash-black seeds di-rectly in the garden as soon as nights are warm, or start them four weeks ahead, covering them lightly. They will sprout in as few as three days. Set the young plants outdoors about 8 inches apart after the last frost. In midsummer, the flower spikes will appear and should be pinched off, as they are unattractive and will inhibit the growth of foliage. The plants are very frost-tender, but leaves can be dried or frozen for use in cooking.

Basil's membership in the mint family *Labiatae* is apparent in its square stems. *Ocimum* is derived from a Greek word meaning an aro-matic herb. The species name, *basili-*

Many edible foliage plants can move gracefully from the vegetable or herb garden to the flower garden. These include parsley, dill, Swiss chard, borage, globe artichoke and cardoon, FACING PAGE, *and one of the most decorative, purple basil,* ABOVE. *Its pungently scented leaves, easy to grow from seed sown directly in early summer, are both pretty in the garden and useful in the kitchen.*

83

cum, means royal or princely. Basil is a native of Southeast Asia.

Beefsteak Plant
(*Perilla frutescens, P. nankinensis*)

Another herb, perilla is a favourite of Oriental cooks, and indeed, the unusual scent of the foliage, redolent of lemon and chervil, brings to mind Chinese and Southeast Asian cuisine. The flavour "may be addictive," says the perilla seed packet from Tsang

and Ma, an Oriental seed house in California, which also points out that the green-leaved form is milder and better for cooking and garnishing, while the purple-leaved type, known in North America as the beefsteak plant, is "slightly more pungent" and preferred by the Chinese for medicines, pickling and flavouring seafoods. In the West, the flavour of beefsteak plant is an acquired taste. Both types grow about 2½ feet tall and 2 feet wide. From strong, self-supporting stems grow large leaves with such a high sheen that they look as though they have been rubbed with salad oil. Flower spikes should be pinched out when they appear.

The seeds will germinate better if placed in the refrigerator for a week before sowing. Sprinkle them on the surface of a well-moistened planting medium – they need light to germinate – six to eight weeks early indoors, or sow them directly in the garden after all frost danger. The seeds will sprout in about 15 days at room temperature. Plant or thin to about a foot apart. Situate the beef-

steak plant near pink, rose or red annuals of similar height. Perilla tolerates heat but needs frequent watering. It will usually self-sow if allowed to flower and set seed.

A member of the mint family *Labiatae, Perilla* is an Asian native. The origin of its genus name is obscure, but *frutescens* means shrubby or bushy, while *nankinensis* suggests a Chinese origin.

Blood-Leaf
(*Iresine lindenii*)

This Ecuadoran member of the amaranth family virtually glows in the garden. Although its flowers are insignificant, the leathery, heart-shaped leaves make up for the floral modesty with bright crimson veins on a chocolate or purple background. Blood-leaf is a fairly small plant, a foot tall or somewhat larger, depending upon growing conditions. The stems are fleshy and self-supporting.

It is propagated by cuttings only, which means that gardeners who want it must first find a specimen from a friend, florist or greenhouse. Thereafter, keep a plant indoors through the winter for cuttings to start early the next spring. Plant in good soil, in partial to full shade, and pinch out the centre to encourage bushiness. Blood-leaf makes a pleasant companion for woodruff, variegated geraniums, the polka-dot plant and ferns.

The genus name, which derives from the Greek word *eiros* (wool), suggests the texture of the flowers. The species name honours Jean Jules Linden, a 19th-century Belgian horticulturist.

Burning Bush
(Kochia scoparia childsii)

Burning bush, like many of the annual favourites in public parks, has been badly handled in the past. Too often, it has been used as a specimen plant, a role it is simply not sufficiently interesting to fill. In the background, however, its dense, oval growth of small, slender, lettuce-green leaves on a closely branching, self-supporting bush can nicely occupy spaces between more vertical plants. It also makes an adequate temporary hedge 2 or 3 feet tall.

Sow the seeds on the soil surface, either directly outdoors when nights are warm or indoors two or three weeks before the last spring frost, setting the pots under plastic in a warm place. Our seeds sprouted in just a day, a sure sign of something with a weedy tendency; indeed, burning bush has become a serious pest on prairie grainfields. Burning bush is one of the few annuals that tolerate saline soil, and it will also endure full sun and drought, though it does best in a fertile place and will not survive soggy ground.

Set the plants outdoors 2 feet apart after frost danger. Burning bush assumes a neat oval shape in the early summer. By early August, our largest was 4 feet tall and 2 feet wide. A couple of weeks later, thousands of tiny green flowers appeared and the plant widened at the top. It then turned magenta-pink—the "burning bush" phase. Stems cut at this time will retain a pinkish colour when dried indoors. Otherwise, the plant soon becomes brown.

Kochia, which is found throughout Eurasia, is a member of the goosefoot family *Chenopodiaceae* and is named for Wilhelm Daniel Josef Koch, a 19th-century German botanist. *Scoparia* means broomlike.

Coleus
(Coleus spp and hybrids)

Coleus is sold in six-packs by practically every garden supplier in spring. What makes this Javanese native so popular is its astonishing range of brilliant colours, patterns and leaf shapes on neat, well-mannered plants. Green, brown, yellow,

Beefsteak plant, FACING PAGE, TOP, *is a favourite herb of Oriental cooks, but its shiny leaves also attractively fill spaces in the flower garden. It can be grown easily from seed, while the leathery blood-leaf,* FACING PAGE, BOTTOM, *best known as a houseplant, must be propagated from cuttings. Easiest of all is burning bush,* LEFT, *whose domed masses of small green leaves turn magenta in fall. It grows rapidly from seed and self-sows prolifically.*

pink, scarlet and maroon appear, often all in the same flat, as seeds are frequently sold in mixtures. Even on a single plant, every leaf is different. Leaves may be unremarkable in shape, they may be as indented as oak leaves, or they may have incredibly ornate, frilled edges. Most plants grow as tall as 18 inches and about as wide, but there are dwarf versions, such as the Fairway series, which are 8 to 10 inches tall, perfect for window boxes.

Gardeners who want an ongoing supply usually take cuttings between April and August and root them over the winter for spring plants or during summer for an increased supply. In the meantime, the rooted cuttings will make nice houseplants. If you want a new type, however, coleus is slow but easy from seeds sown, barely covered, in a cool place (60 to 70 degrees F), where they will germinate in two to three weeks. After the last spring frost, set plants a foot apart in half-shade. Less light will diminish the foliage colours, while too much sun will cause wilting. Pinch back the plant tips at least once to encourage bushiness, and remove the flower spikes that appear in late summer, as the tiny, blue flowers are not spectacular and detract from the effect of the leaves.

Coleus is a good candidate for pot culture, in which case it should be watered daily. Pots can be moved around the garden and brought in-doors before the first frost, as the plant is very frost-tender. Plant coleus alone or with plain green or white neighbours, as its colouring is too bright and complex for competition with most annuals.

Coleus, a member of the mint family *Labiatae*, receives its name from the Greek word *koleos* (a sheath) because of the form of the stamens.

Dusty Miller, Silverdust
(Several genera and species)

More than one plant is known as dusty miller—a good example of the sort of confusion that Linnaeus sought to alleviate with his system of binomial nomenclature. Common names persist for good reason, however; it is far easier to say "dusty miller" than "*Pyrethrum ptarmiciflorum*"—and more descriptive too, for anyone but a Latin scholar. The whitish foliage of the two types signals a plant that endures hot, dry conditions. In fact, dusty miller is a very low-maintenance plant, demanding nothing but admiration once it is set in place, provided only that the soil is not too wet.

Usually seen in North America is *Centaurea cineraria* (also known as *Senecio cineraria*, *S. maritima*, *S. bicolor* or *C. maritima*), which has rounded, indented leaves covered with dense, woolly, white hairs that suggest the genus name *Centaurea*, from a word meaning old man. This plant, actually a tender shrub, may grow into neat mounds as tall as 2 feet. The cultivar 'Silver Dust' is a dwarf that reaches about 8 inches in height. Lightly cover the beige seeds indoors 8 to 10 weeks before the last frost or outdoors in early spring. Germination takes four days to three weeks. Plant or thin to 8 inches apart in the garden .

Chrysanthemum ptarmiciflorum (also known as *Pyrethrum ptarmiciflorum*) is similar, although the leaves have a feathery appearance and a spicy fragrance—a common name is silver feather. (The species name suggests a similarity to the northern

grouse, the ptarmigan, which has white feathers in winter.) This dusty miller grows about a foot tall and almost 18 inches wide. Lightly cover the slim, beige seeds indoors about eight weeks before the last frost. Cover the pot with plastic, and set it in a warm place. Our seeds sprouted in just five days, although sprouting times of up to six weeks have been recorded. Plant outdoors a foot apart after the last spring frost.

In the garden, all dusty millers act as low-growing transitions between bright colours. They can be placed here and there between foliage plants or low flowers of almost any bright or pastel colour. All do well in sun in good, well-drained soil and are suitable for the front of a border. Pinch out any flowers that appear.

Dusty millers are members of the daisy family *Compositae*.

Grasses
(Several genera and species)

Although ornamental grasses have been used in flower gardens for cen-

turies, the entire plant family has only recently recovered, in North America, from the notoriety of quack grass, crabgrass and other invasive members. Some of the less pushy grasses, however, are simply beautiful, and their place in the garden can be filled by nothing else. They whisper in the wind, arch heavily when drenched with rain or dew and lend the flowerbed a graceful, almost vertical element that may be taller than the gardener. Grasses can become dense hedges along stone walls or fences and can take a place within the flower border, overhang a pond and spill over a bank. All do best in full sun, though they will tolerate shade. Leave them in place to highlight the winter landscape with blades of yellow and brown. All grasses should be planted in clumps of at least three.

Among the best of the annuals are several members of the genus *Pennisetum*, the feathertop or fountain grasses (the genus name is Greek for feather). *P. ruppelianum*, which Chiltern Seeds judges "splendid,"

Coleus, FACING PAGE, TOP, *does double duty as a houseplant in winter and a garden occupant in summer. Cuttings can be taken from houseplants, or new plants can be grown from seeds. Dusty miller,* FACING PAGE, BOTTOM, *grown here with ageratum, lends an unusual greyish accent to any sunny spot, while ornamental grasses, including squirrel-tail grass,* ABOVE, *produce seed heads that respond to the slightest breath of wind.*

grows 2 to 6 feet tall, depending largely upon soil conditions, and consists of a loosely gathered circle of slim, wiry, coarse-feeling, pleated leaves that surrounds nodding purplish bottlebrushes 1½ inches wide and as long as a foot. Sown indoors in early April, ours were in flower by mid-August. *P. alopecuroides*, more than 3 feet tall, produces a soft, upright, purplish white, 6-inch-long squirrel tail that turns red in autumn. The leaves are just under half an inch wide but as long as 2 feet. Dwarf feathertop, *P. villosum*, reaches 2 to 3 feet and has graceful, white, 5-inch flower spikes tinged with purple. Start the tiny pennisetum seeds indoors in a warm place about seven weeks before the last spring frost, covering the seeds to their depth. Sprouting takes three days to a week. Transplant into individual pots about four weeks later, and plant outdoors in fertile soil in sun after the last frost.

Quaking grass (*Briza maxima*) grows up to 2 feet tall and bears nodding heads of oval, white spikes, which suit dried arrangements. A small version is *B. minor*. Both are native to Mediterranean regions. Scaly, elongated spikelets half an inch to an inch long, like fat green, white or bronze arrowheads, dangle from threads connected to a slightly bent stem. The faintest breeze causes movement through the grass. Sow the seeds generously in patches of warm soil, thinning to 2 to 4 inches apart. The plants are very fast to flower. Cut the stems early for dried flower arrangements, as the panicles will fall off after the grass matures.

Squirrel-tail grass or foxtail barley (*Hordeum jubatum*)—the genus name means barley, the species, maned or crested—yields a long, barleylike brush of pinkish green. It grows only about 2 feet tall and the same width and thus can take its place in a container or bed of medium-sized flowers. Sow the spiny, beige seeds indoors eight weeks before the last spring frost, covering them lightly and placing the pots under plastic in a warm spot. Seeds should sprout in about two weeks. Set plants outdoors, a foot apart, about two weeks before the last frost. This grass turns brown in the heat of summer.

Panicum violaceum resembles a miniature broomcorn whose 6-inch, drooping, purplish flower heads sparkle in the morning dew. The plant forms a sturdy bush 3 feet tall and wide. The stems are grey and hairy, the leaves an inch wide. Sow the sesamelike seeds one-eighth of an inch deep indoors in warm soil. Seeds sprout in about a week. Set outdoors 18 inches apart after frost.

Everything about bunny tails (*Lagurus ovatus*), from the Greek *lagos* (rabbit) and *oura* (tail), is soft, a delight for children. Sow the small, slippery, beige seeds, lightly covered, 2 inches apart in a warm, sunny spot near the front of a border around the last frost date. Sprouting takes about a week. Thin to 6 inches apart. The leaves are covered with downy hairs, and the seed heads, which appear up to four months after sowing, are remarkably like whitish, slender rabbit tails about 2 inches long and just as soft. They rise to about 20 inches, the foliage just over a foot. This grass is extremely frost-hardy, but as it resembles a clump of any weedy grass when the seed heads are gone, this attribute has less value than it would in a more decorative species.

Phalaris canariensis, whose name

suggests its use for birdseed, grows as tall as 4 feet. Clumps tend to fall over and turn brown early in the season, but seed heads can be harvested for use in dried flower arrangements. Sow seeds about four weeks early, lightly covered, placing the pots under plastic in a warm place. Sprouting occurs in four days to a week. Transplant outdoors two weeks later. Seed heads begin to appear about three months after sowing.

Love grass (*Eragrostis elegans*) produces a small, 1-to-2-foot-high cloud of airy inflorescences. This native of Brazil is easily lost except among small flowers. Sow the tiny seeds indoors on the soil surface eight weeks before the last spring frost. Sprouting takes about two weeks. Transplant outdoors, about 6 inches apart, around the last frost date. Seeds sown in late March will produce tassels in early June.

Believed to be one of the oldest grasses in cultivation, Job's tears (*Coix lacryma-jobi*) yields hard-shelled, pearl-grey, cherry-pit-sized seeds that have been used for rosaries, bead curtains and necklaces, as well as in a sweet-tasting flour. The stems have some value, too, in flower arrangements. In the garden, this grass's decorative merits are limited because the 2-foot-tall plant has a tough-stemmed, cornlike appearance (although Gertrude Jekyll once planted yet another grass, sweet corn, as a decorative

plant at the back of a border). The seeds must be started early in order for the grass to mature by September. Nick them or soak them overnight before sowing them indoors eight weeks before the last frost, setting plants outdoors 2 feet apart after frost. Rich, wet soil is essential—by a stream or close to a dripping tap. Harvest the stems before the seeds turn brown, stand them upright in a vase to dry, and strip the leaves if you want only the seed pearls. When drying, the grass emits a pleasant smell like that of sliced apples.

All grasses are members of the family *Gramineae*.

Jewels of Opar
(*Talinum crassifolium*)

The glory of this plant is not its collection of "jewels"—the tiny, bright pink flowers—but its shiny, deep green foliage, which grows in a neat, circular clump almost 2 feet wide. The laurel-like leaves, as long as 8 inches, form one of the most attractive plain green ground covers in the annual garden. Opar's jewels, on the other hand, are almost inconspicuous blooms on airy panicles held 2 to 3 feet above the leaves. They last a day apiece but are borne in rapid succession, leaving behind branches studded with shiny, round seed balls that are lovely in dried flower arrangements.

Lightly bury the seeds eight weeks

The nodding heads of quaking grass, FACING PAGE, *are attractive additions to dried and cut-flower arrangements. Another foliage plant, also suitable for hot, dry places, is jewels of Opar,* ABOVE, *a relative of portulaca, whose shiny leaves, as long as 8 inches, are far showier than its tiny pink flowers borne above the foliage on the tips of wiry stems. It often self-sows.*

very hardy and showy until late fall.

Sow the seeds one-quarter of an inch deep and half an inch apart in late June in six-packs or flats. Transplant into a sunny place in the garden, a foot apart, when they are 3 inches tall, augmenting the soil with plenty of organic matter. Ornamental cabbage and kale will still be colourful when the snow flies. Infestations of cabbage worms can be treated with *Bacillus thuringiensis* or rotenone.

Ornamental cabbage and kale are members of the mustard family *Cruciferae*. *Brassica* is the Latin name for cabbage; *oleracea* means potherb, a garden herb used in cooking. The species is native to western Europe and the Mediterranean area.

Ornamental Cotton
(*Gossypium* spp)

The cottons are truly beautiful plants in every way. Even northerners, whose season allows them foliage and flowers but not the characteristic puffs of white cotton, are only slightly disadvantaged. This self-supporting shrub, whose stem eventually becomes quite woody at the base, produces shiny, dark green, leathery leaves that have a very decorative, three-pointed, maplelike shape and are held out horizontally from the stem. Even more decorative are the large, hazelnutlike buds, which grow on their own short stems held close to the main stem. These buds are triangular envelopes formed of three sepals, which can be described as fringed, feathered or flame-shaped. After two weeks, the buds open to reveal lovely, 2½-inch-long flowers of densely overlapping petals that never open past a fluted shape. Finally, the petals drop to expose a button within a calyx shell. This button, the cotton boll, gradually expands to fill the calyx and, if the season is sufficiently long, finally bursts to expose the cotton fibres.

G. herbaceum – the species name means herbaceous – one of the species that yields the cotton of commerce, opens creamy yellow flowers which age to a flushed pink and then burgundy on plants 3 to 4 feet tall and almost as wide. *G. hirsutum* – meaning hairy – is a smaller (to 2 feet) Central American native with

before the last frost in a warm place, covering pots with plastic. Sprouting takes about a week; the cotyledons, or seedling leaves, are pinkish, resembling their relatives the portulacas. After the last spring frost, set plants outdoors a foot apart in full sun or partial shade. Blooming begins about four months after seeding. The flower stems reach more than 2 feet tall by early August and are replaced by tiny, rock-hard seeds. The plant is very frost-tender. Jewels of Opar is an excellent temporary ground cover for a dry slope. It also makes a beautiful houseplant.

Talinum, a name whose derivation is obscure, is a member of the purslane family *Portulacaceae*, native to the southern United States and Central America. The species name means thick-leaved.

Ornamental Cabbage
(*Brassica oleracea*)

An amazing variety of differently shaped plants falls within the species *B. oleracea*, including broccoli, cabbage, cauliflower, kale, Brussels sprouts and kohlrabi. In fact, this is the same plant in various disguises. Perhaps none of its manifestations are more unusual than the brightly coloured, so-called "flowering" versions of cabbage and kale. (In fact, the true flowers normally appear only in the second season.) The cabbage has rounded leaves, and the en-

tire plant forms a large, open rosette; ornamental kale is similar but has frilly foliage. Both plants may be pale pink, bright rose or white, always in combination with green. Like all cabbages and kale, they are edible, but their leaves tend to be tough – they have been selected for appearance, not dinner.

Much must be said for anything that continues to be colourful long after the first frost and whose colours brighten as temperatures fall, but placement of these obliging plants in the garden is important. A row by a garden fence, along a driveway or by a house wall or two or three plants in a low container will be more satisfying than attempts to marry these rugged peasant beauties with more refined members of the flower garden. They are attractive, however, in front of artichokes, which are also

creamy white flowers. Sturt's desert rose (*G. sturtianum*), a native of Australia, has bright rose-pink flowers.

The teardrop-shaped cotton seeds are almost as big as corn kernels. Sow them a quarter of an inch deep two months early in 3-inch peat pots; they resent transplanting. Sprouting occurs in less than a week. Alternatively, seeds can be sown directly in warm soil after the last frost. Give the plants rich, moist soil in full sun, setting them a foot apart. Buds form about three months after sowing. Good companions include nicotiana and ornamental grasses. Ornamental cotton is killed by the first frost.

All cottons are members of the mallow family *Malvaceae*. The genus name comes from the Latin word for the plant, *gossypion*.

Our Lady's Thistle
(*Silybum marianum*)

Never did a plant seem to have a greater identity crisis than Our Lady's, or St. Mary's, thistle. Thinking of the shy virgin, we set a seedling into a bed surrounded with ornamental grasses and prickly poppies, and it grew and grew until everything around it had been moved farther away or right out of the bed.

Far more decorative than its kitchen cousin, ornamental cabbage, FACING PAGE, BOTTOM, *offers the same attributes of extreme cold-hardiness and edibility. Another comely relative of a useful plant is ornamental cotton,* FACING PAGE, TOP, *whose beautiful mallow flowers appear infrequently enough that the plant is better known for its lobed foliage. Much larger leaves, some 2 feet long, grow on Our Lady's thistle,* ABOVE, *shown here with the yellow-flowered tripteris.*

Attempts to weed around it brought painful contact with the long thorns. This gorgeous thistle stopped spreading at 4 feet wide in early August, when it began to produce mace-like seed heads. It was eventually armed with a full 20 of them a foot or two above the foliage.

In fact, the common name comes not from an identity problem but from the legend that drops of Mary's milk first made the white markings on the leaves. The plant is medicinal, as were virtually all of the dozens of plants associated with Mary during the Middle Ages. This thistle was considered useful in easing lactation. The roots, flower heads and leaves are all edible.

Growing from a single, huge rosette, the rippled leaves reach up to 2 feet long and have irregular white markings along all the veins. There are sharp needles along the leaf edges, up the stems and on the flower heads, which bloom purple but soon turn brown, later releasing fluffy white seeds that will self-sow in most gardens. Only in late August do the huge, spiny, glossy, marbled leaves begin to fade and shrink. The seed heads, however, are still decorative when the snow falls.

Sow the large, black seeds four weeks before the last frost, covered to their depth. In cool indoor conditions, they will sprout in about a week. Transplant a week later into individual containers, and set outdoors 2 feet apart around the last frost date. The plant tolerates neglect and poor soil but will be larger and more lush in a weeded, fertile spot. Because it is very spiny, it needs a place where it will not be ac-

cidentally brushed. This is an ideal specimen plant for a back corner in sun or shade.

The plant, a native of the Mediterranean area, is a member of the daisy family *Compositae*. *Silybon* is the Greek name for a similar plant, while *marianum* refers to the Virgin Mary.

Polka-Dot Plant
(*Hypoestes phyllostachya,
H. sanguinolenta*)

Rivalling coleus for its fresh, patterned foliage, the polka-dot plant looks as if it has been carefully devised, leaf by leaf, by a very patient artist. Also known as baby's tears or freckleface, it has pinkish spots that shine on leaves whose background colour is medium green when young, darker when old. The largest of the heart-shaped, smooth, papery leaves are about 4 inches long and 2 inches wide. Deep violet, half-inch flowers are sprinkled over the 18-inch plant by late autumn.

As the seeds germinate easily and the polka dots are visible on the second leaves, this endearing plant is a good gardening project for children. Start seeds indoors, lightly covered, three months before the last frost. Sprouting will occur in about a week in a warm place. When plants are about 10 inches tall, pinch out the centre to encourage bushiness. Set plants 6 inches to a foot apart in moist soil in half-day to daylong shade. Move pots indoors before the first fall frost. The polka-dot plant is a lover of shade and so does well as a houseplant or in a shady place outdoors in a pot or at the edge of a flower border accompanying ferns.

Hypoestes is a member of the acanthus family native to Madagascar. The name comes from the Greek *hypo* (under) and *estia* (a house), referring to the bracts that cover the calyx. *Phyllostachya* means "with leafy spikes."

Snow-on-the-Mountain
(*Euphorbia marginata*)

One of our gardens' most impressive foliage plants was snow-on-the-mountain, in part because of its size—around 4 feet, depending mostly upon soil quality and planting

schedule—in part because of the refreshing green-and-white variegated leaves that develop late in the season. When young, the plant looks unpromising, like a milkweed with round, grey-green leaves and a fleshy stem. It needs no staking until early August, when it begins to branch and wind or rain may knock it down. Then small, white flowers and bracts narrowly edged with white appear at the stem tips. At the base of each petal is an olive-green half-bowl filled with nectar that attracts flies, wasps and bees.

Sow the sweet-pea-sized seeds indoors in mid-April, covered to their depth and kept warm and moist under plastic. Sprouts emerge in one to three weeks. After the last frost, move the young plants outdoors, and set them a foot apart in a sunny or partly shady place in fertile or sandy soil. Alternatively, seeds can be sown directly outdoors about two weeks before the last frost. Snow-on-the-mountain will often self-sow.

Grow snow-on-the-mountain as a specimen plant or in groups of three toward the back of the border. It is an excellent plant to mix with cutting flowers, both in the garden and in the vase. The white sap, however, which is as thick as Elmer's glue, can irritate skin or eyes and will turn the vase water milky.

The plant is a North American member of the spurge family *Euphorbiaceae*, named for Euphorbus, physician to Juba, the king of ancient Mauritania. *Marginata* describes the white outlines of the bracts.

Tricolour Sage
(*Salvia viridis, S. horminum*)

Although this plant is now commonly called clary sage, the true clary is a medicinal biennial (*S. sclarea*) and source of the beverage also called clary. *S. viridis*, a lovely hardy annual, does not deserve confusion with any of its cousins, so we prefer the name tricolour sage to describe a plant whose uppermost petal-like bracts are pink, violet, rose, blue or white, all with distinct, contrasting veins. Hairy stems dense with rough-feeling, greyish green leaves branch heavily and reach as tall as 2 feet in good soil, shorter in

poor. The plant creates a massed effect in the garden, filling in to the ground, so it can be positioned anywhere in midborder or left on its own. The small, purplish flowers are hidden in the leaf axils. The colourful spikes are excellent in flower arrangements, either fresh or dried.

Sow seeds indoors 10 weeks before the last frost, pressing them lightly onto the soil surface. Cover pots with clear plastic, and set them in a warm place. Sprouting takes a week or two. Set plants a foot apart in a sunny or partly shaded place after frost. Seeds can also be sown directly in the garden after the last spring frost. Water plants regularly during the hottest weather. Ornamental sage often self-sows, and plants can then be positioned in the garden where they are wanted. Good companions are cloud grass and squirrel-tail grass, which grow to about the same height.

All sages have the square stem characteristic of the mint family *Labiatae*. The name salvia, from the Latin *salvus* (safe), suggests the medicinal qualities of some family members. *S. viridis*, whose species name means green – the colour of the bracts of some plants – is a native of southern Europe.

A twinkle of bright light for a shady corner comes from the polka-dot plant, FACING PAGE, *a delight for children and an adaptable plant that can be moved indoors in fall. Tricolour sage,* ABOVE, *is a lovely, very frost-hardy annual, as tall as 2 feet, with petal-like bracts in pastel shades of pink, violet, blue or white. Excellent in fresh or dried arrangements, it often self-sows, and seedlings can be transplanted easily to new locations.*

Under the Sun

Flowers that flourish in bright light

Sunny gardens are suited to a wide range of annuals, including many members of the daisy family. The name, derived from "day's eye," suggests petals open to the sun, as seen in single flowers like those of many wild species. Double flowers, such as these marigolds and zinnias, have been fashioned by plant breeders to produce more than the usual number of petals.

The sun-loving annuals are a cheery lot. Their innocent and often brightly coloured faces will satisfy any gardener, and they bring a hidden bonus too: self-sufficiency. One way to avoid tedious watering chores in summer follows the principle of the best defence being a clever offence. Some plants simply require less water than others, a fact known and bemoaned by any gardener who has watched dandelions, chicory and hawkweed thrive, growing inches daily, while petunias and snapdragons wither and crackle. The plants that stay green have built-in drought- and heat-tolerance mechanisms that have developed over generations of adaptation to harsh, often semi-desert environments such as those in parts of Africa and the southern United States.

Many of the drought-tolerant plants are members of the daisy family *Compositae*, not only because it is the largest genus of flowering plants but also because its members— including dandelions, hawkweed and chicory—take to full sun, the "day's eye," hence the name daisy. (The name *Compositae*, incidentally, means that the plants have composite flowers—there are two types of flowers involved. Most have centres called discs, which consist of tiny, tubular flowers, each of which has both male and female parts, while the "petals" are properly called ray flowers, each of which has an ovary at its base.)

Many of these sun-loving composite flowers curl closed at night and in overcast weather to protect their pollen when rain might fall and pollinators are not on the wing. Although several of these daisies thrive indoors, they can be disappointing houseplants, as the flowers will stay closed if their situation is not sufficiently bright.

Plants that do well in sun and drought tend to have thicker leaves than those adapted to moisture and shade. Often, the sun lovers are quite hairy too—a self-shading mechanism —so that the foliage appears pale or greyish; the monarch of the veldt, for instance, is almost white with wool, while the silver coat of dusty miller, which protects the plant like the burnoose of a desert caravan driver, can

be scraped off with a fingernail to reveal the vulnerable green tissue underneath. Still other plants, like portulaca, have fleshy stems and leaves that store moisture against times of water shortage. Cool nights and hot days—semidesert weather—suit most of the drought-resistant plants, which may become more energetic after a northern summer's hot, humid nights have passed. Most will even tolerate light frost.

While the following plants require little care other than dead-heading during the summer, all are intolerant of soil that does not drain well and summers that are unrelievedly rainy. Gardeners with clay soil should create raised beds, planters or window boxes filled with a half-and-half mixture of compost and sand to grow the sun lovers.

Besides the flowers listed in this chapter, the following, described in other chapters, are also well suited to sunny places and even dry soil: burning bush, strawflower and all other everlastings, sunflowers, California poppies, dusty miller, Mexican sun-

flower, snow-on-the-mountain, alyssum, verbena and leptosiphon.

African Daisy
(*Arctotis stoechadifolia*)

Among the flowers suited to full sun is a group of daisies that hails from southern Africa: arctotis, dimorphotheca, venidium, tripteris, gazania, mesembryanthemum and the greenhouse specialty gerbera. Most resemble each other, with saucer-shaped, solitary flowers in a range of clear colours including peaches and purples. Their common names tend to become confused because several are dubbed simply African daisy. One African daisy, arctotis, has rosettes of lobed, woolly leaves beneath flowers that bloom in brilliant shades of pink, orange, red, cream, yellow, lilac and plum, always with a contrasting centre ringed with another colour. Each flower, as wide as 3 inches, is borne singly on an upright stem and is open only during daylight. There are some 65 species, which grow from 8 inches to 4 feet tall. The shortest, which spread almost a foot wide, are excellent along borders or in rock gardens. Cut for arrangements, they will last about 10 days.

Sow the fluffy, brown-and-white seeds indoors, just covered, six weeks before the last spring frost. Sprouting can take up to a month, and blooming begins two to four months later. Set outdoors a foot apart. Seeds that we started directly in the garden in mid-May did not bloom by the end of summer, but the plants were potted and brought indoors before frost and bloomed beautifully in a bright window in December. West Coast gardener Helen Chesnut writes that arctotis "bides its time in my garden, to begin flowering in the latter part of summer, almost as though the plants were still held under the spell of their natural flowering time in their homeland." Arctotis is not as appreciative of heat as some of the other African daisies and blooms best in dry but relatively cool conditions. Actually a tender perennial, this plant may overwinter in mild areas and makes a good houseplant.

Arctotis, the genus name of this member of the daisy family, comes from the Greek words for bear's ear because of a supposed resemblance to the scales on the seed. The species name signifies a similarity of the leaves to those of a type of lavender, *Lavandula stoechas*.

Baby's Breath
(*Gypsophila elegans*)

Useful primarily as a garden filler, just as its perennial relative is used in wedding bouquets, baby's breath is

an airy, insubstantial plant—the common name suits it well. It will not, then, provide border impact. The annual types are not very durable as cut flowers, nor are their stems as sturdy as those of the perennials. Still, they can lend a corner of the garden a welcome quietness, and they move with the slightest breeze. Most cultivars are white, although some have red or dusty-pink flowers. Greyish opposite leaves clasp the stem, whose upper part is sticky with a shiny, insect-snaring glue like that of catchfly. The individual, white, pink or rose star flowers, borne in hundreds, are each only about a quarter of an inch wide and shine with a central bead of nectar. As baby's breath is slender and upright, growing to about 2 feet tall, it should be planted densely between stronger stems such as zinnias or cornflowers.

Seeds can be sown indoors, just covered, six weeks early or directly in the garden around the last frost date and, after that, every two weeks until midsummer for a constant supply of stems for cutting. Germination tends to be slow and irregular, and plants flower about three months after seeding. Thin them to stand about 4 inches apart. Baby's breath can be grown in hot, dry places but will also stand partial shade.

Annual baby's breath is a western Asian member of the pink family *Caryophyllaceae*. The genus name comes from the Greek *gypsos* (gyp-

The Dahlberg daisy, FACING PAGE, *is a type of chrysanthemum native to the southern United States and Mexico, while the daisies,* LEFT, *belong to a group that hails from southern Africa. Many of the African daisies resemble one another, with open, upfacing flowers in unusual hues. Annual baby's breath,* ABOVE, *is an airy 2-foot-tall filler for flowerbeds and vases.*

sum, or lime) and *philos* (love), because the plant thrives in alkaline soil. *Elegans* means elegant.

Blanket Flower
(*Gaillardia pulchella*)

This happy flower receives its common name from colours that bring to mind the warmth and brilliance of Navajo blankets. The species, which has 2-inch, yellow-and-dark-orange flowers with rust-brown centres, is one of our favourite annual flowers, very similar to the perennial gaillardia (*G. aristata*) but brighter in colour, standing about 2½ feet tall and 2 feet wide. There are both single and double forms, some with flowers as round as a ball, blooming in one colour alone or in colour combinations such as cream with burgundy in the centre or pale yellow with crimson. The stems and leaves of all species and cultivars are hairy. All make excellent cut flowers, and stems bearing seed balls, which are round and furry like soft green burrs about an inch across, can be used in dried flower arrangements.

Lightly cover the spiny, white seeds about four weeks before the last frost in a cool place indoors. Sprouting takes about a week. Transplant seedlings 2 inches apart a week later. Plant outdoors 12 inches apart after the last frost. Give support in the form of branching twigs pressed into the ground, or set the plants 4 inches apart in the company of sturdier, self-supporting plants. Dead-heading will help to keep blanket flowers in bloom from July until late summer, when cool weather suits them well. All may need watering during the hottest weather. Grow the single types in the perennial garden or with other single composites such as marigolds, cornflowers and coneflowers.

Gaillardias are North American members of the daisy family *Compositae*. The name honours the Frenchman Gaillard de Charentonneau, an 18th-century botanical patron. *Pulchella* means pretty.

California Poppy
(*Eschscholzia californica*)

Gardeners who grow California poppies once are likely to grow them year after year, not only because these satin-sheened flowers are beautiful but also because they tend to self-seed, reappearing in the same beds where they grew the year before. Even seeds sprinkled on the snow in winter will sprout into plants that bloom by mid- to late June and survive several frosts to continue blooming until late fall. Plants grow about a foot high and a foot wide, branching from the base to form a drooping mound of soft, finely cut, grey-green foliage and luminous, four-petalled, 2½-inch flowers centred with a brush of pollen-loaded anthers. The original colour (increasingly scarce in seed catalogues) is medium orange, but hybridists have produced bronze, yellow, cream, red, pink and scarlet forms of California's state flower. Inevitably, there are also double forms with many more petals. Flowering stops in midsummer, but if the plants are cut back, the bright poppies will reappear later in the season. *E. caespitosa* 'Sundew' is a charming dwarf species that grows to about 6 inches tall, with scented, lemon-yellow flowers.

Sow California poppy seeds directly where they will grow, as they resent transplanting. Scatter the seeds on soil or snow, preferably in full sun in a spot where the soil will be dryish in summer. Seeds can be mixed half-and-half with sweet alyssum for an orange-and-white ground cover. Once temperatures reach 55 degrees F, sprouting occurs in about 10 days. Thin seedlings to 6 inches apart. Grow California poppies in masses in a rock garden or along the edge of a border with blue or purple flowers such as Venus' looking glass, dwarf cornflowers, sweet alyssum or Chinese forget-me-nots.

Seldom has such a simple, lovely wildflower been saddled with such a long, difficult botanical name, and as often happens, the genus name has nothing to do with the flower or its origins—the west coast of North America—but rather commemorates a European, in this case a 19th-

century German botanist, Johann Friedrich Eschscholz. The species name, fortunately, is appropriate.

Cape Marigold
(*Dimorphotheca* spp,
Osteospermum spp)

There is something vulnerable and appealing about flowers that look straight up, like the faces of little children. The cape marigold is one of those, a smaller version of the African daisy (arctotis) that is sometimes given the same common name. The flowers, 2 inches wide or bigger, all with a distinct dark circle around the centre disc, bloom in waxen shades of apricot, orange, yellow, rose and salmon, as well as creamy white, the nicest of all. Individual flowers held flat on 5-to-6-inch wiry, upright stems are short-lived, but new buds soon open. The flowers close at night, on overcast days and at the slightest touch of moisture from rain or a sprinkler. The plants, about a foot tall and as wide as 2 or 3 feet, are sturdy and self-supporting,

branching from base to top, although they tend to lean to one side. The foliage resembles that of dandelions.

Start the flat, round, papery seeds directly outdoors after the last frost or indoors in March, lightly covered, and transplant outdoors in May, a foot apart, preferably in full sun. Cape marigold transplants easily. Our seeds sprouted in just three days, though germination can take up to two weeks. Pinch back the plant centre when it is 4 inches tall to spur the growth of side shoots. Blooming, which begins only six weeks later and continues until frost, is especially abundant when the weather is dry and nights are around 50 degrees F. Dead-head spent flowers.

Cape marigold makes a good, dense ground cover. The white cultivars are beautiful in rock gardens with other smallish flowers. In warm places, plants may survive the winter, or they can be brought indoors to do double duty as houseplants in a cool, sunny window.

The cape marigold, which hails

Annual species of gaillardias bring to mind the colours of Navajo blankets. The cultivar 'Double Lorencia,' FACING PAGE, *features different colours in varying patterns and flower shapes. Seeds of blanket flowers can be sown directly outdoors in warm soil, while those of California poppies,* ABOVE, *can be sown on the cool ground of early spring or fall or even on the last snow. They will self-sow generously where they are content.*

from southern Africa, is a member of the daisy family *Compositae*. The name *Dimorphotheca* comes from the Greek words for twice, shape and fruit, suggesting the different types of seed produced by the ray and disc flowers. The Greek words for bone (*osteo*) and seed (*spermum*) make up the name *Osteospermum*.

Chrysanthemum
(*Chrysanthemum* spp)

Although we associate many chrysanthemums with grey autumn months, hospital night tables, stuffy glasshouses and overpriced florists, the new cultivars, offered page after page in good seed catalogues, are dazzling and difficult to resist. All are easy-care daisies that vary from ground-hugging to tall, and all do well in sun. They will bloom from midsummer until after the first fall frosts, provided they are deadheaded faithfully, an easy chore if you cut them for indoors, where they will last well in water. Although some chrysanthemums sold in catalogues are hybrids, the common species include the following:

C. carinatum, the tricolour chrysanthemum, or painted daisy, a native of Morocco, produces 18-to-24-inch stems with flowers 2 inches or wider that are excellent for cutting. Bushy plants resemble small shrubs and, in rich soil, may need support with slender sticks. Discs are purple, while

the showy petals display brilliant bands of contrasting colour. Seeds are generally sold in mixtures of yellows, bronzes, oranges, pinks and crimsons, with either single or double flowers. One of the best mixtures is 'Court Jesters.'

C. coronarium, the crown daisy, a Mediterranean native whose lovely semidouble flowers have yellow discs and golden to white rays, is also about 2 inches wide. The plants grow into dense, rounded shrubs of bright green foliage about a foot tall. Known as chop suey greens or shungiku, this species is a strongly flavoured Oriental vegetable.

C. frutescens, the marguerite or Paris daisy, native to the Canary Islands, has flowers as wide as 4 inches with yellow discs and white rays.

C. municaule forms foot-wide, ground-hugging rosettes of greyish

foliage from the centre of which grow curving, 10-inch stems bearing small daisies that, unfortunately, open only in direct sun. However, the plant's ability to survive the first frosts makes it a welcome bit of ground-covering colour in fall.

C. multicaule is a spreading species. It has small, inch-wide, golden daisies on stems less than a foot long and is an excellent choice for window boxes and containers. The cultivar 'Gold Plate' has somewhat larger flowers.

C. parthenium (also known as *Matricaria capensis* or *Pyrethrum parthenium*) is a type of feverfew, a perennial in some places but often grown as an annual, as it will bloom the first year from seed and may not survive frost. From tiny, white seeds sprinkled on the soil surface, this species produces a mass of half-inch white or yellow rayless daisies on slender, fragrant stems less than a foot long. Feverfew has proven benefits as a soother of migraine headaches. It tolerates mild frost.

C. segetum, the eastern star, or corn marigold (so called because it was once a common weed of British fields), is a very satisfying plant to grow. Planted close to its neighbours in rich soil in full sun, it will form a shrub as tall as 3 feet. The fleshy, bluish stems are almost hidden by emerald leaves and a profusion of 2½-inch, bright yellow daisies. The inner disc is loaded with dark yellow pollen. The wild look of this flower is enhanced by other simple, open annuals such as cornflowers, larkspur and purple cosmos. There are also white cultivars. The corn marigold is pest-free and very easy to transplant. In China and Japan, the petals are lightly boiled and eaten with a vinegar dressing.

C. tenuiloba, the Dahlberg daisy, or golden fleece (also known as *Dyssodia tenuiloba* and *Thymophylla tenuiloba*), produces finely divided, aromatic foliage and a profusion of inch-wide yellow daisies with deep yellow centres on stems 6 inches to a foot tall. The usual cultivar is 'Golden Fleck.' It is a native of the southern United States and Mexico.

All of the annual chrysanthemums can be sown directly in the garden, a quarter of an inch deep, when the soil

is warm. For earlier flowering, sow seeds indoors eight weeks early, where they will sprout in three days to two weeks. Transplant 4 to 18 inches apart, depending upon eventual height, into fertile soil in sun. Chrysanthemums transplant easily. They will tolerate a little shade where summers are hot.

The name of the genus *Chrysanthemum*, a member of the daisy family *Compositae*, comes from the Greek *chrysos* (gold) and *anthos* (flower).

Collomia
(*Collomia* spp)

The collomias produce clusters of tubular flowers on self-supporting stems. *Collomia coccinea* (*C. biflora*) is a low, roundish shrub, somewhat taller than a foot, soft to the touch, with unevenly toothed leaves and violet-brown branches. The sedum-like, half-inch star flowers are borne in a shiny, brilliant red half-globe that is very attractive to bees. The usual cultivar is 'Neon.'

The flowers of *C. grandiflora*, a North American native, are buff or peach-coloured, again borne in clusters atop stems as tall as 2½ feet.

Six weeks before the last spring frost, lightly cover the dark brown seeds indoors in a cool place. Seeds sprout in about 2 weeks, and plants bloom 10 weeks later. Set the young plants outdoors about 6 inches apart around the last frost date, in ordinary

soil in sun. Collomia seeds can also be sown directly outdoors in warm soil. The plant will survive the first fall frosts.

Collomia is a member of the phlox family *Polemoniaceae*. *C. coccinea* is a Chilean native whose species name means scarlet. *C. grandiflora*, whose species name describes its large flowers, is a native of western North America.

Coneflower
(*Rudbeckia* spp)

Like thimbles or jelly candies, the protruding centres of coneflowers are both distinctive and endearing. There are several annual species of rudbeckia, perhaps the best known being the gloriosa daisy (*R. hirta*), with flowers as wide as 7 inches. This domesticated black-eyed Susan grows 2 or 3 feet tall and blooms in artistic colour combinations of yellow, gold, mahogany, red and sometimes bicoloured. The tongue-shaped leaves and stems have a rough texture. The cultivar 'Marmalade' bears marmalade-coloured, black-centred single or double flowers as wide as 4½ inches on a bushy plant about 2 feet tall. Gloriosa daisies will bloom constantly from early summer until the first frost, even without dead-heading, and are visited by honey-bees, wasps and grasshoppers. They are excellent cut flowers.

Although more ephemeral in

The corn marigold, FACING PAGE, BOTTOM, *is an edible chrysanthemum that will form a shrub as tall as 3 feet. Much shorter is collomia,* FACING PAGE, TOP, *whose half-inch star flowers are attractive to bees. Gloriosa daisies,* ABOVE, *are annual coneflowers that will bloom constantly from early summer until the first frost, even without dead-heading.*

reddish on the sunny side and green beneath. There is a double-flowered form. The creeping zinnia is an interesting dried flower; flower heads left unpicked turn papery brown.

Sprinkle the seeds on the soil surface in peat pots six to eight weeks before the last frost or directly outdoors after frost. Sprouting takes about two weeks. Creeping zinnia resents transplanting. Plant in any dryish soil, thinning to 6 inches apart. Flowering commences about two months after sowing and continues until the first frost. Plant creeping zinnia along a garden border or in a rock garden, window box or basket.

This Mexican and Central American member of the daisy family *Compositae* is named for Professor Frederico Sanvitali, an 18th-century Italian botanist. *Procumbens* means prostrate.

Flowering Flax
(*Linum grandiflorum*)

The word flax brings to mind fields of blue flowers, linen fibre and linseed oil, all things associated with the common *L. usitatissimum*, whose species name means most useful. As pretty as it is useful, this soft-looking, broom-shaped plant, 2 or 3 feet tall, also makes a fine ornamental annual. Its periwinkle-blue, half-inch blooms have darker blue veins. The seedpods left behind are excellent for dried arrangements.

Our favourite flax, however, is *L. grandiflorum*, which comes not from the fields of Europe but from North Africa. It is a sturdier, fan-shaped plant that has grasslike stems a foot or two tall and larger and 1½-inch flowers of lustrous carmine-red on the variety *rubrum*. The cultivar 'Bright Eyes' has five pure white petals that meet at a maroon half-inch eye.

Borne one at a time, the flowers of all the flowering flaxes are short-lived and at their best when they open for the first time. After two to four days of closing with the setting sun and opening again with the first sunlight, they lose their lustrous sheen, but other flowers will replace them as more spiky buds wait to unfold. All types of linum are good

bloom, an annual relative that deserves to be better known is *R. amplexicaulis* (*Dracopsis amplexicaulis*), which has goldfinch-yellow flowers about 2 inches across centred with dark brown, inch-high cones so abruptly raised they are almost pointed. There is a brown arrow at the spot where each petal joins the disc. Blue-green, leathery, 2-inch leaves clasp self-supporting stems about 2 feet tall that branch gracefully from the bottom. Cut it back after blooming for another show of flowers in autumn, but save the dry stems. After the petals fall, the central domes, still covered with seeds and securely fastened to the stems, make lovely additions to dried flower arrangements.

Sow the small, ash-black seeds indoors in a cool place a month before the last frost. Seeds sprout in about a week. Plant outdoors a foot apart around the time of the last frost in good soil and sun. *R. amplexicaulis* begins to bloom two months after seeding and finishes about six weeks later, so plant it in a place where

other flowers will fill in the gaps.

A North American genus that belongs to the daisy family *Compositae*, *Rudbeckia* honours Olof Rudbeck, a 17th-century Swedish scientist. *Dracopsis* comes from the Greek *drako* (dragon); the suffix means resembling. *Amplexicaulis* describes the stem-clasping quality of the leaves. *Hirta* means hairy.

Creeping Zinnia
(*Sanvitalia procumbens*)

Among edging plants for dry places, the creeping zinnia is one of the most cheerful choices. It is a low daisy with few requirements other than warmth and room to ramble. Even if neglected, the plant is long-flowering, although occasional watering brings denser, more lush growth. Individual plants spread as wide as 2 feet, forming 9-inch mounds of small, oval, green leaves covered with three-quarter-inch zinnias whose gold or orange petals surround a dark brown centre. The slightly hairy stems, which branch throughout, are cut flowers, but as each bloom lasts just a short while, cut a stem with plenty of buds.

As soon as the ground can be worked in spring, scatter the seeds over a well-drained, finely worked garden plot in full sun. Sprinkle a thin layer of soil over them, pressing lightly with a board or your hands. When the seeds sprout, prick out the weakest seedlings for a spacing of 5 to 8 inches. Sow more seeds at intervals of three weeks for flowers over a long season, since the plant is short-lived. Flowering flax does best with cool nights and some moisture. We sowed seeds directly in the garden May 30, as seedlings do not transplant well. Seeds germinated in six days, and plants were in flower by July 21.

Instead of staking flowering flax with twigs, position it between stronger-stemmed companions. The plant needs the support, as it reacts to the slightest breeze and will droop when touched by mist or rain. Excellent companions for both types of *L. grandiflorum* – the variety *rubrum* and the cultivar 'Bright Eyes' – are cornflowers and deep blue statice, which can also be harvested as everlastings. Flowering flax often self-sows.

Flowering flax is a member of the flax family *Linaceae*, most of whose members are native to the area around the Mediterranean. Both genus and family names come from the Latin word for flax. *Grandiflorum* means large-flowered.

Gazania
(*Gazania* spp)

Although the gazanias that first caught the eye of botanists in Africa were orange-flowered perennials, most seeds sold today are hybrids of several species, either annuals or tender perennials. They bloom in every colour except true blue, and most have a blotch of contrasting colour where the rays meet the pollen-bearing centre. Like most African daisies, the flowers, which sit on individual upright stalks, close with the lightest mist as well as at night and when skies are overcast – a challenge to plant breeders who are working to develop a gazania that remains open more dependably. The leaves, green above and grey-white beneath, form a circular, 14-inch-wide clump. Individual flowers are short-lived, so dead-head for continued bloom throughout the summer.

Sow the greyish, cylindrical seeds an eighth of an inch deep indoors about eight weeks early. They should sprout in about a week in a warm place. After the last spring frost, transplant 8 inches apart in a sunny, well-drained place. Or sow directly in the garden in the warm soil of late May or early June for blooms from mid-August until after the first frosts. Gazanias transplant easily and make acceptable houseplants indoors, where they will bloom on a sunny windowsill. Cuttings can be taken in August and rooted in a greenhouse or sunny window for planting out the following spring.

The gazania is a southern African member of the daisy family *Compositae* and named for Theodore of Gaza, who translated the botanical works of Theophrastus during the 15th century.

Hawk's Beard
(*Crepis rubra*)

As self-reliant as a dandelion and similar in appearance, save for the scores of pink flowers in place of yellow ones, hawk's beard toughs it out through summer's heat and fall's early frosts to continue blooming into

Creeping zinnia, FACING PAGE, is a good choice for sunny border edges, where its small daisies brighten 2-foot-wide mounds of oval green leaves. The larger-flowered gazania, LEFT, glows in full sun but tends to close in the lightest mist or when skies are overcast. Both creeping zinnia and gazania can be sown directly on the warm soil of late spring but will bloom sooner if started early indoors.

October. Each 18-inch plant branches profusely from the base, producing many ridged, vertical flower stems, each of which holds a single, upfacing, 1½-inch-wide bloom high above the mound of toothed foliage. The flowers turn into creamy white clusters of downy seeds.

After the last frost, sow the half-inch, needlelike seeds in shallow rows in any well-drained soil in sun. Or start them six to eight weeks early indoors. Sprouting may take as little as two days in warm soil. Thin to 6 inches apart. Blooming commences about two months after sowing, so hawk's beard can be sown late in open patches for fall colour. For a long-lasting picture, plant it behind Virginia stocks and sweet alyssum and in front of single asters.

A European member of the daisy family *Compositae*, hawk's beard takes its genus name from the Greek word for boot, for unknown reasons. The species name means red, in reference to the flower colour.

Livingstone Daisy
(*Mesembryanthemum* spp,
Dorotheanthus bellidiformis)

This African daisy received its common name—which recalls David Livingstone, 19th-century Scottish missionary of "Dr. Livingstone, I presume" fame—after an English seedsman saw the plant growing as a weed in the Kirstenbosch Botanic Garden in Cape Town and decided it needed an English name to gain popularity. More descriptively, it is often called ice plant, because its greyish, succulent foliage has a distinctive crystalline sparkle. As mesembryanthemum grows only a few inches high but can spread to about a foot wide, it is used to great effect as a ground cover and front-of-the-border plant in dry places. The flowers, which bloom in brilliant shades of pink, apricot, maroon, white, violet, buff, yellow and rose, usually with contrasting centres, close at night and on cloudy days and are most abundant during the cool weather of early and late summer.

Sow seeds indoors three months before the last frost date. Seeds should be sown on the soil surface but require darkness for best germination, so cover flats with cardboard or black plastic and set them in a warm place. Check the flats daily after a week, as sprouting usually takes two to three weeks. When nights are dependably warm, set plants out 6 inches apart in full sun in the well-drained soil of a rock garden, border edge, pot or window box. Plants may overwinter in mild climates.

The genus name *Mesembryanthemum* means flowering at midday. The plant is a member of the carpet-weed family *Aizoaceae*. *Dorotheanthus bellidiformis* honours Dorothea, the mother of Dr. Martin Henry Schwantes. The species name suggests that the plant resembles bellis, a perennial daisy.

Marigold
(*Tagetes* spp)

Marigolds are somewhat confusing, because they have been divided into French and African types, although all are, in fact, New World natives; indigenous people of Central and South America had already selected large-flowered strains before the arrival of Columbus. Because marigolds naturalized rapidly in Africa after their introduction there, they were mistaken for wildflowers when discovered by botanists during the 16th century. An early interest in the flowers in France further clouded the issue of origin. But the New World has reclaimed the marigold, which is now one of the top three annual bedding flowers sold in North America because the plants are self-supporting, easy to grow from seed and bloom profusely and continuously, if dead-headed, until frost. Also appealing are their sunny shades of yellow, orange, gold and red, although there are now white cultivars as well.

The genus *Tagetes* includes about 40 species, the best known of which are *T. erecta* (the African, or now, American, marigold), *T. patula* (the French marigold), *T. tenuifolia* or *T. signata* (the signet, with small, single flowers) and *T. filifolia* (Irish lace, grown for its lacy foliage). Many new releases are hybrids, including some sterile triploids, which bloom without interruption through hot or cool weather but have a lower germination rate, often only 50 percent.

Tallest of the marigolds are *T. erecta* cultivars, at 1 to 3 feet, depending upon cultivar. These need the warmest weather to germinate and flower, with minimum night temperatures of 50 degrees F and a recommended seeding temperature of 75 to 80 degrees. Most are double-flowered.

The French marigolds are smaller, most under a foot, and tolerant of lower temperatures for germination — about 60 degrees F — and flowering. In fact, French marigolds suffer during the hottest summers. Although most are double, single-flowered cultivars such as 'Golden Gate' and 'Granada' are becoming increasingly popular. Less showy than its brighter kin yet more charming is *T. tenuifolia*, which produces a mound of finely divided foliage —

each small branchlet resembles a television aerial — and single, five-petalled flowers that are less than an inch wide and borne singly at the branch tips. Irish lace (*T. filifolia*), only about 6 inches tall, is grown just for its foliage, as the white flowers are few and tiny.

Sow marigold seeds directly where they will be growing, an inch apart and one-quarter of an inch deep, in a sunny or partly shaded place in any soil. In warm soil, seeds will sprout in about a week and bloom 5 to 10 weeks after sowing — a longer period for cooler temperatures and taller flowers. Or start six weeks early indoors, transplanting out after the last spring frost. Thin to 6 to 12 inches apart, depending upon the size of the mature plant. Dead-head about once a week to encourage blooming and to keep the plants looking attractive. Marigolds have few disease or pest problems. In fact, some, especially *T. patula*, repel harmful soil nematodes. Consider a drift of tall marigolds for the back of a border, perhaps interplanted with zinnias and

Good ground covers are the lesser-known small single cultivars of marigold, such as 'Granada,' FACING PAGE, which are easy to grow from seed sown directly in the garden. Another ground cover for sun is the Livingstone daisy, LEFT, which grows only a few inches high but can spread a foot wide. This African native is sometimes called ice plant because of its grey foliage.

calendulas, and smaller versions for sunny pots and window boxes. All can also form a temporary hedge. Although marigolds are long-lasting as cut flowers, many have an unpleasant scent best left outdoors.

Marigolds, native to the area from Argentina to Arizona, are members of the daisy family *Compositae*. *Tagetes* comes from Tages, an Etruscan deity who sprang from the ploughed earth. *Erecta* means erect, *patula* spreading, *filifolia* thread-leaved, *tenuifolia* finely divided leaves. The name marigold indicates that this was a plant dedicated to the Virgin Mary, hence Mary's gold.

Mexican Tulip Poppy
(*Hunnemania fumariaefolia*)

The Mexican tulip poppy is somewhat like a more substantial version of the California poppy. The canary-yellow flowers, up to 3 inches wide, are borne atop wide, bushy plants 1 to 3 feet tall, with leaves that are feathery and greyish but broader than those of California poppies. Tuliplike flowers bloom all summer long. In the garden, partner this plant with dark background foliage such as heliotrope or with other grey-green plants such as catchfly, evening primrose or snow-on-the-mountain — or with California poppies. Tulip poppies are good cut flowers.

Since, like those of all poppies, the seeds are difficult to transplant, sow the round, black seeds either directly in warm garden soil or about four weeks early in individual peat pots. Seeds sprout in about three weeks and bloom some five weeks later. Mexican tulip poppy does best in well-drained soil in sun.

H. fumariaefolia, the only species in the genus, is a tender perennial that takes its name from 19th-century English botanist and bookseller John Hunneman. The species name suggests that the foliage resembles that of fumaria, or fumitory. It is a Mexican member of the poppy family *Papaveraceae*.

Monarch of the Veldt
(*Venidium fastuosum*)

If hairy foliage indicates a plant well equipped to handle drought, venidium must be the Boy Scout of annuals, the best prepared in the garden. This African daisy, whose flower is much like that of a calendula, is so woolly that its buds, its deeply serrated leaves and its ribbed, hollow stems look white. When young, it is almost cuddly. The plant also has a sticky texture, a sign of predator defence. The 2-inch-wide, solitary, upfacing flowers close at night. At their best for two or three days, they consist of double rings of petals, the outer held flat and the inner raised. The usual colour is bright yellow-orange, although there is also a white variety. Both types have a dark centre and a dark spot at the base of each petal of the inner ring. The monarch of the veldt grows about 30 inches tall, branching from the base but tending to flop unless staked or surrounded within a wire cage when young. Dead-heading is necessary because the spent flowers become unattractive brown globes.

Sow the tiny, beige seeds an eighth of an inch deep either directly in the garden after frost or about four weeks early, keeping the soil moist at cool room temperature. Sprouting takes about a week. Plant outdoors a foot apart after the last spring frost in full sun and well-drained soil. The first flowers appear about three months after sowing. Venidium may survive a light frost, although it will cease blooming.

The genus name of this southern African member of the daisy family *Compositae* comes from the Latin *vena* (a vein), referring to the ribbed fruit or seeds. *Fastuosum* means proud.

Portulaca, Moss Rose
(*Portulaca grandiflora*)

Softly reclining plants with succulent stems, fleshy leaves and jewel-bright colours reminiscent of those of cactus flowers define the portulacas. Both single- and double-flowered forms are available in brilliant shades of yellow, orange, pink, scarlet and violet as well as white, all with a cen-

tral cluster of yellow stamens. Seemingly fashioned from tissue paper, the roselike flowers open in the morning and bloom till midafternoon, but most close with the heat of the day. Some newer cultivars such as 'Cloudbeater Mixed' stay open on overcast days. They have flowers as wide as 2½ inches, much bigger than the standard old-fashioned single, whose flowers are an inch wide. One plant covers more than a square foot of ground and grows 8 inches tall.

Sow the fine seeds thinly in shallow rows in a sunny place after the last spring frost. Thin gradually to stand about 10 inches apart. Or sow in a warm place indoors eight weeks early, pressing the seeds lightly into the soil surface and covering pots with clear plastic. Our seeds sprouted in three days, although they can take as long as three weeks. Thinnings may be eaten in salads or in soups, where they have a slight thickening effect—as does the plant's weedy relative purslane. Flowers appear about eight weeks after an outdoor sowing. Portulaca self-sows if it is content, which is most likely in well-drained, sandy soil in a sunny place. We have seen it come back repeatedly along the inhospitable-looking edge of a gravel driveway. The flower can also be propagated by cuttings, as we demonstrated by taking lengths of leafy stem from a window box while on a trip. After the cuttings had travelled in a moist plastic bag for 10 days, they were immediately planted in soil in a clay pot and bloomed a month later. Plants can be potted before frost in the fall and brought indoors for sunny windowsills.

Portulaca, the Latin name for purslane, is a member of the purslane family *Portulacaceae*. The species name *grandiflora* suggests large flowers. The species is native to South America.

Prickly Poppy
(*Argemone grandiflora, A. mexicana*)

Never have poppies been as well armed as these ones—more than two feet of prickly stems and thorny leaves as indented as holly. The flower buds are like spiny little cucumbers—hence another name for

A. mexicana, devil's fig—which eventually become thorny seedpods. The lustrous flowers are notably delicate by comparison, like fragile ladies protected by an entire garrison. These poppies are 4 inches wide in the case of the 2-foot-tall *A. grandiflora*, whose flower colour is indicated by cultivar names 'Yellow Lustre' and 'White Lustre.' Both have sharply toothed leaves, dark green with a bluish silver finish, as though they have been washed in milk; these are truly decorative foliage plants even before the spiny buds and poppies appear.

The flowers, like wide-open, six-petalled tulips, are lemon-yellow and 2½ inches wide on the smaller and thornier *A. mexicana*, which grows about 18 inches tall and 2 to 3 feet wide. The honeybees love its abundant pollen. This unusual poppy was praised by botanist Carolus Clusius when it was introduced to Europe in the late 16th century, and Chiltern Seeds picks up the theme, calling the flower "splendid: if you don't normally bother with annuals (you should, of course!), do try this one." The leaves are greyish underneath and dark green on the upper surface, with veins outlined smartly in white. The sap is bright yellow. Seedpods open at the top in early fall to release seeds that may self-sow. Desert plants, the prickly poppies tolerate heat and dry, sandy soil. There are additional species available from specialist seed houses, and all are well worth growing.

Sow the small, round seeds, lightly covered, three to a peat pot, in a warm place. After germination occurs in four to six weeks, thin to the

The unusual daisies of monarch of the veldt, FACING PAGE, consist of two rings of petals, the outer held flat and the inner raised. The deeply serrated leaves, hollow stems and buds are so hairy that they are almost white, a sign of a plant well equipped to handle drought. Also suited to dry conditions is portulaca, ABOVE, whose succulent, low-growing stems and leaves are capable of storing water.

strongest seedling per pot. After the last frost, transplant outdoors, 2 feet apart, in well-drained soil in a sunny place. Staking may be necessary. The prickly poppy is a good companion to Our Lady's thistle, various grasses and any white flowers. It will survive the first light frost.

A Central American member of the poppy family, argemone takes its name from the Greek *argemon*, cataract of the eye, because its sap was once used to treat the disorder.

Prince's Feather
(*Amaranthus* spp)

The most stately amaranths are described in chapter four, but more often grown is prince's feather (*A. hypochondriacus, A. hybridus erythrostachys*), represented by such cultivars as the all-green 'Green Thumb' or the red 'Pigmy Torch.' This is a tidied-up version of a close relative, pigweed. Prince's feather is a 2-foot-tall plant that is half stem and half fuzzy flower spike. It tends to flop over if unstaked, making the related and self-supporting *Celosia argentea plumosa* (also called prince's feather) a better bet for places where a medium-height plant is wanted.

In warm soil, lightly buried, the seeds germinate almost immediately, just like those of pigweed, appearing above the soil in about three days. The seedlings grow so quickly that if started indoors, they should not be given too much warmth or they will become leggy; keep them at cool room temperature in a bright place. It really makes more sense to sow the seeds directly outdoors, thinning to 6 inches apart. The amaranths do well in full sun but will tolerate some shade.

Prince's feather belongs to the family *Amaranthaceae*, whose name comes from the Greek *amarantos* (unfading) because of the long-lasting nature of the flowers. *Hypochondriacus* suggests former medicinal uses for the plant, which is indeed edible; *erythrostachys* means red-spiked.

Salvia
(*Salvia* spp)

There are several salvias, or sages, that add vertical notes of season-long colour to the annual garden without requiring staking. All have spikes of tubular flowers and soft, attractive, aromatic foliage that brings to mind their relative, culinary sage.

The best known of these is scarlet sage (*S. splendens*), which is always available in flats from garden stores in spring and whose spires of purple, red, white, violet, salmon or pink flowers bloom continuously, like well-fuelled torches, from June until the frost in fall. Although the flower is overused and is too clashing and spiky for many situations, it nevertheless can be a welcome addition to a garden—provided that it is liberated from the usual public-park rows —planted in informal groups among complementary dark greens and heavy blues or among the lush, oval leaves of nicotiana. We planted the bright reds with heliotrope and golden ageratum for a beautiful combination that flowered all summer. Cultivars grow from 10 inches to 2 feet tall.

S. farinacea, blue salvia, or mealycup sage, is a taller tender perennial with a thick, strong central stem that branches all the way up to form as many as 10 beautiful spires 2 to 4 feet tall. The flowers, smaller and more delicate than those of scarlet sage, are loved by bees. The greygreen leaves are smooth, with a slender heart shape as long as 4 inches. They contrast beautifully with pale, soft-looking, lilac-coloured buds that become dark purple when open. There is also a creamy version. The plant makes a good companion for celosia, scarlet sage, snapdragons or bergamot. Blue salvia may overwinter in warm places.

Texas sage (*S. coccinea*) is a wild species that grows 2 feet tall and just as wide and produces loose spikes of small, scarlet flowers on dark stems.

Sow salvia seeds indoors 10 weeks before the last frost. As seeds, especially those of red-flowering types, need some light to germinate, press them lightly into the soil surface. Cover pots with clear plastic, and set them in a warm place. Sprouting takes a week or two. Seeds can also be sown directly in the garden after the last spring frost. Set plants a foot apart in a sunny or partly shaded place after frost danger, and they will fill in the gaps between. Water plants regularly during the hottest weather.

All sages have the square stem characteristic of the mint family *Labiatae*. The name salvia suggests the medicinal qualities of some family members. *S. splendens* is a Brazilian native whose species name means splendid. The species name of *S. farinacea*, a native of the southwestern United States, means mealy or starch-containing.

Sun Lovers
(*Heliophila longifolia*)

Literally "lover of the sun," according to the genus name, this is one of the few blue flowers that prefer a shadeless spot in the garden, though paradoxically, it closes at noon and remains closed until the following morning—a reason to surround this flower with more colourful choices. British gardeners do not report this daytime closing phenomenon, so perhaps the flower stays open all day in that cloudier, more northerly place. In any case, in full blue sail, it buzzes with honeybees. It grows about a foot tall, forming racemes of half-inch, four-petalled, blue flowers with white eyes reminiscent of flowering flax. Four plants set together will create a wall 2 feet tall and 4 feet wide that is soon matted with slender 2-inch seedpods resembling braids. Try planting sun lovers in front of nicotiana or mingled with catchfly.

Sow the small, sesamelike seeds indoors in a cool place four weeks before the last spring frost. Seeds sprout in about a week. Set plants outdoors 10 inches apart after danger of frost is past in full sun and average

soil, where they will begin to bloom around mid-June and finish two months later. Young plants can also be left indoors to bloom in a sunny window or greenhouse.

Heliophila, which suggests a love (Greek *philo*) of the sun (*helio*), is a southern African member of the mustard family *Cruciferae*. *Longifolia* describes the relatively long leaves of one species.

Swan River Daisy
(Brachycome iberidifolia)

In our garden, some self-sown chamomile seedlings came up between the young brachycome plants, and for a time, the two looked quite alike, with their finely divided, greyish foliage on trailing stems. But the brachycome eventually distinguished itself by bursting into a huge crop of delicately scented blue daisies. The inch-wide flowers, which resemble cineraria, also bloom in shades of lilac, pink, white and deep violet. Contrasting central rings enhance the disc flowers. Unlike many other daisies, brachycomes stay open even after watering as well as at night. They also make excellent and long-lasting cut flowers on their attractive, gently curving stems.

Sow the seeds about eight weeks before the last frost, keeping them in a fairly cool place indoors. Germination takes about two weeks. When nights are warm, set the plants outdoors 6 inches apart in full sun in soil that is well drained and not too rich. Alternatively, sow seeds directly outdoors around the last frost date. Plants should bloom about two months later. Pinch out the tips to encourage bushiness. Staking with brushy twigs will help keep the plants upright if you desire. Blooming may cease during summer's hottest weather, so cut the plants back entirely then, and water them well for a crop of fall flowers. Brachycome is a good plant for the front of a border, or it can be grown directly behind a border of sweet alyssum.

Brachycome is a Western

Several ornamental sages add vertical notes of colour to the garden without requiring staking. Best known is scarlet sage, also simply called salvia, FACING PAGE. *Its spires of flowers are common in public parks. An appealing companion for low-growing sun lovers is the Swan River daisy, or brachycome,* ABOVE, *whose mats of small white, blue or purple blossoms, like those of the cultivar 'Purple Splendour,' are good choices for pots and the fronts of borders.*

Australian member of the daisy family *Compositae*, whose name derives from the Greek *brachys* (short) and *kome* (hair) because of the short bristles on the pappus. *Iberidifolia* means that the leaves are similar to those of candytuft (*Iberis*).

Sweet-William Catchfly
(*Silene armeria*)

Some of the most interesting flowers in the annual garden are those that have devised their own means of predator protection. Most have thorns or bristles, but the catchflies receive their common name from a ring of glue that encircles each flower stalk to snare aphids and other small pests. In some species, this ring is more obvious than in others. *S. armeria* has a brown band that is quite evident against the greyish stems, while on the related viscaria (described in chapter eight), the ring is transparent.

Another notable attribute of catchfly is its 2-inch clusters of bright magenta-pink, five-petalled flowers, each with a deep, three-quarter-inch throat, attractive to pollinators such as hawk moths. The opposite, wing-like leaves are bluish with a matte finish. The plant has sturdy, self-supporting stems that will grow up to 2 feet tall.

Catchfly is an easy plant to grow and tend. Sow the fine seeds directly outdoors in a sunny place in spring, lightly covered, in any soil that is not waterlogged. Or sow the seeds indoors in a cool place two months before the last frost, transplanting outdoors, 6 inches apart, around the last frost date. The bright flowers complement white gypsophila and white or blue flax.

Silene, a member of the pink family *Caryophyllaceae*, has the Greek name for viscaria, which is now sometimes applied to all plants in this genus. *S. armeria* is a native of southern Europe. The species name is the Latin word for a type of dianthus.

Tahoka Daisy
(*Aster tanacetifolius*, *Machaeranthera tanacetifolia*)

A delight for hot, sunny border edges is the Tahoka daisy, an aster whose flowers, with lilac-blue rays and pale yellow centres, follow the sun by day and close at night. The 6-to-8-inch-tall rosette of finely divided, grey-green, ruelike foliage feels a bit sticky to the touch and has a fresh, piny fragrance when crushed. If the soil is too rich, the foliage will grow taller than the flowers, leaving them peeking coyly out from underneath.

Break the dormancy of the seeds by mixing them with moist peat moss and refrigerating them for two or three weeks before sowing indoors in a cool place. Sprouting takes about a week. Transplant seedlings 6 inches apart in well-drained soil after the danger of frost has passed, or sow directly outdoors in full sun or half-shade as soon as the ground can be worked in spring. Blooming begins about three months from sowing and continues until frost. Dead-heading during summer will prolong flowering. This daisy goes well with alyssum at a border's edge or in a container and is an excellent cut flower.

The Tahoka daisy is, as one might expect, a member of the daisy family *Compositae*. It is a native of the southern United States and Mexico, named for the small town of Tahoka, Texas. The genus name *Machaeranthera* is derived from Greek words suggesting that the anthers are sickle-shaped. The species name compares the leaves to those of tansy.

Tassel Flower
(*Emilia javanica, E. flammea, Cacalia coccinea*)

With its slender stems and small blooms, the tassel flower suits a wild garden and, in fact, can simply be sown *in situ* and left pretty much on its own. Its best feature is its crop of half-inch tassel flowers in jewel-like colours of scarlet, orange and gold. The flowers, composed of tiny, tubular florets borne in clusters, bloom singly on their own branches. Smooth, grey-green, alternate leaves, which are edible, grow about halfway up the 2-to-3-foot stems.

In mid-May, sow the seeds directly in a sunny, well-drained or dry spot, thinning to 6 inches apart. By early July, ours were in flower, and by the end of the month, some were in seed, producing tiny, dandelionlike parachutes. Grow this with strawflower and coneflower, which are also directly sown in the garden.

The origin of the genus name is unknown. *Emilia* is a member of the daisy family *Compositae*. The species name *javanica* refers to its origin in Java.

Tripteris
(*Tripteris hyoseroides*, *Osteospermum hyoseroides*)

This bushy annual has a scent some books optimistically describe as fresh or haylike. We were less enthusiastic. One of us found the fragrance of tripteris acceptable but bitter and somewhat rhubarblike, while the other found the scent obnoxious and discovered that a fluid on the greyish stems and leaves was capable of producing an allergic reaction—sneezing, burning skin and watery eyes. The daisy is nevertheless worth growing because of its continuous, season-long production of neon-orange flowers, about 2 inches wide, borne singly at the ends of erect stems 2 feet or taller. Instead of closing in dark weather like most light-sensitive daisies, these peculiar flowers roll their petals backward, leaving only the brown discs and a circle of orange showing until the petals unroll again the next sunny morning. If cut, the flowers last well in water, although they will stay open only in bright light. Again, the fragrance may bother some people. 'Gaiety' is the usual cultivar.

Sow the large, beige, winged seeds indoors, lightly covered, in a cool place about four weeks early. Sprouting takes four days to a week or more. Set the young plants outdoors a foot apart after the last frost in a spot in sun in well-drained, fairly fertile soil. For easier flowers, tripteris can also be directly sown in warm soil. Ours, transplanted outdoors on June 7, bloomed July 25. Dead-head only when the flowers are fully open; otherwise, you will find it difficult to distinguish the finished blooms from the closed ones.

Tripteris, a southern African member of the daisy family *Compositae*, takes its name from the Greek *tri* (three) and *pteron* (wing) because of the shape of the seed.

Ursinia
(*Ursinia anethoides*)

Before the flowers developed, this low-growing, foot-tall bush of feathery, dill-like foliage put us in mind of a delicious potherb that smelled like tansy when crushed. We did not anticipate the beautiful crop of vividly coloured, 2-to-3-inch, daisylike blooms that would soon appear on long, wiry stems. The petals of the flowers are intense yellow or orange, and at the point where they connect with a dark disc ring, a small bluish black circle sets the two orbits off strikingly. The blossoms have a friendly, sunny look, but unfortunately, they will not stay open during overcast or moist weather. On such days, their closed petals make them look offended. Do not dead-head them, however, as they will open again. A white, papery star is left behind after the seeds have dispersed. Ursinia also makes a long-lasting and beautiful cut flower.

Ursinia is easy to grow. Sow seeds indoors, just covered, six weeks before the last frost date. Seeds sprout in two or three weeks in somewhat cool soil, and plants bloom about three months later. After the last frost, set plants outdoors, 6 to 9 inches apart in rather poor soil in full sun. Ursinia does best in warm, somewhat dry summers.

Ursinia is a southern African member of the carrot family *Umbelliferae* that is named for Johann Heinrich Ursinus, a 17th-century botanical author. *Anethoides* suggests a resemblance to dill (*Anethum graveolens*).

Tassel flower, FACING PAGE, has 2-foot windblown stems, bright half-inch flowers and carefree habits well suited to wild gardens. On the other hand, foliage is one of the attractions of the more substantial Tahoka daisy, LEFT, an aster which follows the sun by day and closes by night. It is an excellent cut flower that grows only 6 to 8 inches tall, making it suitable for sunny border edges.

In the Shade
Selections for sunless places

Shady gardens need not be without flowers. Both wax and tuberous begonias, for instance, are well suited to sunless corners and window boxes, where they will produce brightly coloured blooms all summer. Plants that are adapted to shady conditions usually require fertile, somewhat moist soil and as a rule make good houseplants.

Many gardens lack full sun, and every garden has at least a bit of shade. Shade accompanies houses, trees, fences, walls and even flowers. In the city, the shade of neighbouring buildings and trees may extend from one end of the yard to the other. The garden repertoire is somewhat limited in such situations—as it is limited by any difficulty with soil, climate or space—but many flowers grow contentedly in a shaded environment. In fact, most garden plants do best with at least a little shade—vines and foliage plants such as coleus and polka-dot plants especially so. Many others, such as alyssum and candytuft, will grow well in shade, although flowering will be less prolific. In any garden, trees, fences and trellises not only add visual interest but also provide the shade and shelter required by flowers native to the forests of the world.

There are varying degrees of shade. The sort of dappled shade caused by deciduous trees is often termed light shade, as compared with full shade, which endures all day under evergreens or beside walls, and the half-shade of a bed exposed to full sunlight for part of the day. There, shade is movable, leashed to the Earth's own turning; places briefly illuminated fall again into relative darkness.

Shade-loving plants have a few things in common. Many have glossy leaves suited to shedding the plenti-ful rain that falls in their native habitats. Many have seeds that germinate only in the presence of light; in nature, they fall and sprout directly on the forest floor. Shade-loving plants tend to do poorly in dry or infertile soil. What they need is humus, a wonderful substance that holds moisture and nutrients remarkably well. The United States Department of Agriculture once demonstrated that while 100 pounds of sand holds 25 pounds of water and the same amount of clay holds 50 pounds of water, 100 pounds of humus holds 190 pounds of water, just the thing for shade lovers. Humus stays aerated, allows for the easy movement of roots and tends to be about neutral or slightly acidic in pH, ideal for most annuals. Compost, well-rotted manure and dampened peat moss are all forms of humus, or organic matter. Mulching with hay, straw, grass clippings or composted leaves—good treatment for shade lovers in any case, as it keeps the ground cool and moist—also increases the soil's humus content. An extra layer of humus is especially important directly under trees whose shallow roots may take nutrients and water from the annuals.

Watering is necessary for all plants, but the shade lovers are among the least drought-tolerant garden occupants. A deep watering of about an inch once a week is preferable to several light ones, and apply-ing water directly to the ground is better than sprinkling, which not only wastes water, much of which is lost to evaporation, but also encourages fungus diseases. Drip systems or buckets of water poured on the ground work more efficiently. If you can supply water that is not ice-cold, so much the better. Water last thing in the evening to make the most of the cool night.

One side benefit of all the tender-perennial shade plants is that their tolerance of low light makes them excellent houseplants. Browallia, impatiens, Persian violets, wishbone flowers and fibrous-rooted begonias, all lovers of shady places, are residents of the annual garden well suited to indoor flowering. By the same token, certain houseplants, such as ferns, caladium, weeping fig, dieffenbachia and spider plant, can move into the shady garden for the summer. All, of course, must be moved indoors before the first fall frost if they are to remain undamaged and continue to live indoors for another winter.

As well as the flowers listed here, nicotiana, black-eyed Susan vine, Persian violet, coleus, cup flower, polka-dot plant and the violas, all described in other chapters, are also suited to shade. Most white flowers, too, are good choices for shady places, where they shine as though illuminated by the moon.

Baby Blue Eyes
(*Nemophila* spp)

The white petals of *N. maculata* are distinguished by purple dots that have led to another name for this species, fivespot. Each silken three-quarter-inch flower grows on its own little stalk from a leaf axil or from the tip of a slender, fragile stem, which trails about a foot—perfect for containers. The large seeds form in globular seedpods. California bluebell (*N. menziesii, N. insignis*) has larger, inch-wide flowers with white centres and blue margins and lacks the spots of *N. maculata*.

Sow the seeds directly in the garden, as baby blue eyes suffers in transplanting. Give it rich, moist soil in a sheltered place with dappled shade or a little afternoon sun, and

thin to 6 inches apart. Dead-heading will produce a second crop of flowers in late summer. This is a good plant for pots and planters and the edges of shady beds. Be sure, however, to plant it at least a foot back from the edge so that it can recline forward. The plant does best in cool weather and survives light frost. It will also flower in pots in a cool greenhouse.

Baby blue eyes is a member of the waterleaf family *Hydrophyllaceae,* most of whose members are North American natives. Both species of nemophila are natives of California. Their genus name comes from the Greek *nemos* (a wooded place or grove) and *philo* (to love), because the plants thrive in shade. *Maculata* means spotted; *menziesii* honours Archibald Menzies, a botanist who collected in North America around the turn of the 19th century.

Begonia
(*Begonia* spp)

There are two types of begonias, both of which thrive in full shade.

One is the tuberous begonia, which, true to its name, grows from a round, flattish, brown tuber. Sumptuous, tropical-looking flowers and big, toothed, hairy leaves have made it a favourite for pots and window boxes for generations. The other is the wax begonia, which has smaller flowers, a fibrous root system and leaves with such a shiny finish that they look wet. In both cases, each flower grows on an individual, fleshy stem that originates in a leaf axil, and leaves have a characteristic lopsided heart shape. Both types of begonia need humus-rich soil, little sun and cool temperatures. They will drop flowers when the weather is hot or windy. Both are ideal container flowers, although they can also take their place in a border – the wax begonia is an alternative to impatiens in that role. Both species are commonly available in pots and flats in garden nurseries every spring.

The tuberous begonia (*B. x tuberhybrida*) is a hybrid derived from several wild species. There are two types: upfacing and downfacing (or

There are varying degrees of shade. The California bluebell, FACING PAGE, *here growing in company with another North American native, meadow foam, is a type of nemophila that grows happily in dappled shade or partial sun. The wax begonia,* ABOVE, *easily grown from seed or cuttings, will bloom all summer even in full shade and can be brought indoors as a winter houseplant.*

115

cascading). Flower colours include red, pink, yellow, salmon, orange and white, and the top flower is larger than those farther down the stem. Foliage may be green or bronze. The tuberous begonia is a particularly good plant for shady window boxes, where an elevated situation shows off the big flowers well. It also makes a good cut flower floating in a bowl of water with a bit of foliage.

In spring, about six weeks before the last spring frost, plant the tubers in pots of moist peat moss, hollow side up and only about half an inch deep. Alternatively, set the tubers directly in warm soil after the last frost. Leave the plants in the garden until after a frost or two, to give them as much time as possible to store nutrients in the tubers. Then dig the tubers, pull off any remaining foliage, let them dry, and put them in paper bags in a place that is dry and cool but not freezing. Humidity suits these plants, but water on the leaves does not, as it fosters mildew.

The wax begonia (*B. semperflorens*) has 1½-inch-wide, sparkly, double or single flowers – two large petals north-south, two small ones east-west – with a central tuft of yellow stamens. The plant forms a roundish bush, 8 to 12 inches high and equally wide, that is covered with flowers in the white-through-pink-to-red range from summer until the first frost. Foliage may be green, bronze, mahogany or variegated. Before fall

frost, pot them up, divide them into sections or take cuttings and root them in water for splendid houseplants during the winter and cuttings for the next spring.

Both types of begonia can be grown from seed, although some tuberous begonias are difficult and will not bloom the first year. The wax begonia is slow but easy from seed, and growing it this way provides a wider range of combinations of flower and leaf colour than one is likely to find at the neighbourhood plant store. In January or February, sprinkle the dust-fine seeds on the soil surface. Cover pots with plastic, and set them in a warm place, bottom-watering or misting if necessary to ensure that the soil never dries out. Seeds sprout in one to three weeks, producing threadlike seedlings. Transplant into individual containers or six-pack cells four weeks later. If you are growing a colour mix, take care to keep some of the smaller as well as the larger plants, as white-flowering types grow faster than the others. Planted 6 inches apart in warm soil well after the last frost, wax begonias will form a solid, ever-blooming ground cover by midsummer. The first frosts will damage and gradually kill them.

Begonia is the largest genus – with some 900 species – of the family *Begoniaceae*. Both the genus and family take their name from Michel Bégon, a French patron of botany and gover-

nor of New France in the 18th century. *B. semperflorens* – the species name means ever-flowering – is a native of eastern South America.

Browallia
(*Browallia speciosa*)

We were impressed by browallia – from summer, when the flowers looked like children in snowsuits with upraised arms, until winter, when it graciously assumed the role of a splendid houseplant covered in flowers. Outdoors, browallia is a cool accent for a shady corner, where it forms a low, spreading shrub about 8 inches high and more than a foot wide decorated with 2-inch trumpet blooms all summer. There are white-flowered cultivars, but more valued are the periwinkle blues. The foliage is soft and has pronounced veins underneath. Browallia dislikes heat and drought and fades after even a single afternoon of bright sun.

Although it is often sold in greenhouses, browallia is easy to grow from seeds sown on the soil surface eight weeks before the last spring frost. Place the pots in a warm place under clear plastic, where sprouting takes one to three weeks. After the last frost, set plants outdoors 12 inches apart in pots, window boxes, rock gardens or at the border front, in any good, moist soil in partial shade. Blooming begins about three months after germination. Do not

overfertilize, since, like other members of the tomato family, browallia is apt to produce foliage at the expense of flowers. Pinch plants when they are 4 inches tall to encourage bushiness. Pot up a few plants in fall for a cool, bright window. In pots, browallia is fine alone or married with nemesia, polka-dot plants, white begonias or petunias (see planter illustration on page 19).

Browallia is a Colombian member of the nightshade family *Solanaceae* and takes its name from Johan Browall, an 18th-century Swedish botanist. *Speciosa* means showy.

Foxglove
(*Digitalis purpurea*)

Foxgloves are magical-looking plants, with foot-long, velvety leaves and finger-shaped flowers that produce digitalin, a substance that is both medicinal and poisonous. Most foxgloves are biennial, with seeds that grow foliage the first year and flowers the next. But 'Foxy,' a relatively short cultivar (to 4 feet), is a true annual that flowers about five months from sowing. From snout-like, greenish buds open 2-inch downward-pointing trumpets in shades of yellow, white, pink, rose and purple, all of them with inner surfaces of cream and lilac decorated with dark red freckles and long, white hairs, guides for the honeybees that visit faithfully in warm weather. Flower spikes bloom from the bottom of the stem up for about a month, after which no more flowers appear.

Sow the tiny, round, caramel-coloured seeds on the moist soil surface about three months before the last frost. Cover pots with clear plastic, and keep them in a warm place indoors. Seeds sprout in about a week, and plants can be transplanted into individual pots a month after sprouting. In late spring, set outdoors 18 inches apart in fertile, moist soil in partial shade; plants are frost-tolerant. As foxgloves will blow over in wind and may be knocked down by heavy rain, either grow them in a sheltered place or stake them. Castor beans provide an attractive backdrop and welcome shade.

The name *Digitalis* derives from the Latin *digitus* (a finger), referring

to the shape of the flower. The plant is a European member of the figwort family *Scrophulariaceae*. *Purpurea* (purple) describes the flower colour of the wild species.

Impatiens, Busy Lizzie
(*Impatiens* spp)

In warm climates, busy Lizzie (*I. wallerana*) has become something of a pest, the fate of a few flowers so dependable they are almost overly eager to please. Impatiens flings its seeds far and wide from ripe, bursting pods—hence another common name, touch-me-not. In North America, the plant has colonized just as successfully but with human help. During the early 1980s, impatiens, a rare flower as recently as the 1930s, overtook the petunia as the continent's most popular bedding plant. One chief reason is that impatiens blooms beautifully in shade. In fact, it blooms constantly from spring until frost on neat, shrubby plants yet requires almost no maintenance; deadheading is unnecessary, as the spent flowers simply fall away. Watering alone will maintain a lush, thick carpet of foliage and flowers.

Single or double flowers bloom in shades of orange, scarlet, crimson, rose, pink and white, either alone or bicoloured, with contrasting central stars. The white and pale pink cultivars are especially luminous under trees and in other shady places. The

Browallia flowers, FACING PAGE, BOTTOM, *bloom in glorious masses all season, and plants can be brought indoors in fall. Vertical elements in shade come from annual foxgloves,* FACING PAGE, TOP, *which produce the typical elongated bells about five months from sowing. Although New Guinea impatiens,* ABOVE, *is more tolerant of heat and sun than the other impatiens species, it will also thrive in light shade, where it is a popular choice for containers.*

117

glossy, pointed foliage may be green or bronze. Plants grow as tall as 2 feet, although the smooth, translucent, juicy stems are somewhat reclining, so they are best at the edge of a bed. Impatiens is also an excellent choice for a pot. One healthy transplant will fill a 10-inch container in four weeks. In larger pots, use more plants, or combine them with browallia, salvia and begonias.

Impatiens is available as a bedding plant in spring, the usual way to grow it. If you choose to start it from the tiny, hard seeds, sow them on the soil surface two to three months before the last spring frost. Cover pots with plastic, and keep them in a warm place. Sprouting takes one or two weeks. Alternatively, take cuttings before the first fall frost and root them in water for winter houseplants that can themselves become the source of cuttings for the late-spring garden; impatiens is actually a tender perennial. Plant in good soil in at least partial shade. As with aloe, the juice can soothe the effects of contact with nettles or poison ivy.

Balsam impatiens (*I. balsamina*) is a vertical version, as tall as 3 feet, that is an old-fashioned favourite, with waxy, single or double flowers borne within the leaf axils on the top two-thirds of the stem. From early summer until frost, inch-long stalks bear loose-hanging, lightly scented, 1½-inch flowers in pink, red, white, lavender or yellow, either single or double. This is also a good foliage plant: the lance-shaped leaves, about 4 inches long and an inch or so wide, are produced densely, especially toward the top.

Sow the seeds directly outdoors in warm soil. Grow these larger plants 18 inches apart. Balsam impatiens is effective when planted with single forms of *I. wallerana*. Although both types of impatiens are appreciated for their ability to flower freely in shade, they will also tolerate full sun, provided they have humus-rich soil, cool roots and plenty of water. Apply mulch. In a cooler climate, they can take more sun than in hot places.

New Guinea impatiens (*I. hawkeri, I. petersiana*) is similar in form to busy Lizzie but is both taller and wider, about 2 feet both ways, with impressive variegated foliage. The flowers are bigger too – 2 to 3 inches wide – in electric shades of pink, violet, red and orange, but they are sparser than those of *I. wallerana*. New Guinea impatiens hybrids could formerly be grown only from cuttings, but that ended in 1988 with the release of 'Tango,' an All-America Selection. Its seeds, like small, flat apple seeds, should be lightly covered and kept moist in a warm place. Seedlings are stocky and treelike. Set plants about 18 inches apart in sun or partial shade, where they will bloom in 10 to 12 weeks from sowing, provided they have plenty of warm weather. New Guinea impatiens branches from the base.

A genus that belongs to the balsam family *Balsaminaceae, Impatiens* takes its name from the explosive release of the "impatient" seed capsule when it is touched. *I. wallerana* is an East African native whose species name honours Horace Waller, a 19th-century missionary in Africa. *I. balsamina* is a Southeast Asian native whose name means "bearing balsam." *Hawkeri* commemorates Lieutenant Hawker, who collected plants from the South Sea Islands.

Lobelia
(*Lobelia erinus*)

This delicate-looking little plant with its jewel-like violet, blue, magenta, lilac or white flowers, is a traditional favourite in hanging baskets and window boxes, and so it should be. Lobelia blooms most abundantly in the cool weather of early summer and early fall. The bright, half-inch flowers – twice as wide in some new cultivars such as 'Blue Moon' – have three large lower petals and two small upper petals. The soft, sometimes slightly toothed leaves are small and few.

There are both mounding and trailing types. The former (*L. erinus compacta*) grows into small, neat hills about 6 inches tall and wide, while the latter (*L. erinus pendula*) has smooth, 10-inch stems that curve down, then up, covering pot edges, box corners and border edges. English gardener Vita Sackville-West

recommended that "really generous patches" of the blue cultivars be combined with violet or purple alyssum so that "the blue of the lobelia mixes into something very sumptuous with their mauves and purples."

Sow the dust-fine seeds about eight weeks early by pressing them into the surface of moist growing mix. Cover pots with plastic, and set them away from direct sunlight. Sprouting occurs in two or three weeks. Keep the pots in a coolish place indoors. Three weeks later, transplant small clumps into pots or flats. Around the last frost date, set them outdoors 6 inches apart in very rich soil in partial or full shade. Blooming, which begins about eight weeks after sprouting, slows or ceases with hot weather but resumes grandly with the cool weather of late summer. In the interim, plants may become unsightly and brown and should be cut back.

A southern African member of the bellflower family *Campanulaceae*, lobelia is named for noted 17th-century Flemish botanist Mathias de l'Obel, who was a physician to King James I of England. *Erinus* is the Greek name for a plant.

Madagascar Periwinkle
(*Catharanthus roseus, Vinca rosea*)

This lovely tender perennial made its first European appearance in the Paris Jardin des Plantes in the 18th century, when Madagascar was a possession of France. The native plant grown then was an open, 2-foot-tall bush with flat, pink flowers and the typical lush, oily-looking foliage of the perennial periwinkle (*Vinca minor, V. major*). Vincristine, a chemical extracted from *Vinca rosea*, is used in cancer treatment. Thanks to the work of plant breeders, gardeners can now grow bushier, more dwarf forms of Madagascar periwinkle, as small as 10 inches, with rose, pink or white flowers, sometimes with a centre of one of the other colours. Flowers, which appear in the crown and leaf axils, resemble single impatiens about 2 inches across with a small hole in the centre where the stamens and pistil hide. The underside of the petals is almost white. The shiny, lance-shaped leaves, about 3½ inches long and an inch wide, have a pronounced white central vein and become deep green with age. Stems are reddish brown.

Sow seeds, completely covered, about three months early in a warm place. Germination may take three weeks, and seedlings grow very slowly, especially at cool temperatures. After the last spring frost, set plants outdoors 10 inches apart in well-drained soil in half-shade or sun; in the latter case, watering must be generous. Choose a protected place, as strong winds can tear off the flowers. Flowering begins about four months after sowing and continues until frost. Pinch back

Lobelia, FACING PAGE, *is one of the best-known flowers for hanging baskets and window boxes, where its tiny, jewel-like flowers bloom on trailing stems. Here, it accompanies viscaria and geraniums. More substantial is Madagascar periwinkle,* ABOVE, *an annual type of vinca which forms a glossy shrub covered with flat, 2-inch flowers. Brought indoors in fall, it makes a beautiful houseplant.*

composed of five joined petals. The cultivar 'Calypso,' available in several colours, has won many awards from England's Royal Horticultural Society, as it is more compact than previous hybrids, which tended to be straggly. The shiny, medium green foliage has serrated edges. Green to reddish fleshy stems trail and then point upward to form a good ground cover about 5 inches high. A bell-shaped calyx is left after the flower falls.

Sow the tiny, brown seeds on the soil surface about eight weeks early, covering the pots with clear plastic and keeping them in a cool place indoors. Seeds sprout in one to three weeks. Transplant outdoors 6 inches apart after the last frost, in moist, fertile soil in semishade, in pots, window boxes or garden beds. Although mimulus will bloom in shade, it also tolerates sun, provided soil is humus-rich and moist. Blooming begins about eight weeks after sprouting and will stop with the onset of hot weather, when plants become a bit leggy. They can be encouraged to resume flowering if they are clipped back and kept watered—this is a plant that should never dry out. Plants will survive the first few fall frosts but may not continue blooming. Bring them indoors as houseplants. A gentle trailer, mimulus is a good candidate for baskets in half-shade.

Mimulus, a tender perennial member of the figwort family *Scrophulariaceae,* is native to the west coast of the United States and South America.

Saponaria
(*Saponaria vaccaria,* *Vaccaria pyramidata*)

Saponaria produces one of the whitest whites in the garden, bringing Ivory Snow to mind, yet it is sheer coincidence that the plant name means soap (Latin *sapo*). The name really comes from a soapy substance that can be pressed from the roots of some species of saponaria. There is another sense in which saponaria has a cleansing effect: its expanse of white flowers can quiet any bed cluttered with brilliant reds, oranges and blues. It will grow in both shade and sun.

Although we prefer the sudsy white type of saponaria, there is also

plants when they are 4 inches tall to encourage branching. Dig entire plants to bring indoors as houseplants, and take cuttings the following spring; the variegated Madagascar periwinkle will grow from cuttings only. Grow some in pots in summer, three plants per 8-inch pot, and move them indoors in fall for beautiful houseplants for the winter.

A member of the dogbane family *Apocynaceae, Catharanthus* is native from Madagascar to India and derives its name from the Greek *katharos* (pure) and *anthos* (a flower). The name *Vinca* originates in the Latin *vincio* (bind), referring to the use of the stems in wreath making. Both species names mean red.

Monkey-Flower
(*Mimulus* spp)

Both the common and genus names of this shade lover come from wild relatives with flower markings that do resemble simian faces. Hybrid monkey-flowers do not but are only slightly less charming for the lack. Flowers up to 2 inches wide bloom in shades of yellow, orange, red, brownish and cream, all with freckles and splashes of colour on the lower surface of the throat, which is

a pink: "This is one of those plants that appear to have gone completely out of fashion," notes the Chiltern Seeds catalogue. "Once very popular, now very few catalogues appear to list it. Very easy to grow, almost in the sow-and-forget category, it is in fact a very attractive and showy annual with graceful sprays of deep pink flowers." Both the pink and white forms become small, beautiful bushes, about 18 inches high, covered with a drift of sweetly scented flowers that move with every breath of wind. Planted in masses, they are excellent substitutes for baby's breath. The leaves are long, triangular and grey-green, while the somewhat drooping flowers resemble three-quarter-inch buttercups, with five round petals that swell into five-sided, lanternlike seed capsules. These last are good for dried flower arrangements and will supply the next year's seeds.

About eight weeks before the last spring frost, chill the brown seeds in the refrigerator for 10 days before sowing on the soil surface. Sprouting takes two days to three weeks in a warm place. Set plants outdoors a foot apart around the last frost date in full sun or partial shade. They will bloom 8 to 10 weeks after sprouting. Branches break easily, so keep the plants in a sheltered place and stake with twigs to help keep them upright. For a pleasant border, plant the pink- and white-flowered culti-

vars together in the company of low-growing blue bachelor's buttons.

Saponaria is a European member of the pink family *Caryophyllaceae*. *Vaccaria* derives from the Latin *vacca* (cow), because the plant was used at one time for forage; another common name is cowherb.

Venus' Looking Glass
(*Specularia speculum*,
Legousia speculum-veneris)

Although the common name of this beautiful annual is said to come from the shiny, round seeds that someone fancied resembled mirrors, the flowers are as blue as tiny ponds in which one might imagine a goddess admiring her reflection. The five-petalled flowers, about three-quarters of an inch wide, are purple at the edge and have blue centres. They grow on somewhat stiff stems that are about a foot long and curve and turn upward so that the plant is only about 9 inches tall. The fine little pointed leaves are lightly bristled along the edges.

Sow the reddish seeds directly outdoors around the last frost date. Seeds sprout in about a week. Thin seedlings to stand 4 inches apart. Flowers bloom less than two months after germination and have more or less finished blooming before summer's end. For an earlier start, the seeds can be sown indoors, lightly covered, four weeks before the last

Monkey-flower forms ground-covering clumps of soft foliage and unusual 2-inch blooms. The cultivar 'Calypso,' FACING PAGE, has won awards for its particularly compact growth. Venus' looking glass, ABOVE, is named either for its shiny round seeds or for the petals which are as blue as tiny ponds. Here, it shares a sheltered corner with California poppies.

frost; for later flowers, sow outdoors at the end of June. Choose a spot with moist soil in partial shade. Venus' looking glass is lovely with California poppies, which grow to about the same height.

Venus' looking glass is a European member of the bellflower family *Campanulaceae*. *Specularia* and *speculum* both refer to a looking glass.

Viscaria
(*Viscaria* spp)

These lovely plants produce a gentle drift of single flowers on slender, windblown stems about 2 feet long and somewhat reclining. The narrow, greenish grey foliage recalls viscaria's relatives, the carnations. There are bluish, magenta, pink, lilac and white flowers, some with black or maroon centres, but all are five-petalled and three-quarters of an inch wide, each one on a long calyx on its own short stem.

Sow the fine, dark brown seeds by pressing them into the soil surface and keeping them at room tempera-

ture until they sprout in about a week. Plant 6 inches apart after the last spring frost in well-drained soil in shade or partial sun. Sow seeds or transplant seedlings in large patches. Ours bloomed on July 8 after an April 17 indoor sowing.

The plants are soft enough to blow in the lightest breezes and thus are attractively fronted by similarly willowy, pink-flowered Virginia stocks. They are also excellent in baskets and as cut flowers and look fine next to larkspur or zinnia 'Green Envy.' Viscaria will withstand the first few fall frosts.

Viscaria is a member of the pink family *Caryophyllaceae* and is sometimes included in the genera *Lychnis* and *Silene*.

Wild Foxglove
(*Ceratotheca triloba*)

Flowers that look like bridal white foxgloves come from a plant that is not a foxglove at all but a relative of sesame. One distinguishing feature of this flower, which is attractive to bumblebees, is a long, tonguelike petal that extends 2½ inches from the flower base. This landing platform rolls tightly into a funnel until the flower is ready for pollination and only then unfurls, letting pollinators dive to the four dark brown anthers that fold around the long pistil. Only one or two flowers on each plant are ready to be pollinated at the same time. The succulent, 4-to-6-foot stem bears serrated, opposite leaves that are heart-shaped and hairy but soft to the touch. Wild foxglove is a good companion for ferns and is attractive in front of castor beans, trees or any dark background.

Lightly cover the seeds, which resemble small, ash-coloured apple seeds, eight weeks early in a cool place indoors. Our seeds, sown April 17, sprouted May 5, and plants bloomed August 1. After the last frost, set the plants a foot apart in rich soil in light shade. Staking may be necessary.

The genus name of this little-known annual comes from the Greek *keras* (a horn) and *theke* (a case), in reference to the horned shape of the fruit. A member of the pedalium family *Pedaliaceae*, the wild foxglove is a

native of southern Africa. *Triloba* means three-lobed because of the shape of some of the leaves.

Wishbone Flower
(*Torenia fournieri*)

Peek into the throat of the wishbone flower, and you will see two distinctive wishbone-shaped stamens that join at the tip, giving this flower its common name. The stamens spring apart when the flower is ready for pollination. Torenia would be the answer to any gardener's wish for a classic and elegant flower equally adaptable to garden beds, pots and indoor window ledges were it not for one great weakness—its vulnerability to aphids, whiteflies and almost every other indoor pest.

The flowers resemble those of its relatives—foxgloves, snapdragons and monkey-flowers—blooming in velvety shades of light blue, dark blue and deep rose, all with a yellow throat; there is also a white form. Plants grow 8 to 10 inches tall and about 6 inches wide, with toothed leaves that are about 1½ inches long.

Sprinkle the sandlike seeds on the moist soil surface four months before the last frost, keeping the pots in a warm place with diffuse light until sprouting occurs in one to three weeks. Bottom-water or mist to keep the soil moist. Transplant into individual peat pots when the second leaves appear. When night temperatures stay above 60 degrees F, set outdoors 6 inches apart in rich soil in a semishaded or totally shady border. If torenia has the high humidity and plentiful water supply that suit this tropical native, it will begin blooming three to four months after germination.

In containers, torenia partners well with yellow pansies and blue lobelia. For houseplants, dig entire plants before the first frost. Before you bring them indoors, spray them with insecticidal soap, then water, and continue to spray from time to time.

A Vietnamese member of the figwort family *Scrophulariaceae*, torenia is named for Olaf Toren, chaplain of the Swedish East India Company in the 18th century. The species name *fournieri* commemorates 19th-

century French botanist Pierre
Nicolas Fournier.

Woodruff
(Asperula azurea setosa, A. orientalis)

With its whorled leaves on square
stems, annual woodruff has a cool,
fresh look that brings to mind its perennial relative, sweet woodruff (*A.
odorata*), the May-flowering ground
cover of European woods. Annual
woodruff is equally beautiful and
redolent of spring—evocative of
cowslips, bedstraw and spring
beauty. One of the few hardy annuals
with fragrance, woodruff forms a low
mound about a foot tall and produces
masses of clustered flowers that
resemble forget-me-nots from a distance. The tiny, four-petalled trumpet flowers, which open bright blue
and gradually fade to pale lavender,
grow in clusters at the ends of
branching stems like bursting fire-
works. Woodruff is best in mass
plantings, edging its perennial relative, sweet woodruff, or other shade-
and moisture-tolerant plants such as

wishbone flower, impatiens, violas or
blood-leaf, whose red nicely complements the blue of woodruff. It makes
a good cut flower too, if you can bear
to reduce the lovely mound of bloom.

Chill the seeds in the refrigerator
for two weeks before pressing them
into the moist soil surface. Cover
pots with plastic, and place them in a
cool place away from direct sun.
Sprouting occurs in six days to four
weeks, and flowering begins about
two months later. Or sow seeds
thinly outdoors in a moist, shady
place as soon as the soil can be
worked in spring, raking the seeds
into the soil and eventually thinning
seedlings to stand 4 to 6 inches apart.
Pot some plants for fragrance indoors in fall. Woodruff may self-sow
in favourable locations.

Woodruff is a Caucasian member
of the madder family *Rubiaceae*,
which includes gardenias, coffee
trees and cinchona, whose bark
yields quinine. *Asperula* derives from
the Latin *asper* (rough), referring to
the texture of the stems. *Orientalis*
means eastern, *azurea* blue.

Gentle drifts of viscaria, FACING
PAGE, *produce flowers a little less than
an inch wide resembling those of its
relatives, the pinks. Slender stems
grow about 2 feet long. The shorter
wishbone flower,* ABOVE, *takes its
name from its distinctive stamens,
which are joined at the tip until the
pollen matures, when they spring apart
to reveal the stigma underneath.*

Sweet Scents
Fragrance for day and night

Perfumed flowers, the essence of gardening, recall an era when plants were grown for utility more than for decoration. Flowers with sweet scents, such as alyssum and some petunias, FACING PAGE, could be used for potpourris, bouquets or colognes, but even in the garden, they were considered therapeutic, a benefit now confirmed by scientists.

Centuries ago, flowers were more highly valued for medicine and scent than for ornament. Sweet scents were, in fact, considered therapeutic—they "banished melancholy," as the early herbalists put it—an idea that science now confirms. Flowers were cut, mixed in potpourris, spread on the ground to perfume the indoors or dried and carried in sachets. A Dutch visitor to England in the 16th century wrote, "Their chambers and parlours strawed over with sweet herbes refreshed me; their nosegays finely intermingled with sundry sorts of fragraunte flowers, in their bedchambers and privy rooms, with comfortable smell cheered me up and entirely delighted all my senses." Many of the garden's most sweetly scented flowers are, then, traditional favourites.

Today, gardeners are more sensitive to visual stimulation and have all but forgotten the temptations of floral perfumes. Hybridists, for their part, turn out ever bigger and brighter blooms, longer-flowering and more abundant, but the scent of many new cultivars of even the most dependably fragrant flowers—roses, carnations, pansies, sweet peas—has been lost. Without perfume, these flowers somehow lack heart. Certainly, they lack much of their appeal to moths and bees.

After all, their silently miraculous sweetness, their curative love-on-the-breeze is produced not for nosegays or depressives but for pollinators. Most pollinating insects have scent organs in their antennae. Bees, which rely primarily on colour for finding suitable flowers, are nevertheless able to take advantage of scent as a tracer. It is carried back with them to the hive so that when they perform the detailed dance that points to the source of nectar, their sister bees can pick up not only visual cues but also odoriferous ones. For moths and butterflies, scent is a powerful attractant. Evening flowers such as evening-scented stocks, four-o'clocks and datura entice winged passersby with some of the strongest fragrances in the garden. The trumpet structure of many of the night-blooming flowers excludes most insects except the long-tongued moths best suited to pollination. Humming-

birds, too, will come to deep-throated, scented flowers such as four-o'clocks and nicotiana.

The scents themselves are unromantic in composition, as they result from a combination of sugars, enzymes and scented alcohols that turn into aldehydes when exposed to the air. Aldehydes may be as much as 20 times as fragrant as the original alcohols. The scent molecules are not only powerful but also large, so they tend to stay fairly close to the ground, one reason flowers smell best on warm, still days. They release less scent on cold days, when pollinators are less likely to fly, and their scent is quickly dissipated in hot or windy weather. Scented flowers, then, should be grown close to the house or near pathways and patios. The scent of the smaller ones is most noticeable when they are raised off the ground and planted closer to nose level in pots or window boxes.

As well as the flowers listed below, several annuals described in other chapters are also remarkable for their scent: basil, pincushion flower, sweet peas, moonflowers, saponaria, woodruff and some violas.

Alyssum
(Lobularia maritima, Alyssum maritimum)

The commonness of alyssum may turn some flower lovers against this little ground cover. Yet alyssum has much to recommend it and few shortcomings. It blooms quickly from seed in both sun and shade, is a good cut

flower, harmonizes with almost everything and lasts long past the first frosts. Its honey scent – the plant is often labelled sweet alyssum – is apparent both in the vase and on the ground, although you may have to get onto your knees to sniff it. Alyssum often self-sows to reappear in the same spot next year. If you want plants in a different location, cut the flowers when they are in seed, shake them over newspapers, and sprinkle the seed where it is wanted, or spread spent flower stalks in bare garden patches.

Although the flower spikes reach up only 3 to 5 inches, the soft, trailing stems extend about 10 inches, so do not sow alyssum too close to the edge of a bed unless you want the clusters of quarter-inch, four-petalled flowers on the lawn or pathway. Blooming continues even after more than 100 seeds have set on the stem but may cease during summer's hottest weather, especially if plants are grown in full sun – some cultivars such as 'Snow Crystals' are more heat-resistant. There are white, rose, light purple and dark purple cultivars. The purple should be used with discretion, since it can contrast harshly with many other flower colours. Mixed with white, however, or sown between stretches of white alyssum, it can be beautiful, especially in front of larkspur. Since alyssum starts blooming early, it is an excellent companion for California poppies. *L. maritima minima* (*A. benthamii*) is an almost prostrate, white-blooming species about 3 inches tall. It also is wonderful in containers, hanging baskets and rock gardens, between flagstones and as a ground cover under leggy plants such as hollyhock or Mexican sunflower.

Sprinkle seeds on well-drained soil in sun or light shade anytime in spring, cover them lightly, and after they sprout, thin the seedlings to 3 inches apart. Alternatively, sow indoors four weeks early. Alyssum sprouts in a few days and blooms about six weeks after sowing. After flowering, shear the plants back lightly to coax more flowers. Sow some in autumn in the greenhouse for fragrant bouquets and a white cloud next to the geraniums and other houseplants in March.

Alyssum, a southern European member of the mustard family *Cruciferae*, takes its genus name from the Latin *lobulus* (a small pod), referring to the small, round seed-pods. *Alyssum* comes from the Greek *a* (not) and *lyssa* (madness), because the plant, also dubbed madwort, was once thought capable of calming anger or curing madness. The species name suggests a native habitat near the sea.

Cladanthus
(*Cladanthus arabicus, Anthemis arabica*)

A pinch of the leaves of this unusual flower, also known as Palm Springs daisy, releases the plant's secret: an unusual, spicy fragrance. The foliage is remarkable in appearance too – the finely pointed, slender, bluish leaves become warmer green in the late-evening shadows. In bright contrast are 2-inch, golden yellow daisies. At first, they are nestled within the branches, but the plant repeatedly branches and buds just below the flower head so that flowers eventually cover the 2½-foot globes of foliage. Without the flowers, cladanthus would be decorative enough, but its blooms give it an exotic alpine look.

Sow the tiny, dark brown seeds indoors on the soil surface about eight weeks before the last frost date. They will sprout in as few as three

Although perfumes are enjoyed and exploited by humans, the scent of flowers such as nicotiana, FACING PAGE, TOP, *is actually there to attract pollinators—in this case, hummingbirds and moths. A favourite of bees, alyssum,* FACING PAGE, BOTTOM, *is one of the best edging annuals. It blooms quickly from seed sown directly in the spring garden and often self-sows. Cladanthus,* LEFT, *which also reappears on its own, bears orange daisies nestled in spicy-scented foliage.*

days. Transplant outdoors around the last frost date or a little before. Plants are frost-hardy but will not grow much until the weather warms. They can also be sown outdoors but may not sprout for four weeks. Plants should be thinned to a foot apart in full sun or partial shade, in any soil that drains well. They begin to bloom about three months after sprouting, stop in midsummer and then bloom again until frost, although the later flowers are smaller.

Cladanthus, a native of Spain and North Africa, is a member of the daisy family *Compositae*. The genus name derives from the Greek words for branch and flower because the flower heads are produced directly on the shoot ends. *Arabicus* and *arabica* mean Arabian.

Datura
(*Datura* spp)

The delicious scent of datura, almost overpowering when the plant is too close to a bedroom window, advertises a flower that is not only ir-resistible to moths but has also been known as a human intoxicant for centuries. Datura contains an alkaloid, hyoscyamine, that is both hallucinogenic and toxic. This is a plant best left out of gardens frequented by children. The scent of the sacred datura *D. meteloides* (*D. inoxia*) is described by Chiltern Seeds as "subtle to an extreme and quite unlike that of any other flower, one that leads you to seek it more whilst giving you no hope of fulfillment." The shrubby plant grows about 3 feet tall and 6 feet wide.

In late afternoon, the upright, tightly rolled, cigarlike buds unfold from a tubular calyx for their one-night performance of hawkmoth seduction. In the morning, scales from the moth wings left inside the long, upfacing trumpet flowers betray a secret night life, while unvisited flowers still hold a pool of nectar. The flowers then shrivel and are best picked off. The leaves are dark green and soft, like those of the related potato, and release a strong smell when touched.

Although you will have to search the seed catalogues for them, there are several species for the annual garden, including *D. arborea*, with 8-inch, white flowers and smooth leaves; *D. metel*, a native of China, with 10-inch, single or double flowers in shades of white, yellow, purple, red or pink on 3-foot plants; *D. sanguinea*, with orange flowers on 4-to-6-foot plants; *D. stramonium*, thornapple, or jimson weed, with upright, white, 4-inch flowers and prickly, egg-shaped, hedgehoglike fruits on 3-to-6-foot plants; and *D. suaveolens*, from Brazil, with pendant, white flowers on 10-foot plants.

Sow the seeds one-eighth of an inch deep in peat pots in a cool place indoors two or three months before the last frost. Sprouting takes as long as six weeks. Thin to one plant per pot. When nights are warm, plant the pots outdoors 2 feet apart. Tender perennials, they can be kept going with cuttings taken in early summer, potted and kept indoors in a cool, bright place. After the nights have warmed the next spring, prune plants and set them back outdoors in warm, somewhat spare soil in sun. Too much fertilizer may produce foliage at the expense of flowers. Depending upon species, plants may grow as tall as 10 feet.

Datura is a native name for these members of the nightshade family *Solanaceae*.

Dianthus
(*Dianthus* spp)

The genus *Dianthus* includes a number of plants best known by their common names—pink, carnation and sweet William. Pinks, once called gillyflowers or clove gillyflowers because of their spicy fragrance and their habit of flowering in July, have been beloved as garden flowers for centuries. In the 17th century, William Lawson wrote that "of all the flowers (save the damask rose), they are the most pleasant to sight and smell . . . their use is much in ornament and comforting the spirits, by the sense of smelling." The pink's relation to etymology is evidence of long use and appreciation—this is the garden's only flower that has given rise to a verb, a noun and an adjec-

tive. One can "pink" the edge of fabric to make it resemble the jagged flower petals, and the colour of the flower is, of course, pink.

Not all of today's cultivars are scented, however (check catalogue descriptions). To add to the confusion, there are annual and perennial species and cultivars of both pinks and carnations and both annual and biennial forms of sweet William. Pinks are smaller-flowering types derived from many species. An annual cultivar of *D. laciniatus*, 'Double Gaiety,' produces plants about 18 inches tall and 8 inches wide, with sweetly scented, double flowers in a range of shades. Also scented are 'Mrs. Sinkins,' 'Doris,' 'Loveliness' and 'T&M Frosty Mixed,' as well as many more.

Carnations derive primarily from the species *D. caryophyllus* and have slender stems holding relatively large flowers that need staking on all but dwarf selections. Fragrant selections include 'Giant Chabaud,' the Knight series and anything with "clove" in the name. Sweet Williams are forms of the species *D. barbatus*, which produces its fragrant flowers in clusters. Although they are hardy biennials, they will bloom the first year if the seeds are sown in early spring. All types of dianthus have silky, overlapping, fan-shaped petals and are beautiful cut flowers that bloom in shades of pink, rose, white and maroon, often changing toward

the centre. The bluish foliage resembles broad blades of grass.

Dianthus grows quickly from an outdoor sowing. Or sow indoors eight weeks early, with seeds barely covered. Germination takes as long as four weeks at about 70 degrees F. All types will tolerate poor, relatively dry soil and full sun if the weather is not too hot, and they are good companions for godetia and catchfly. The low cultivars are excellent at the edge of a border.

Dianthus species are Eurasian members of the pink family *Caryophyllaceae*. The genus name comes from the Greek *dios* (divine) and *anthos* (flower)—literally, flower of the gods.

Evening Primrose
(*Oenothera* spp)

A sweet scent similar to that of orange blossoms comes from some species of evening primrose, flowers whose common name hides the fact that many bloom by day. The big, fragile, poppylike, four-petalled flowers are yellow or white, sometimes fading to pink, and face directly upward. Each is borne on its own smooth, succulent stem. *O. odorata*, *O. deltoides* and *O. pallida* are all fragrant.

Sow the small, thin seeds, lightly covered, about eight weeks early in a warm place indoors. Our *O. pallida* seeds sprouted in four days, pro-

The sacred datura, FACING PAGE, *is poisonous, yet its sweet perfume is almost overpowering on a summer evening. Buds unroll in the late afternoon, bloom all night and shrivel in the morning. Sweetly scented by day are many cultivars of dianthus. The annuals, called pinks,* ABOVE, *form attractive clumps of flat, open flowers in many shades.*

ducing pale pink seedling leaves followed by a greyish rosette of foliage. The plants continued to be attractive at every stage. Around the last frost date, set them outdoors 6 inches to a foot apart, depending upon the size of the mature plant, in a warm, sunny or slightly shady place with well-drained soil. Evening primrose is attractive when planted with lavender.

Oenothera is a member of the evening primrose family *Onagraceae*. The name comes from *oinotheras*, the Greek name of a plant. Most are natives of North and South America.

Four-O'Clock
(*Mirabilis jalapa*)

Named for its intriguing habit of opening as daylight wanes, this Victorian favourite forms a dense shrub studded with slender, tubular flowers of yellow, red, rose, pink, salmon or white, sometimes more than one colour on a single plant and sometimes striped, mottled or splashed with contrasting shades. A flower that opens around suppertime one day and closes before lunch the next may seem unappealing, but mirabilis is an attractive shrub even when the flowers are closed, with its deep green, heart-shaped leaves. As a bonus, flowers do stay open late in the morning on overcast days, and on especially gloomy days, they may even stay open all day. The shrubby plants

can grow 3 or 4 feet tall and just as wide from tubers, but they will be smaller from seed. When open, the flowers exude a heavenly, cowslip perfume that is strongest at twilight, although the fragrance remains all night. We have observed hummingbirds visiting the flowers by day and a great variety of moths by night.

Four-o'clocks can be grown from seed or tubers or bought as bedding plants. The advantage of purchased tubers over seeds is a 3-foot-tall bush in flower by early summer rather than a foot-tall plant still in bud. The disadvantages are greater expense and a narrower range of colours. Set tubers or bedding plants in the garden after the last frost in well-drained soil in half-shade. If you elect to grow from seeds, soak them for two days in tepid water before sowing them half an inch deep directly in the garden after the last frost. Sprouting occurs in about a week and blooming two months later. Or sow a month earlier indoors in peat pellets, and plant out 18 inches apart when nights are warm. Both seeds and seedlings need temperatures of at least 70 degrees F to thrive. Blooming is continuous until frost. Water plentifully and fertilize monthly. Four-o'clocks may self-sow. After the tops are blackened by frost, dig the dark maroon tubers to store in dry peat moss in a cool place.

Plant four-o'clocks as a fragrant hedge, and set some in large pots for scent at the doorstep or wherever there are noses and eyes to enjoy them. The yellow-flowering types are an excellent background for purple basil and beefsteak plant.

Mirabilis, a member of the four-o'clock family *Nyctaginaceae*, was brought to Europe by the Spanish in the 16th century. The genus name is Latin for wonderful. The species name refers to Jalapa, Mexico, which may be the place of origin.

Heliotrope, Cherry Pie
(*Heliotropium arborescens*, *H. peruvianum*)

This plant fairly exudes the air of Victorian society, with its dark leaves suggesting drawing rooms and potted plants and its flowers blooming in a colour popular for ladies'

dresses a century ago—indeed, it was in the 1880s that the word heliotrope joined the vernacular to mean deep purple. In *The Canadian Fruit, Flower and Kitchen Garden* of 1872, heliotrope is one of the annuals most highly recommended, although as "a plant valued for the sweetness and delicacy of its perfume more than for the beauty of its flowers." In fact, the dark purple heliotrope cultivars, those carried by most seed catalogues today, have very little scent, while the lilac or violet strains carry the sugary fragrance that gave the plant the common name cherry pie. There are also white cultivars, although they are seldom available.

Despite the 19th-century remark that heliotrope is best grown for its perfume, we found the quarter-inch flowers, which bloom ceaselessly until frost in trusses 6 to 9 inches wide, beautiful enough even without fragrance and attractive to both butterflies and bumblebees. The deeply ribbed, suedelike leaves are dark to medium green and strongly veined underneath. Plants grow about 2 feet tall and wide and branch all the way up. Dead-head to remove the spent brown flowers.

Sow the seeds, lightly covered, in a warm place indoors about three months before the last frost. Sprouting may take as long as six weeks. Plant a foot apart in dryish soil in sun or half-shade after all frost danger has passed. Blooming begins about four months after sprouting. As heliotrope is actually a tender evergreen perennial, the gardener can take cuttings in late summer or lift entire plants and prune them to overwinter in a bright room whose tem-

perature does not fall below 45 degrees F. Because of its shrubby shape, heliotrope can be used as a temporary hedge (as it is used permanently in its native Peru) or can be clipped to form a standard. To do this, remove the lower branches, stake the plant and prune out the tip so that the top will become bushy. Accompany heliotrope in a garden bed with pink poppies, four-o'clocks or blue salvia, or grow it as a container plant. In a tub, it will subdue the clashing reds of salvia or celosia.

Heliotrope is a Peruvian member of the borage family *Boraginaceae* and takes its name from the Greek words *helios* (sun) and *trope* (to turn), in reference to an old belief that the flowers followed the sun across the sky. *Arborescens* describes its tree-like shape.

Lemon Mint
(*Monarda citriodora*)

Lemon mint, also called purple lemon mint and lemon bee balm, is one of the newest farm crops on the Canadian prairies, where it is grown for its scented oil, thymol, used commercially in the manufacture of cosmetics. Present in all parts of the plant but especially on the surface of the flowers and leaves, the oil gives lemon mint a strong flavour and scent, and the plant makes a delicious, fragrant tea. Aside from these plusses, lemon mint is also hardy, heat-tolerant and decorative, producing clusters of deep purple bracts and toothed, opposite green leaves on strong, self-supporting, square stems 1 to 3 feet tall. The mature seed heads can be used in dried flower arrangements.

Sow the small, brown seeds indoors, lightly covered, eight weeks early. Seeds sprout in about a week. Around the last frost date, set transplants 8 inches apart in ordinary soil in sun or partial shade. Lemon mint often reseeds itself. It is best grown in masses in midborder.

The genus *Monarda* is named for Nicholas de Monardes, a 16th-century Spanish botanist who never visited North America but wrote an

Named for its habit of opening in late afternoon, the four-o'clock, FACING PAGE, TOP, *is a South American native that forms a dense shrub 3 or 4 feet tall and just as wide. It can be grown from tubers or, more slowly, from seed. Heliotrope,* FACING PAGE, BOTTOM, *is a Victorian favourite, while lemon mint,* ABOVE, *is an annual version of the better-known perennial monarda. Its scented leaves, too, can be used for tea.*

account of its plants, *Joyfull newes out of the newe founde world*. A member of the mint family *Labiatae*, monarda is native to North America and Mexico. *Citriodora* means lemon-scented.

Mignonette
(*Reseda odorata*)

If it weren't for its knockout fragrance, no one except the occasional botanist would bother with mignonette, so unassuming are its spikes of greenish, broccoli-like flowers. Yet mignonette (literally, little darling) was beloved of Josephine, wife of Napoleon, a choosy flower collector if ever there were one and so jealous of her acquisitions that she sometimes prohibited their culture by commoners. Mignonette, however, became all the rage for Parisian balcony pots of the 18th century, although the plant needs sun to be fully fragrant. Vincent van Gogh apparently had a small plot.

The quarter-inch flowers grow in clusters at the tips of succulent stems about 20 inches tall and well suited to a border edge. Pumpkin-orange stamens hang inside the fringed, feathery petals. The light green leaves are soft and paper-thin.

As soon as the soil can be worked in spring, sow seeds directly in the garden on the raked soil surface. Sow in drifts, then thin plants to 6 inches apart. Or start seeds indoors in 3-inch peat pots, thinning to three seedlings per pot. Pinch back plant tips early to promote branching – or create a tree mignonette, popular in Edwardian times, by training a plant as a standard in the fashion of heliotrope, described above. Plant mignonette in the company of showier plants such as schizanthus. The plants do best in cool weather or with some shade in the afternoon.

Mignonette is a North African member of the mignonette family *Resedaceae*. The genus and family names, from the Latin *resedare* (to heal), suggest medicinal value. *Odorata* means fragrant.

Nicotiana
(*Nicotiana alata, N. affinis*)

Although they have always been overshadowed in the annual garden by their relatives the petunias, the bedding nicotianas not only have a more sophisticated elegance but also offer the ever-blooming qualities of their better-known cousins. Nicotiana, or flowering tobacco, needs neither dead-heading nor staking. Furthermore, nicotiana can bring height to the garden, with species and cultivars from 15 inches to more than 5 feet tall (described in chapter four).

It is an interesting flower to watch growing. The low crown of leaves that first develops sits in the garden for some time, seemingly spaced too far from its neighbours. Once the weather warms and the central shoot decides to grow, however, the gardener can almost see its daily progress. The stalk bears hairy, somewhat sticky, paddle-shaped leaves. Along side branches and at the tips, nearly horizontal flower buds open continuously until frost.

Flowers, up to 2 inches wide, comprise five or, rarely, six fused petals that form 3-inch-long trumpets – like a neater, more substantial petunia – sought out by hummingbirds and moths. The pistils and anthers are black. Pure white or violet-tinged cultivars are the most fragrant, but there are also mauves, violets, purples, reds and pinks, all with paler undersides that create an interesting double exposure when the flowers are blown by the wind. All have some sweetness, especially at night, and all are beautiful cut flowers.

The species *N. affinis* is a white, evening-scented type that grows about 2½ feet tall. *N. alata* is available as a bedding plant every spring, but if you wish to start your own, sow the dust-fine seeds on the moist soil surface about eight weeks early. Cover pots with plastic, and keep them out of direct sun until sprouting occurs in one to three weeks. After frost danger, plant in full sun or light shade in deep, rich, moist soil.

A South American member of the nightshade family *Solanaceae*, nicotiana is named for Jean Nicot, who introduced the tobacco plant to

France in the 16th century and whose name is also remembered in the alkaloid nicotine (which is present in both nicotiana and tobacco). *Alata* means winged, describing the shape of the petioles.

Persian Violet
(*Exacum affine*)

The Persian violet is one of those rare plants that almost always look neat, tidy and colourful—the kind you want to touch to make sure they are real. It has glossy little heart-shaped green leaves and perfectly formed half-inch flowers of lavender, blue, rose or white, depending upon cultivar. But nothing synthetic could smell as sweet, and the flowers are too complex to be artificial, with bright yellow-orange anthers and a pale green pistil that curves up over them like an elephant's tusk. From propellerlike buds, flowers grow individually on stalks that originate in the leaf axils. The stems are fleshy, ribbed and self-supporting. Persian violets are now available in many places in spring as large potted plants, and they can be left in their containers, but they also do beautifully transplanted along a border. Depending upon cultivar and growing conditions, plants can grow 4 inches to 2 feet tall. They have only recently become popular for outdoor gardens, so new forms will undoubtedly be appearing for years to come.

Persian violets grow very slowly from seed, but they demand more patience than skill. Sprinkle the dust-like seeds onto the moist soil surface four months early, and place the pots under clear plastic in a warm place. Sprouting takes one to two weeks, although the cotyledons are so tiny that gardeners may not realize the seeds have sprouted for a few days. Six weeks after sowing, our plants were still only about an eighth of an inch across. The Persian violet seedlings pick up speed when the weather is warm and the days are long. They like plenty of moist, fertile soil and shade. Set plants in individual 8-inch pots or 8 inches apart in the garden. Soil must be perfectly drained but never dry enough to make the plants wilt. Flowers bloom constantly until frost. Before then, bring plants indoors for reincarnation as excellent houseplants. Root short tip cuttings for additional plants.

The Persian violet, which comes from the island of Socotra, in the Indian Ocean, is a member of the gentian family *Gentianaceae*, and its genus name comes from *exacon*, the Gallic name for another plant. *Affine* means "related to."

Petunia
(*Petunia* spp)

Although it has now been eclipsed by impatiens, the petunia was North America's favourite bedding flower

Nicotiana, FACING PAGE, *available now in most places as started plants, is a tomato relative that blooms all summer and makes a beautiful cut flower. The half-inch flowers of Persian violet,* LEFT, *a plant that seems too perfect to be real, glow on a small, round shrub that makes an excellent plant for shade or indoors.*

in the 1950s and 1960s. It is long-blooming, comes in a wider range of colours than any other flower, is not particular about soil and blooms throughout the summer, surviving fall's first light frosts. Only where rain is heavy do petunias become blowsy and unattractive – the flowers close when wet, though some strains are more weather-resistant than others. Plants about 2 feet tall and wide bear soft trumpet flowers. Singles consist of five joined petals, while the doubles look fluffy. Stems and leaves are dull green, fuzzy and slightly sticky.

What is surprisingly little known about petunias is that many have an intoxicating perfume. Fragrance is such a low priority, however, that gardeners searching for scented petunias will have quite a challenge. The current seed catalogues do not mention fragrance at all in individual petunia descriptions. In our experience, however, the white, blue and mauve shades are most apt to be fragrant. If you grow these flowers on a balcony or porch or by a window, you will enjoy their sweetness, which is strongest in the late afternoon and evening. A variety of night-flying moths comes to gather the nectar.

There are two principal types of petunias – grandifloras and multifloras – and both may be scented. The grandifloras have fewer but larger flowers, to 5 inches wide. Multifloras are better choices all around, because they are bushier and their flowers, about 2 inches wide, recover more quickly after rain. There are single and double selections of both types. Petal edges may be frilled or fringed. There are also cascading petunias for hanging baskets.

If you choose to grow petunias from seed, press the tiny seeds lightly into the soil surface – they need light to germinate. Cover the pots with clear plastic, and set them in a warm place. Our seeds sown March 24 sprouted April 3 and bloomed in early June. Keep the seedlings in a cool, bright place after sprouting because their growth is influenced by temperature and day length. When the weather is cool and days are short, petunias are compact and branching, but when the temperature rises above 75 degrees F, they

become leggy, producing just a single flower on each stem. Pinch back and transplant outdoors after the last frost, about a foot apart, in rich soil in sun or partial shade. Dead-head regularly, and pinch the plants back again in late summer.

Petunias can be potted up around the time of the first fall frost to overwinter indoors. The gardener can then take cuttings from the plant for an easy supply of spring flowers. Cut sections of stem with three leaf joints, trimming off flower buds and lower leaves. Insert the bottom inch or two in moist growing mix, covering a leaf joint. Set the cuttings into individual pots as soon as new growth begins.

Petunias are excellent container and window-box flowers, but keep them out of deep shade, or they will become leggy. They also make good cut flowers, but try to cut as much stem as possible. Use petunias, too, in their traditional role to edge beds of annuals or perennials.

Petunia is a tender perennial South American member of the nightshade family *Solanaceae*, and its name derives from the word *petun* (tobacco) of the Tupi Indians of Brazil.

Schizopetalon
(*Schizopetalon walkeri*)

Aside from its sweet scent, what is most interesting about this little-known flower is the intricately cut shape of its petals. The white flowers, as wide as an inch, have petals so deeply indented they resemble aerials. They grow in exquisite, orchidlike groups on the upper half of fragile stems that tend to flop to one side and wander, reaching 6 to 12 inches in height. The rough-feeling leaves are lobed and clasp the stems.

Sow the tiny, round, brownish seeds in peat pots or pellets, as the plants suffer if their roots are damaged during transplanting. Seeds sprout in about 10 days. Plant pots or pellets 6 inches apart in a sunny place in good soil where the flowers can glisten white against a dark background. Or sow seeds directly in the garden about two weeks before the last spring frost for flowers six weeks later. Flowering does not last long; our plants had entirely gone to seed by late August, leaving us with a crop of long seedpods. However, schizopetalon will flower again if cut back. This is a good companion for nolana in a rock garden.

The name of this Chilean member of the mustard family *Cruciferae* comes from the Greek words for divided petals.

Stock
(*Matthiola longipetala, M. incana*)

There are two types of stock whose sweet scent earns them a

place in the fragrant garden. Like mignonette, the evening-scented stock (*M. longipetala*, formerly *M. bicornis*) offers perfume rather than visual impact. In the early evening, when the plants "pour out upon the still night air a lavish gift of sweetest fragrance," as Gertrude Jekyll wrote a century ago, "the modest little plant that in strong sunlight looked unworthy of a place in the garden now rises to its appointed rank and reigns supreme as its prime delight."

Strong praise from one of the foremost English garden designers, yet the evening-scented stock, whose half-inch, white-to-purple flowers curl into unsightly brownish specks by day, has impressed generations of garden visitors. When the flowers open in the evening, "the scent will reach you, sweet and mysterious," writes 20th-century English gardener Rosemary Verey. "One moment it will be with you and the next will have vanished. So elusive is it that you must move along the path to find it again." This intriguing, slender plant grows a foot or two tall, branching from halfway up. The slender, toothed, greyish leaves are covered with fine hairs. Young seedpods arch upward, ending in a whalelike tail.

The common stock (*M. incana*), once called stock-gillyflower, is an old-fashioned, short-lived perennial grown as an annual and is so hardy that it provides some of the best late colour in the annual garden. Most frequently grown are the so-called 10-week stocks, which come into flower in about that length of time. They produce shrubby, self-supporting, foot-tall plants whose spires of four-petalled, single or double flowers bloom in warm shades of yellow and pink through red and purple. There are also creamy whites. All make excellent cut flowers.

Both types of stock can be sown directly in the garden, barely covered, as soon as the soil can be worked or as late as June. *M. longipetala* will flower less than two months later, *M. incana* about 10 weeks later. As they have taproots, stocks do not transplant well. Sow evening-scented stocks in full sun close to the house to enjoy their beautiful scent, but scatter the seeds between patches of their diurnal counterparts, Virginia stocks, or among other day-flowering plants such as salpiglossis, salvias and petunias. Otherwise, the result may be unappealing stretches of dead-looking flower heads until sunset. Plants may self-sow, so we gather armloads of seed-covered branches to spread here and there for bloom the next spring.

Matthiola, a member of the mustard family *Cruciferae* native to the Mediterranean regions, is named for 16th-century Italian doctor and botanist, Pierandrea Mattioli. The species name suggests the two-horned shape of the seedpods.

Petunias, FACING PAGE, are some of the most popular annuals in the garden because they are long-blooming, shade- and heat-tolerant and come in almost every colour. Many are sweetly scented. They are also easy to grow from seed and sometimes self-sow, although seeds should be started indoors, unlike those of the intoxicating evening-scented stock, LEFT, whose tiny unassuming flowers bloom from seeds sown outdoors in spring.

The Cutting Garden
Flowers for designs and arrangements

Flowers for cutting can be grown in regular garden beds and picked judiciously so that the outdoor effect is not spoiled, or they can be grown in special rows, perhaps as part of the vegetable garden. If the flowers are kept picked, new ones will continue to take the place of the old. The best cutting flowers have long stems for design flexibility and are capable of enduring a long time indoors.

The best cutting flowers are movable pleasures. Outdoors, they are the most faithful producers of season-long colour. Indoors, unlike the flowers that quickly wilt or decorate the floor with a blizzard of petals when cut—morning glories and many poppies, for instance—these flowers bloom on and on, rootless, as though time has slowed. Sometimes they grow new roots into the vase water.

Snipping these flowers from the annual bed can leave gaps, of course, especially if you have a small garden and a large appetite for floral arrangements, so some gardeners plant a separate cutting garden. Here, flowers are grown in rows or beds, just like carrots and onions—and sometimes shoulder to shoulder with them. This arrangement not only encourages gardeners to pick their flowers for indoors but also adds summer-long beauty to the vegetable garden. May Sarton writes in *Plant Dreaming Deep*: "There are gardeners who cannot bear to pick. I am not one of them, so it has been a boon to have that plot at the back, a kind of kitchen garden, stuffed with lettuce and annuals that I can plunder without a qualm."

Patches of the same flowers can also go into more permanent or more decorative beds. There, an occasional picking will keep the plants fresh. Flowers for indoors will, of course, be picked in the bud or at their peak, but pick those past their prime too. Once flowers are "blown," as gardeners used to say, they should be dead-headed (removed from the stems). Leaving the spent flowers on the plant allows it to mature its seeds, which slows or stops flower production—flowers are produced by the plant for the purpose of making seeds. If the flowers are kept picked, however, new ones will continue to take their places. Both cutting and dead-heading are refreshing for most annuals, as well as for herbaceous perennials and roses.

When cutting flowers for indoors, carry a big jar of body-temperature or even hot water into the garden. Cut the flowers in the morning when they are dry, and plunge them immediately into the jar so that the water comes right up to their necks.

Using warm water in the jar is the first stage in the important process of conditioning, or hardening off. (The latter term is also used for the quite different process of acclimatizing plants on their way outdoors in spring or indoors in fall.) Conditioning cut flowers ensures that they will last as long as possible and makes a remarkable difference to the longevity of some types. Judges at flower shows can almost always tell the conditioned flowers from the unconditioned ones, which quickly wilt in the heat and bright lights of the judging areas. The second step in conditioning involves placing the jug of flowers in a cool place such as a basement for several hours or overnight. The next morning, cut the stems once more under running water, removing all the leaves that will be underwater in the vase.

There are many schools and types of floral arranging. Some, such as the Japanese ikebana, are very formal. Victorian parlour arrangements, which create a massed effect within a rounded or triangular outline, are also stylized, with established proportions of vase height to flower height. A contemporary school stresses the natural-looking bunching of flowers in whatever way suits one's own preference. In any case, the so-called rule of three almost always applies: odd numbers of one colour or type of flower will arrange themselves more artfully than even numbers—that is, until you get to the point where the exhausted eye stops counting. The overall aim is joy; a flower's own simple beauty is brought indoors to please once more.

Besides the flowers mentioned here, other excellent cutting choices include all the plants mentioned in chapter eleven as well as alyssum, blanket flower, browallia, canary creeper, celosia, Chinese forget-me-not, larkspur, love-in-a-mist, marigold, nasturtium, nicotiana, phlox, rudbeckia, salvia, sweet peas, the smaller sunflowers, tidy tips, ursinia, Mexican sunflower and the taller cultivars of ageratum. Snow-on-the-mountain can also be used as a cut flower, but since its sap clouds the

the water, it is best to put it in an opaque vase.

Blue Lace Flower
(*Trachymene caerulea*)

This unusual flower, with its umbels of lilac-blue stars resembling 2-to-3-inch circles of lace, marries well in the vase with all kinds of other cut flowers, its long, curved stalks providing a gentle contrast with stiffer stems. Lace flower stems, about 2 feet long and gracefully bending, produce just a few branches and beautiful, deeply lobed leaves similar to dill. In the centre of each flower is a prominent, bright yellow stamen.

Sow the seeds directly, just covered – they need darkness for germination – in warm soil after the last frost in semishade or full sun, thinning to 8 inches apart. Germination takes two or three weeks. Or seeds can be sown in peat pots or peat pellets indoors about eight weeks early. Blue lace flower will tolerate poor, dry soil, although it does better in humus-rich ground. In the garden, it is attractive with other umbels such as bishop's flower or coriander and also complements Johnny-jump-ups and other wild-looking flowers.

Blue lace flower is a Western Australian member of the carrot family *Umbelliferae*. The genus name comes from the Greek *trachys* (rough)

and *meninx* (a membrane), referring to the fruit of some species. *Caerulea* means blue. The plant used to be known as *Didiscus caerulea*.

Butterfly Flower
(*Schizanthus pinnatus,*
S. x wisetonensis)

"As a cut flower, schizanthus has few rivals for delicacy of tones or beauty in form," wrote Richardson Wright in *The Practical Book of Outdoor Flowers* of 1924. A member of the nightshade family, schizanthus is unusual because it resembles an orchid more than it does its cousins the petunias and salpiglossis. A common name is poor man's orchid, and like many orchids, schizanthus simulates a display of abundant pollen with a patch of speckles on the uppermost petal. The true pollen is

There are many schools and types of floral arranging, but the overall aim is joy. FACING PAGE: *a flower's simple beauty is brought indoors to please once more. A rare treat in a bouquet is the blue lace flower,* LEFT, *whose lacy circles of petals top 2-foot stems. Schizanthus,* ABOVE, *also known as poor man's orchid, is a cutting-garden favourite that grows best when nights are cool and may be sown more than once for summer-long bloom.*

hidden, however, on saucer-shaped anthers tucked beneath a divided lower petal that projects from the flower like a platform. When an insect lands on the platform, the anthers spring out, throwing a shower of pollen over the pollinator. The insect proceeds to another flower and crawls over a long, extended stigma that picks up pollen from its body. Schizanthus neatly avoids self-pollination by having the stigma emerge only after the pollen has already scattered.

One-to-two-foot self-supporting stems are covered with flowers just wider than an inch, coloured pink through crimson-violet to purple, with contrasting veins. There is also a pale yellow. The leaves are soft, fernlike and deeply indented.

Sow the tiny, round seeds eight weeks early, lightly pressing them into the moist soil surface. Cover pots with cardboard or black plastic, as they need darkness to germinate. Ours sprouted in four days and bloomed two months later, although sprouting may take two weeks or more. Set outdoors 6 inches apart after the last frost, in rich soil in partial shade. Butterfly flower can also be sown directly outdoors in the cool soil of late spring for cut flowers in summer. It does best when nights are cool. Water well, especially in hot weather. As flowering otherwise continues for only a month or so before the plant goes entirely to seed,

you may want to make a later sowing for continued bloom. Schizanthus is an excellent container plant.

Schizanthus obtains its name from the Greek *schizo* (to split) and *anthos* (flower) because of the divided lower petal. It is a Chilean member of the nightshade family *Solanaceae*. *Pinnatus* refers to the shape of the leaves.

Calendula
(*Calendula officinalis*)

Freshly cut flowers for the Thanksgiving centrepiece—and perhaps a few petals in the salad—are the gifts of calendula, or pot marigold, a truly long-lasting flower not only in the vase but also in the garden, where it survives repeated frosts in the company of just a few other annuals. The harvest of daisies in warm shades of orange, copper and reddish, as well as the original sunny yellow, appears on stalks of varying lengths, because the first flower opens at the end of the self-supporting 1-to-2-foot stem, while later flowers appear on smaller branches that emerge from it. Slightly sparkly, butterknife-shaped leaves grow 8 inches long at the plant base but much smaller toward the top. We set the plants close together, about 8 inches apart, to let them grow into each other like a low hedge. There are scores of cultivars varying in height from 8 inches to 3 feet, with both single and double

flowers, but we prefer the original pot marigold because it is tall, informal and healthy. Some types self-sow, but gardeners who collect the seeds will be sure of having bright spots in next year's garden.

Sow the large seeds, which look a little like curled, beige caterpillars, a quarter of an inch deep in a warm place. Sprouting takes three days to two weeks. Around the last frost date, set the young plants outdoors 8 inches apart in any soil in a sunny or partly shaded place. Calendula also grows dependably from seeds sown directly in the garden—"sow and forget," direct Chiltern Seeds, who also note that this is one of England's most popular hardy annuals. The flower comes into its own in the cool weather of late summer but suffers and may die in prolonged heat. If the summer is hot and calendula ceases blooming, cut the flowers back to help the plant cope until cool weather resumes. Try sowing drifts of this amenable flower directly in the garden with masses of zinnias or 'Giant White Hyacinth' candytuft or with any purple flower, such as China aster or Tahoka daisy.

The genus name of this southern European member of the daisy family *Compositae* derives from the Latin *calendae* (the first day of the month), suggesting the long flowering period. The species name *officinalis* indicates that the plant was once used as a medicinal herb. The flowers are edible, and petals can be used as a substitute for saffron.

Candytuft
(*Iberis umbellata*)

As carefree a plant as calendula, candytuft is also reliable from a direct garden seeding and continues to bloom long after the first fall frost. Clusters of small, sweetly scented flowers bloom in candy shades of white, light pink, mauve, deep magenta and salmon pink, each 1½-inch floral platform supported on its own 2-to-3-inch stalk. Candytuft can grow up to a foot tall and 8 or 9 inches wide, branching from the bottom up to form a ground-covering mass of mixed petal colours and deep green foliage perfect for the front of a border. Dwarf cultivars such as

'Fairy Mix' and 'Brilliant Mixture' grow 8 to 10 inches tall; 'Super Mixture' is a foot tall; 'Flash' is also a foot tall with especially bright colours.

'Giant White Hyacinth' (sometimes considered a member of a different species, *I. odorata*) is an especially beautiful candytuft, one of our favourites both for the garden and for cutting. Attractive combined with almost any brightly coloured flower of medium height, this dignified candytuft looks like a slender white hyacinth or a giant alyssum with gently bending, foot-tall spires of half-inch, snowy, four-petalled flowers. The rough, greyish leaves are shaped like fork handles.

Candytuft can be sown directly outdoors a quarter of an inch deep anytime after the soil can be worked—we sowed 'Giant White Hyacinth' in early June for late-summer flowers. Sprouting takes about 10 days, and blooming occurs about six weeks after outdoor sowing. Seeds can also be sown early indoors. Our 'Brilliant Mixture,' sown March 7 and set outdoors 6 inches apart on April 25, was in bloom by June 15. Choose a spot in well-drained soil in sun or partial shade. Candytuft is a fairly faithful self-sower, if some flowers are allowed to

The old-fashioned calendula, FACING PAGE, *known, for cooking purposes, as the pot marigold, is one of the cutting-garden occupants that will survive repeated frosts, providing bouquets until Thanksgiving. Candytuft, too, is frost-tolerant. The cultivar 'Giant White Hyacinth,'* ABOVE, *lends a beautiful touch to both the garden and arrangements, where its foot-tall spires of snowy flowers provide a note of refreshing calm.*

141

turn brown. Let the seeds fall where they may, or gather entire plants when the seeds are mature and scatter them in areas where you would like to see these cheerful flowers next year.

Iberis is a European member of the mustard family *Cruciferae*. Its genus name refers to the Iberian Peninsula, and the species name indicates that the flowers are borne in umbels.

China Aster
(*Callistephus chinensis*)

Most asters bloom in a cool colour scheme from white to blue through lilac to bluish pink and red, although the garden annuals called China asters add yellows, oranges, peaches and bicolours to the palette. Among the traditional choices for Japanese flower arrangements, these Oriental beauties are valued for their strong stems and long-lasting, upfacing flowers, both single and double. Even if they are not picked, however, they will contribute colour to the garden from late July or early

August until frost, brightening the late-summer doldrums when most perennials are spent and some early-blooming annuals have gone to seed. Furthermore, China asters stay open during showers and in the strong July sun, unlike some of the more weather-conscious daisies.

There are both single and double flowers, including powderpuffs, pompons and spider asters, which have needlelike petals. China aster stems grow from 6 inches ('Pinocchio') to 3 feet tall ('Super Giants,' 'Mixed Powderpuffs,' 'Crego Finest'). Gertrude Jekyll warned her readers away from the dwarf forms: "Here is a plant (whose chief weakness already lies in a certain overstiffness) made stiffer and more shapeless still by dwarfing and by cramming with too many petals."

No one could accuse our favourite, the lovely 'Single California Giant Finest,' of having too many petals. Its 3-inch-wide, single, pink, violet and magenta daisies with yellow centres bloomed in late August from a late-May seeding. By the end of August,

we counted about 15 flowers per plant—a bouquet on its own. Plant these 8 inches apart with bells of Ireland or lavatera 'Mont Blanc.' The 2-to-3-foot stems will stay upright if crowded among other plants but will require staking in open situations. We also liked 'Gusford Supreme,' with balls of tight, white centres surrounded by bright scarlet petals. This is beautiful in an arrangement with 'Giant White Hyacinth' candytuft and geraniums.

Sow the light brown, teardrop-shaped seeds of China asters an eighth of an inch deep at room temperature, either indoors three or four months early or, for later blooms, directly outdoors around the last frost date. Seeds will sprout in one or two weeks. Transplant 2 inches apart when seedlings are three weeks old. They should bloom about two months later. Outdoors, sow the seeds after frost danger, thinning to 6 to 12 inches apart, depending upon eventual plant height. Choose a spot in full sun or partial shade. Asters will tolerate hot, dry soil, and colours may be brighter in poor soil. The insect-borne disease aster yellows, which makes plants unsightly, can be avoided if the gardener plants asters in a new place each year. The singles are reliable self-seeders for us and bloom from early August until a few weeks before frost.

Asters are members of the daisy family *Compositae*. Their name derives from the Latin *astrum* (star), because of the shape of the flower. *Callistephus*, native to Japan and China—hence *chinensis*—takes its name from the Greek words *kallos* (beauty) and *stephanos* (a crown) because of the beautiful flowers.

Chinese Houses
(*Collinsia heterophylla*)

The inch-wide, bicoloured snapdragon flowers of this fancifully named little plant are arranged in whorls around the upper stem. The lower two petals are violet; the upper two are white and fold tightly over the lower after pollination or in moist conditions. Between the lower petals lies a hidden fold containing the anthers and pistil. Stems hung with

these intricate flowers and the complementary, slightly toothed green leaves are lovely on their own in vases or in combination with other delicate white or purplish blooms. Chinese houses are also excellent container plants in shade.

Sow the seeds directly in a place that receives afternoon shade, covering them lightly. Germination takes about two weeks. From a late-May sowing, ours were in flower by the end of July. Thin to 6 inches apart. The 1-to-2-foot stems may need staking. Hot weather stops the blooming of Chinese houses, but flowering will resume in September even if the stems are not cut back. Plants will withstand the first frosts and will self-sow in many gardens.

Chinese houses is a California member of the figwort family *Scrophulariaceae*. The genus name honours 18th-century Philadelphia botanist Zaccheus Collins. *Heterophylla* indicates that the plant has variable leaves.

Clarkia, Godetia
(*Clarkia* spp, *Godetia grandiflora*)

Along with California poppies, clarkia and its cousin godetia are among the most appealing North American natives for the annual garden. Both are excellent cut flowers either bunched on their own or in bouquets with other medium-sized, cool-coloured, soft flowers such as alyssum and eustoma. A single branch of clarkia in a slender glass vase looks as exotic as an orchid. Godetia also holds up well in a vase while exhaling the light honey fragrance of sweet clover. In the garden, both clarkia and godetia will bloom all summer, provided the temperature is not too high—they may expire in a hot, sunny spot—and will survive the first fall frosts.

C. elegans, the popular clarkia, or garland flower, offers stiff spires of bright flowers in white through pink to rose, salmon, orange, scarlet and purple. Conelike buds open into flowers from the bottom of the spike upward. Flowers, pollinated by bumblebees, have four outer petals and four smaller inner ones with a big, white, woolly stigma in the middle. Clarkia grows as tall as 2 feet and about a foot wide (although in rich

Most asters, FACING PAGE, *bloom in a cool colour range, with pinks, violets and purples predominating. Clarkia,* ABOVE, *combines well in a bouquet with other soft flowers such as alyssum and eustoma, while the curious Chinese houses,* LEFT, *makes a fine bouquet on its own or with other delicate white or purplish blooms.*

143

soil, some gardeners have reported stems as tall as 4 feet). *C. pulchella* is a shorter, more slender flower, about a foot tall, with flower spikes in such pastel shades as lilac and pink. *C. concinna*, called eucharidium or red ribbons, produces rounded, bushy plants about a foot tall with feathery, rose-coloured flowers. Satin flower (*C. amoena, G. amoena*) bears the single, satiny flowers typical of the godetias on plants as tall as 3 feet.

Godetia, or farewell-to-spring (*G. grandiflora, C. amoena whitneyi*), yields candlelike buds that open into beautiful five-petalled silky cups more than an inch wide, like single roses or poppies, in shades of white, pink, crimson, salmon and rose with splashes of darker shades and frilled petal margins. There are also double selections. The flowers close at night and in overcast weather. The lush, bushy plant grows 1 to 3 feet tall, depending upon cultivar.

Sow clarkia and godetia seeds directly outdoors, barely covered, in early spring in sun or partial shade. Choose a sandy loam or otherwise well-drained spot out of the wind. Sprouting takes about a week, and flowers appear about three months from sowing. Thin the seedlings to 6 inches apart for a mass effect. Let the soil dry out between waterings. A later sowing in mid-June produces flowering godetia by September. Potted up, the flowers will continue to bloom as houseplants.

Clarkia and godetia, natives of western North America and Chile, are members of the evening primrose family *Onagraceae*. Clarkia takes its name from Captain William Clark, co-leader with Captain Meriwether Lewis (genus *Lewisia*) of the first expedition (1804 to 1806) to cross North America from Missouri to the mouth of the Columbia River.

Cosmos
(*Cosmos* spp)

Gardeners who haven't much time for a large plot but want to have a summer-long supply of long-stemmed flowers for cutting might buy a couple of packets of cosmos seeds and scratch them into any bare, well-drained patch of watered soil in spring. With scarcely any more attention than that, cosmos will produce a mass of slender stems and airy foliage decorated with daisy flowers until frost. This easy flower is early, fast and heat-resistant and comes in many different colours and shapes. It is pest-free and usually self-supporting. In bouquets, cosmos looks wonderful with snow-on-the-mountain, which will last in a vase for about the same length of time.

There are two species commonly grown in northern gardens, both excellent for cutting and both with open, dome-centred flowers. *C. sulphureus* blooms in warm tones of yellow, orange and flame-red. Most flowers are about 2 inches wide, although cultivars with larger and semidouble flowers have been developed, including the Sunny series, 'Sunny Red' and 'Sunny Gold,' which grow about 15 inches tall. Eight plants make a solid, 2-by-2-foot mound of orange and green. 'Sunset' is much taller. Its sturdy, 3-to-4-foot, self-supporting stems are an inch across at the base and then branch to form a bush about 2 feet wide. The deeply lobed leaves of *C. sulphureus* resemble those of ragweed. All types of *C. sulphureus* are good companions for zinnia 'Sombrero' edged with dusty miller.

Cool shades of white, pink, rose and crimson come with *C. bipinnatus*, another Mexican native. This species produces wider flowers on taller plants, generally about 4 feet. The foliage is much airier and finer than that of *C. sulphureus*. Most flowers are about 3 inches wide—such as

those of the commonly grown 'Sensation.' 'Sea Shells' has uniquely rolled petals that add a distinctive touch to floral arrangements, while 'Candy Stripe' has flowers variegated crimson and white, difficult to integrate into the garden and unappealing in the vase. On the other hand, the all-white 'Purity' is a quiet flower that looks harmonious in any colourful garden corner.

Cosmos is reliable from direct seedings and easy to transplant when young, should you find that you have sown it too thickly. Sow the seeds outdoors, lightly covered, at the end of May. They should sprout about a week later, and plants will bloom by the end of July. Even seeds sown in July will produce flowers before frost. Or sow the seeds indoors six weeks early, and set transplants 8 inches to a foot apart in a sunny part of the garden when nights are warm. Staking with twigs may be necessary for tall plants in windy places. Deadhead every few days, as cosmos goes to seed quickly. Save some seeds for next year, or let the plant mature a few flowers so that it will self-sow.

Cosmos is attractive in masses by itself – this is a good medium-height plant for bedding in front of a house – or it can contribute colour to a spent perennial border. Single plants are decorative as well.

Cosmos is a tropical and subtropical American member of the daisy family *Compositae*, and its name comes from the Greek *kosmos* (beautiful). *Bipinnatus* means with bipinnate, centrally divided leaves. *Sulphureus* describes the sulphur-coloured flowers.

Dahlia
(*Dahlia* spp)

Florists love dahlias for their contribution of bright, long-lasting colour to arrangements. Gardeners need not be intimidated by these amenable daisies, which are long-blooming, weather-tolerant and brilliantly coloured. The fastest way to grow them is to purchase potted plants in spring, but they are just as easy, if somewhat slower, from roots,

Cosmos is one of the easiest, most gratifying flowers in the garden. There are two species commonly grown: the warm-toned Cosmos sulphureus, *such as 'Sunny Red,'* FACING PAGE, TOP, *and the cooler-coloured* C. bipinnatus, *whose most popular cultivar, 'Sensation,'* FACING PAGE, BOTTOM, *self-sows generously. The two types are sown directly in the garden for tall stems and bright colour just a few weeks later,* ABOVE. *Deadhead every few days, as cosmos goes to seed quickly.*

and some types can be grown from seed, the slowest but least expensive route. All will yield a crop of roots that can be harvested in fall for blooms the following summer.

The popularity of dahlias is reflected in the vast selection available. The American Dahlia Society recognizes 12 different groups based on form and flower structure. Anemone-flowered dahlias, for instance, have large, tubular petals that form a disc in the centre of the flower. The mignons have single flowers on stems 12 to 20 inches long. Dahlias flower in all shades but blue—especially orange, light yellow, deep magenta, pink and white—each lush bloom on its own stalk overlooking a mound of thick, leathery foliage that is green above and silvery beneath. Both leaves and the succulent, self-supporting stems have a spicy smell when crushed. The plant branches throughout, and the shortest selections form attractive mounds. The tallest cultivars require staking— 'Cactus Flowered Exhibition,' for example, grows 6 feet high.

Both potted plants and roots can be set outdoors in a sunny place in rich, well-drained soil after the last spring frost. Set dwarfs a foot apart, larger dahlias 18 to 24 inches apart. If you elect to grow dahlias from seed, sow the spoon-shaped, papery brown seeds a quarter of an inch deep about two months early, keeping them at room temperature. Ours sprouted in three days (although sprouting can take as long as three weeks) and bloomed three months later. Transplant the seedlings into individual pots when they are 3 inches tall, and move them outdoors when nights are warm. Dead-head throughout the summer. Blooming may be sporadic during the hottest, most humid weather, and if dahlias stop flowering because of too little water, it will be nearly impossible to coax them to start again. A mulch of grass clippings or straw will help. If slugs are a problem, grow dahlias in pots.

After they have been blackened by the first frost, dig up the roots (often and erroneously called tubers), which look like small seed potatoes or slender radishes. Shake off the loose soil and dry them in the sun. To prevent them from drying and shrivelling, pack them in moist vermiculite, sawdust or peat moss, and keep them in a very cool but not freezing place. The following spring, divide the roots so that each piece has an eye at the crown—new growth comes from buds at the base of the old stem. If the eyes are difficult to detect, put the roots in a warm spot for a week until sprouting begins. Then plant the roots horizontally, with the eye up and the crown exposed, in warm garden soil, or start them earlier in pots indoors. Keep them moist and warm in good light.

Dahlias are not only good bedding plants but are also well-suited to containers and window boxes. They will bloom continuously in a flower basket with pinks, verbena and lobelia.

Dahlias are natives of the cool highlands of Mexico and Central America. These members of the daisy family *Compositae* derive their name from Dr. Anders Dahl, an 18th-century Swedish botanist.

Eustoma, Lisianthus
(*Eustoma grandiflorum, Lisianthus russellianus*)

Eustoma is a flower that nature seems to have designed just for cutting. Each plant, about 2 feet tall, is a bouquet of lovely, waxen, greyish leaves and big, long-lasting, silken flowers that, according to Park Seed Co., "resemble roses at first, open to tulip form and at maturity look like poppies." From buds that look like perfect minarets unroll seven or eight of these 3-inch-wide, five-petalled flowers in shell-like shades of pink, lilac, rose, cream and deep gentian-blue, each on its own greyish stem. There are also double forms. All stay fresh in the vase for more than three weeks.

In the garden, where bumblebees collect the golden pollen and the flowers close somewhat in overcast and wet weather, eustoma is difficult to place because of its distinctive yet delicate appearance. Plant a group by the front door, backed with foliage plants such as ferns and snow-on-the-mountain, or accompany eustoma with pink or white saponarias. In front of it plant alyssum, baby's breath or 'Giant White Hyacinth' candytuft.

Eustoma grows slowly from seed. Plan to start it at least three months before the last spring frost; some gardeners aim for the end of December. Seeds sown in February will flower in July. Sow the drab, dust-fine seeds on the soil surface, cover the pots with plastic, and set them in a warm place. Germination takes two or three weeks. In five weeks, the still tiny seedlings can be pricked out into individual pots of rich soil. Pinch the growing point to encourage branching. After frost danger, set transplants a foot apart in a sunny or partly shaded spot in good, moist soil. Leave some in pots too—one to three plants per 12-inch pot of rich, humusy soil—to be brought indoors before the first fall frost.

Eustoma was so recently brought into cultivation that it does not appear in many garden guides, and some catalogues refer to it as lisianthus, an older name. *Eustoma* is a North American member of the gentian family *Gentianaceae*, and its name derives from the Greek words for beautiful countenance. *Grandiflorum* describes the large flowers.

Geranium
(*Pelargonium* spp)

The ease of growing geraniums from cuttings has endeared this decorative tender perennial to gardeners for well over a century. In 1872, *The Canadian Fruit, Flower and Kitchen Gardener* called geraniums "too well known to need particular description." For only a little trouble and no expense, one could have a perpetual supply of long-blooming plants, which hold hand-span clusters of flowers high above decorative, skirt-shaped, leathery leaves. And anything that takes to growing from cuttings this well is sure to be a good candidate for the vase, where it will look fresh for weeks and may even take root if some leaves and a long enough stem are attached. Pick them when the inch-wide, five-petalled flowers are just beginning to bloom, and the flowers will open indoors. The brilliant reds have always been favoured, but geraniums also bloom in shades of cream, light pink, neon-pink, purple, salmon, orange and bicolours. Except in the case of white flowers, leaves are usually zoned with a horseshoe of a darker hue.

There are more than 10,000 cultivars of geranium—or, rather, pelargonium, for the true geranium is a different but related plant. (The struggle to introduce pelargonium as the common name for this plant is an old one. The 1872 book quoted above mentions the debate and concludes that "the name geranium has been so long used . . . that it is quite too late to unsettle long-established public custom.") Most plants grow about 18 inches tall on slightly hairy, succulent stems. *P. x hortorum* is the common garden, or zonal, geranium.

Dahlias can be grown from tuberous roots, but a few smaller-flowered types such as 'Collarette,' FACING PAGE, will bloom in a season from seed, leaving a harvest of roots for next year's cutting garden. Eustoma, LEFT, is a flower almost too exotic for the garden but wonderful in the vase, where it will continue to look fresh for more than three weeks.

The multiflora strains grow about a foot tall and branch from the base, while the dwarfs, about 4 inches shorter, are good choices for pots and window boxes. *P. x domesticum* is the Martha Washington, or regal, geranium. Especially good for window boxes and hanging baskets are cultivars of the ivy geranium (*P. peltatum*), which has ivy-shaped leaves and a trailing or spreading habit. 'Summer Showers' is the first ivy geranium available from seed.

Geraniums are so easy to grow from cuttings that few gardeners bother to start them from seed, which has been possible only since the 1960s. Yet this is a good way to obtain new colours and to refresh one's stock. Sow the reddish brown seeds an eighth of an inch deep in a warm place (about 75 degrees F) two or three months before the last frost. Alternatively, seeds can be sown in fall and the seedlings overwintered on a cool, bright windowsill. Seeds sprout in a week or two and bloom about three months later. Transplant the seedlings into individual containers when they have four or five leaves, and plant them outdoors a foot apart after the last spring frost in a sunny or partly shaded place in rich soil with plenty of water. Buds form only if temperatures are above 56 degrees. Prune the dead flowers, and encourage branching by pinching back the shoots.

For an ongoing supply of a choice plant, take cuttings in August—in time for them to form sturdy plants for overwintering. Choose short pieces of nonflowering stem tip with a leaf attached, and place them in small pots of wet soil mix or vermiculite. When the cuttings begin to grow, set the plants into larger pots. Take new cuttings in March to multiply plants for the garden. Entire plants can also be dug in fall and set in large pots for blooms all winter in a bright window.

The genus *Pelargonium*, a member of the geranium family *Geraniaceae*, is a native of southern Africa.

Painted Tongue
(*Salpiglossis sinuata*)

The first time we saw salpiglossis in its glorious shades of red-brown, deep blue, purple, rose and yellow was in a tropical garden where the flowers looked so exotic that we asked a friend to identify them. It turned out she had ordered her seeds from Stokes, a Canadian seed company. Back home in Canada, salpiglossis was on the top of our seed list, and the flowers turned out to be as beautiful in our northern gardens as they had been in the south. Salpiglossis is a native of Chile, but it must come from the mountain slopes, as it is quite cold-hardy. The seeds sprout even after lying dormant outdoors all winter. Salpiglossis also turned out to be an excellent cut flower, either in a bouquet on its own or combined with peaceful whites and greens. Pot a few plants in fall before the first hard frost for many more weeks of flowers indoors. We transplanted some in bud from the garden to an indoor windowsill in October, and by mid-November, they flowered beautifully.

Salpiglossis is a little like a petunia that has been to finishing school: more delicate, upright and distinctive, around 2 feet tall and 6 inches wide. The slender, green, hairy leaves—toothed on the lower part of the plant, smooth-edged higher up—are sticky and resinous. Grow it where you might otherwise grow petunias. Its trumpet flowers, about 2 inches wide, have contrasting veins that inspired the common name painted tongue, and the upper throat glows yellow as though illuminated. Flowers open from the bottom of the stems up and will bloom forever, it seems—even indoors in the fall. If painted tongue is grown in a container, a role that suits it well, the move to indoors will be much easier.

Sow the seeds six weeks early indoors or in a cold frame, pressing them into the soil surface and covering the pots with cardboard or black plastic, as the seeds need darkness. They will germinate in about three weeks. Transplant into the garden a foot apart when the weather has settled; they transplant easily. Seeds can also be sown directly in the garden around the last frost date. Painted tongue prefers good soil in sheltered half-shade. Pinch out the central stem when the plant is about 5 inches tall to encourage bushiness. Stake with twiggy branches. It makes a nice container plant by itself or bordered with alyssum and lobelia. Painted tongue often self-sows, but the colour range is apt to be less exciting.

Salpiglossis is a Chilean member of the nightshade family *Solanaceae*. Its name comes from the Greek *salpinx* (trumpet) and *glossa* (tongue). *Sinuata* means wavy-edged.

Penstemon
(*Penstemon* spp)

Resembling a small foxglove, to which it is closely related, the lovely

penstemon adds an unusual touch to flower arrangements, with its long-lasting spires of tubular flowers in shades of deep magenta, pink, salmon-red, lavender and white. Like foxglove, penstemon's first flowers appear on the top third of the stem and open upward, one at a time, each on its own 1-inch stalk. The five-petalled flowers, 1½ inches wide, point directly outward from the stem, their petals curving backward and marked inside with white lines that lead pollinators into the central tunnel. Pressed to its walls are four bluish anthers and one bearded, sterile anther—source of its common name, beard-tongue. Plants grow 18 to 24 inches tall, branching from the base. The lance-shaped leaves are a semigloss green, about 3 inches long and an inch wide, and have a light central vein. Several annual species are available, the most common of which is *P. gloxinioides*, in a wide range of colours (cultivar 'Sensation').

Sow the small, brown seeds indoors on the soil surface about eight weeks early; the seeds need light to germinate. Ours sprouted in about three weeks and bloomed 3½ months later. Set outdoors a foot apart after frost danger in rich soil in full sun. Penstemon is best planted in groups, alternating with lower-growing plants such as desert marigolds, with their silvery foliage and bright yellow flowers.

Penstemon is a member of the figwort family *Scrophulariaceae*. Most species are native to North America. The genus name comes from the Greek *pente* (five) and *stemon* (a stamen), a distinguishing feature of the flower.

Snapdragon
(*Antirrhinum majus*)

Many flower gardeners are not enthusiastic about the formal, rigid spikes of certain ornamentals. We know people who do not like foxgloves, lupins, certain salvias or snapdragons. Someone likes them, however, because snapdragons are among the top 10 annuals in North

Picked when the flowers are just beginning to open, geraniums, FACING PAGE, *will bloom in the vase and may even take root. Painted tongue,* ABOVE, *is a little like a petunia that has been to finishing school: upright, delicate and distinctive. Flowers, which open from the bottom of the stem upward, seem to bloom forever, even indoors.*

dwarf or carpeting types, as small as 6 inches in height, are excellent for rock gardens and border edges. The taller types will stay upright in a sheltered place but will require staking with twiggy branches in a windy spot or where rains are heavy. Side shoots alternate with leaves. The flowers form in clusters on stem tips, the top ones opening last. The satiny-feeling leaves are long, narrow and dark green and grow thickly up the stems for a massed effect.

Sow seeds indoors six to eight weeks early by sprinkling the seeds on the soil surface—they need light to germinate. They will sprout in one to three weeks. Pinch plants back when they are a few inches tall to encourage bushy growth. After the last spring frost, plant snapdragons 6 inches apart in clumps, in rich, well-drained soil in half-shade to full sun. Seeds can also be sown directly in the garden when the soil has warmed in spring. Snapdragons do best in cool weather.

Antirrhinum is a tender perennial member of the family *Scrophularia-ceae*. The genus name derives from the Greek *anti* (like) and *rhin* (a snout) for the shape of the flower. The species name of *A. majus*, which originates in the Mediterranean, means large.

Zinnia
(*Zinnia* spp)

Whether elegantly single or as fully double as snowballs, zinnias make beautiful, long-lasting cut flowers that are especially nice in joyous combination with other bright daisies such as asters and calendulas. Cut the stems when the flowers are newly opened or not quite open, and they will last for weeks. In the garden, all zinnias demand is well-drained soil, hot weather and sun.

Zinnia flower shoots emerge from leaf axils, and buds that resemble art-nouveau lampshades become baskets of sepals to hold the petals, which vary from cream through pale green to flamboyant yellow, orange, red, purple and bicolours. In size, the flowers range from barely an inch across in some species to saucer-sized, single or double. Do not judge zinnias by flower size alone, how-

American gardens today. A century ago, Gertrude Jekyll judged them as "one of the best and most interesting and admirable of garden plants." Snapdragons are easy from seed or transplant, they often self-sow, they are very frost-resistant, and they bloom in a range of colours: red, white, yellow, orange, bronze, purple, rose and, less fortunately, bicolours. (As Katharine S. White wrote in one of her garden columns for *The New Yorker*, "The snapdragon is a very complicated flower form to start with, and it has style. Fuss it up, and it becomes overdressed.")

The snapdragon, or figwort, family includes many genera. Some, like mimulus, penstemon and torenia, have almost bell-shaped lobes with exotic markings, whereas toadflax and snapdragon have bunny faces, with two upright petal "ears" above the "face." The complex little jaws can be squeezed open, a delight for children. Snapdragons make beautiful cut flowers, although indoors and out, the plain colours are easier to work with than the bicolours.

In the garden, the usual full-sized plants produce clumps about 16 inches tall and a foot wide. Cultivars 3 feet tall are spectacular, and the

ever, as the singles and the smaller flowers often have more grace and better proportions for both the garden and the vase. Depending upon cultivar, stems may be less than a foot tall (the dwarfs) to more than 3 feet. The taller ones may need staking. There are types for border edges, walkways, pots and the back of the border.

We recommend the following common zinnia (*Z. elegans*) cultivars:
• 'Border Beauty Scarlet' has rich scarlet, double flowers on 2-foot stems.
• 'Dream' has 3-foot stems supporting giant, dahlia-flowered, deep purplish pink flowers with lime-yellow discs. The sturdy, well-branched plants grow to a foot wide and are very adaptable to windy places.
• 'Dreamland Scarlet' has 3-inch double red flowers on foot-tall stems well suited to a position just in front of 'Border Beauty Scarlet.'
• 'Envy,' with pale, yellow-green dahlia flowers on 2-to-3-foot stems, is striking in semishade and in cut-flower arrangements.
• 'Rose Pinwheel,' the first mildew-resistant zinnia, has single rose-coloured flowers on 12-to-18-inch stems.

Z. haageana (*Z. angustifolia, Z. linearis*) 'Classic' or 'Orange Star,' a different species, which forms a bush-shape of distinctive narrow foliage, grows less than a foot tall. Its daisies are golden orange and about an inch wide. It tolerates poor soil and hot, dry conditions as well as light frost. Additional cultivars include the taller 'Old Mexico' and 'Persian Carpet.'

The slowest but cheapest way to get zinnias for cutting is to sow the seeds outdoors, lightly covered, in the warm soil of late May or early June. The soil should be well drained and rich in organic matter. Choose a spot in full sun—even partial shade reduces flowering and weakens stems. Seeds sprout in a few days to a week, and blooming takes place about 10 weeks later. Thin according to eventual stem height. For a pleasantly crowded look, 18 inches apart is about right for 3-foot stems—zinnias look best when massed. For earlier flowers, start the seeds indoors six weeks early, two or three seeds per recycled foam cup or six-pack cell, thinning to the strongest seedling. Transplant outdoors carefully, watering both before and after, as zinnias resent being moved. Sown April 12, our zinnias began flowering by early July. They do best when summers are hot, dry and long. Dead-head the faded flowers.

A member of the daisy family *Compositae*, zinnias are native to Mexico, Central America and the southwestern United States and named for Johann Gottfried Zinn, an 18th-century German professor of botany who grew *Zinnia peruviana*.

Snapdragons, FACING PAGE, which are easy from seed and often self-sow, make beautiful cut flowers, although both indoors and out, the plain colours are easier to manage than the complex bicolours. Zinnias, ABOVE, are easy garden flowers too. Their range of bright colours makes them attractive in the garden and in vases, especially with other daisies such as asters and calendulas.

Annuals Forever
Everlasting flowers from the garden

Certain annuals dry well enough, without any complicated procedures, that they will continue to be colourful all winter and often beyond. Here, statice, celosia and strawflowers are combined with the perennial yarrow for a bouquet that needs no further care. For highest quality and the most long-lasting colour, these flowers must be picked at the peak of perfection, dried quickly and kept out of direct sun thereafter.

153

Anything that breaks the barriers of the growing season is welcomed by northern gardeners, and nothing does so as gently as the enduringly bright flowers called everlastings or immortelles. These unusual blooms, which carry their colours into winter like small memories of summer past, need no special preparations or processes in order to stay beautiful. Even in the garden, they are surprisingly dry.

In many cases, this is because the coloured part of the flower is not made up of petals, which would fade and perhaps fall, but of papery little leaves playing the colourful pollinator-attracting role of petals. These modified leaves are called bracts. A disproportionate number of the best of the brightly coloured bract flowers come from Australia, many of whose plants and animals are somewhat out of step with the rest of the world. Fewer plant genera are found in Australia than on any other continent. The everlasting Australian daisies include Swan River everlasting, ammobium and, the most popular of all, strawflower. All have bracts in place of the usual ray florets—the circle of petals of most daisies—although these Australian daisies do maintain the softer disc florets, which form the centre of the flower.

While they are both unusual and useful, everlastings are not the most attractive flowers in the annual garden. Their stems are often thick and long, bearing just a few smallish flowers. There are many showier daisies, not to mention hundreds of other brighter flowers for the annual garden. We often start the everlastings directly in the garden from seed, since we are growing them not for summer colour but for a crop to harvest, and other gardeners may want to grow them in rows or in their own place, like the flowers for cutting described in the previous chapter. Then, you can cut the everlastings at will without destroying the effect of your garden design. As D.W. Beadle wrote of everlastings a century ago in *The Canadian Fruit, Flower and Kitchen Gardener*, "They do not appear to any advantage in the garden when it is gay with summer flowers, but when wintry winds toss the seared leaves above the flowerbeds, then the everlastings play an important part in the Christmas decorations and, mingled with the ornamental grasses, make charming bouquets of rare beauty." We could imagine a small indoor evergreen tree decorated only with everlastings.

Rare beauty will result, however, only if the gardener picks the flowers at the right stage of growth and prepares them quickly for drying. The best stage for picking each type is described in the plant list that follows. In general, flowers for drying should always be picked when they are dry, preferably in midday or during the afternoon of a sunny day. Strip the lower leaves, tie the stems in small bunches with string or rubber bands, and hang them upside down in a dry, airy place out of direct sun. Some sturdy types such as globe amaranth, grasses and starflowers can be left upright in baskets or empty vases to dry. You may elect to wire some flowers or to tape the stems just below the flower heads to hold them securely upright for flower arrangements.

As well as the following plants, other annuals that dry well but are described fully elsewhere in the book include amaranths, grasses, calendula, dusty miller, blanket flower, larkspur and tricolour sage. Keep an eye out, too, for attractive seedpods. Some of the best are listed at the end of this chapter.

Ammobium
(*Ammobium alatum*)

Ammobium, or winged everlasting, partners with strawflower and rose everlasting to form a trio of durable daisies whose petal-like, papery bracts surround a central disc of soft florets. In this case, the flowers, about an inch wide, have silvery white bracts surrounding yellow centres that often turn brown when dried. The young plant resembles a dandelion or salsify, with a basal cluster of floppy, woolly leaves that are silver underneath. Later, the sturdy flower stem shoots straight up to 1 to 3 feet tall, bearing the distinctive ripply wings that give the plant its common and Latin names. In proportion to the width of the stems, the flowers seem inappropriately small, although the usual variety sold, *A. alatum grandiflorum* —the variety name suggests flowers larger than usual—bears daisies almost 2 inches wide. The flowers fold tightly closed at night.

The easiest route to flowers involves sowing the seeds directly in the garden around the last frost date. Choose a sunny spot with ordinary soil, where germination will take as long as two weeks. Thin to 9 inches apart. Alternatively, sow the seeds in a cool place indoors about six weeks early, and set the transplants

outdoors around the last frost date. Ammobium will survive the first fall frosts.

To harvest winged everlasting, pick each flower on its own short stem before it is fully open. Even the buds dry well. Bunch and hang in an airy, dry place as soon as possible.

Winged everlasting is an eastern Australian member of the daisy family *Compositae*. Its genus name comes from the Greek *ammos* (sand) and *bio* (to live), in reference to its native habitat. *Alatum* means winged.

Bells of Ireland
(*Molucella laevis*)

Irish only in colour, this unusual plant is a 2-to-3-foot spire of cone-shaped calyxes arranged around the upper part of the stem like densely tiered rings of bells. The flowers, held deep within each calyx, are as insignificant as tiny dolls in deep cradles. The toothed leaves grow opposite one another on long peti-oles, with the whorls of flower bells emerging from leaf axils.

Because bells of Ireland resents transplanting, the large seeds are best sown directly in the garden after the last frost, when the weather has warmed. Choose a spot in sun or partial shade with rich, moist soil. Press the seeds into the soil surface, as they require light. Germination is uneven, taking one to three weeks. If you want an earlier start, sow the seeds indoors four weeks before the last frost, three seeds to a peat pot or peat pellet, thinning to one seedling per pot. After frost, set the plants out 8 inches apart. Bells of Ireland requires staking unless the spikes are cut before they fall under their own weight. The plants are good garden border companions for soft plants such as clarkia or balsam impatiens, fronted by salvias. Bells of Ireland self-sows in our northern gardens.

Cut the stems as soon as the calyxes are fully open. Indoors, bells of Ireland should be kept out of the light, but in any case, the green bells will eventually fade to pale beige. Handle the stems with care, as the little bells are very fragile when dry.

Ammobium, FACING PAGE, *produces its 2-inch daisies on disproportionately fat stems. For drying, the flowers are best picked before they are fully open. Bells of Ireland,* ABOVE, *is a fresh apple green, which fades to a parch-ment shade when the delicate calyx funnels dry. This everlasting is easily grown from seeds sown outdoors and often self-sows.*

155

Bells of Ireland is a Mediterranean to western Indian member of the mint family *Labiatae*. Its genus name is obscure in origin. Possibly it derives from the island of Molucca, Indonesia, source of one species. *Laevis* means smooth.

Bupleurum
(*Bupleurum rotundifolium*)

Bupleurum is a little-known plant with several virtues, we discovered. This "plant with an identity crisis," as Thompson & Morgan describes it, is "more like a euphorbia than a euphorbia in flower, yet it has leaves like a eucalyptus." It also makes an excellent and unusual cut flower, with self-supporting stems as tall as 2½ feet, very attractive, leathery, greyish platform leaves and star-shaped green bracts holding tiny yellow umbel flowers that glisten with nectar. Not until late summer did it become apparent that it is also a fine everlasting: the bracts, which dry to a light straw colour, hold the black seeds fast, like jelly beans within papery nests.

Lightly cover the carawaylike seeds, five per peat pot, eight weeks before the last spring frost. Seeds should sprout in about two weeks.

Plant 18 inches apart in well-drained soil in sun so that the fan-shaped plants can overlap to produce the effect of a lacy hedge.

The genus name of this member of the carrot family *Umbelliferae* derives from the Greek words for ox and rib, although the reason is unknown. The species name describes the round foliage. *B. rotundifolium* is an Old World plant that has naturalized in the eastern United States.

Celosia, Cockscomb
(*Celosia argentea*)

There are two very different members of this species, both good for drying. The most familiar is prince's feather, the variety *plumosa*, which produces woolly spires of hundreds of tiny, often brilliantly coloured flowers that are as attractive in the garden as in a vase or dried arrangement. The central plume sits deeper in the plant than the side candles. Cockscomb, the variety *cristata*, is a mutant that frankly looks like one, with a broad, ridged stem and flowers in dense, convoluted ridges that resemble a furry brain—not our idea of floral beauty. Cockscomb is prized, however, for some Japanese arrangements.

Both varieties of celosia bloom in bright shades of red, yellow and orange, although there are also cream selections, and a recent rose-pink *plumosa* cultivar, 'Pink Castle,' is a welcome addition. *Plumosa*s may be as tall as 3 feet, while the *cristata*s are generally under a foot tall. Both have medium green, pointed, deeply ribbed leaves, both are self-supporting, and both stay brightly coloured until frost. They are suitable for a position just back of the border edge, although the brighter cultivars can be difficult to combine with other plants.

Start the shiny, round, black seeds six weeks early, lightly covered in a warm place indoors, where they should sprout in about a week and bloom some two months later. Set the plants into larger pots as they grow, because growth will be checked if they become pot-bound. Plant in the garden after the last frost. Alternatively, seeds can be sown outdoors around the last frost

date for flowers in midsummer. Thin dwarfs to 8 inches apart, larger plants to a foot. Celosia does best in fairly rich, moist soil in full sun or light shade. It also makes an excellent pot plant and an interesting cut flower surrounded by soothing 'Giant White Hyacinth' candytuft.

Because celosia has a high moisture content, it should be dried as quickly as possible in a warm place such as a spot over a hot-air vent or wood stove.

Celosia is a member of the amaranth family *Amaranthaceae*. Its genus name derives from the Greek *kelos* (burned), because of the flower colour. *Argentea*, the name of the tropical Asian species, refers to the silvery flowers of the wild species. *Plumosa* means feathered, *cristata* crested.

Globe Amaranth
(*Gomphrena globosa*)

It is said that the Greeks covered the body of Achilles with globe amaranth flowers to signify his immortality. Certainly, this colourful plant has a long history of use as an everlasting. It was called English clover in the 19th century, and it does indeed resemble clover, although the flower heads, half an inch across or a little wider, are much more durable. They are composed of tightly shingled bracts, soft and prickly to the touch. These little hedgehoglike globes make natural hiding places for tiny beetles and for the flowers – pale yellow miniature trumpets that shoot out between the papery layers. There is no scent – even if you prick your nose on the globe trying to find one. The flowers are traditionally purple, orange, pink and white, although lilacs and reds have been introduced. The orange-blooming types are leggier than the others. There are both standard (12 to 18 inches) and dwarf (6 inches) cultivars; the former are more versatile for arrangements because of their longer stems. Unlike many other everlastings, the globe amaranth is showy in the annual garden, where it contributes bright colour all season.

Like all the everlastings, globe amaranths are most easily started by sowing seeds directly in the garden, lightly covered, around the last frost date. The seeds sprout in 10 or 20 days. Thin to 6 inches apart. Alternatively, sow the flat, beige seeds indoors by pressing them into the surface of a moist growing medium six weeks before the last spring frost. Cover the pots with black plastic or cardboard – the seeds require darkness to germinate – and set the pots in a warm place, where the seeds will sprout in 10 to 20 days. After the last frost, set outdoors in well-drained soil in sun.

Let the side shoots and buds develop fully before you pick the entire

Although the upright, feathery forms of celosia are best known, the type called cockscomb, FACING PAGE, *is prized by some flower arrangers. The globe amaranth,* ABOVE, *is an everlasting that is as attractive in the garden as indoors. The domes of papery bracts, soft and prickly to the touch, dry fully outdoors, so the stems need only be picked while still fresh and bright for winter-long colour.*

157

plant for drying. Do not leave them in the garden too long, however, or the flower heads will begin to look shaggy as they slowly elongate and the lower bracts fall off. The stems are durable enough that globe amaranth can be dried upright in a basket or laid loosely in a box.

Globe amaranth is a member of the amaranth family *Amaranthaceae*, which grows in the Tropics worldwide. The genus name is the Latin term for a type of amaranth. *Globosa* means spherical, in reference to the shape of the flower heads.

Golden Ageratum
(*Lonas inodora, L. annua*)

Flattened clusters of golden, quarter-inch flowers, beautiful in the garden, in vases and in dried arrangements, identify a plant also known, confusingly, as African daisy – golden ageratum is a daisy but not African. On sturdy, light green stems, it produces foliage so lush and healthy that it looks like a crunchy salad green, the lower leaves deeply lobed and antler-shaped, the upper ones linear. The stems, which grow about a foot tall, branch from the base and turn purplish with age. The individual flowers are grouped in yarrowlike heads about 2 inches wide early in the season but diminish in width as the summer progresses.

Sow the parachutelike seeds directly in the garden in spring around the last frost date in well-drained, moderately fertile soil. Or start seeds eight weeks early in a cool place indoors, covering lightly. Seeds sprout in about a week. Set transplants outdoors 6 inches apart in sun. Golden ageratum is a good companion for anchusa, whose bright blue nicely complements the sunny yellow. Try a combination of primary colours – red celosia or salvia, blue heliotrope and yellow ageratum – in a large container.

The flowers in the clusters of golden ageratum mature simultaneously, which makes harvesting easy. Wait until all are fully open and golden, then pick the entire stem and hang to dry. If the flowers are picked before the seed ripens, they "will hold their brightness for years," as Thomas Fessenden wrote in 1843.

Golden ageratum is the only species in the genus *Lonas*, the origin of whose name is unknown. *Inodora* means without odour, *annua* annual. It is a Mediterranean member of the daisy family *Compositae*.

Immortelle
(*Xeranthemum annuum*)

"In order to have a few blue flowers to add to the winter collection," states a century-old garden book, "it will be necessary to grow the xeranthemum." In truth, salvia and statice also contribute good blue everlasting flowers, but the immortelle is the only member of the trio that is a daisy and thus a good basketmate for yellow strawflowers and pink rose everlasting. This erect annual, branching stiffly upward from the base to a height of about 2 feet, has solitary, papery flowers 1 or 2 inches wide in not only blue but also rose, cobalt-violet and white. The small, greyish leaves are only about 2 inches long with downy undersides. In the garden, immortelle looks attractive with baby's breath, cornflowers or golden ageratum.

Immortelle is best sown directly in the garden around the last frost date. Another sowing by mid-June produces a September harvest – immortelle is quite frost-hardy. Seeds sprout in 2 to 10 days. Thin to 6 inches apart. Immortelle will tolerate any soil, although it is most productive with some moisture.

The wiry stems and delicate roots mean that you must use pruning shears or sharp scissors to cut immortelle. Harvest the flowers at just the stage you want for dried arrangements, as they neither open nor close after picking. Tie them immediately in small bunches and set them upright in a container or hang them to dry, as the flowers will otherwise retain any shape into which they are pressed. They will turn brownish as they dry but will nevertheless remain attractive.

Immortelle is a southern and eastern European member of the daisy family *Compositae*. The genus name comes from the Greek *xeros* (dry) and *anthos* (flower).

Love-in-a-Mist
(*Nigella* spp)

Love-in-a-mist, like immortelle, is an old-fashioned favourite. This is one of the flowers grown by Catharine Parr Traill in her 19th-century backwoods Canadian garden, and in the same century, Gertrude Jekyll called it "a plant I hold in high admiration." An erect, branching, wiry-stemmed annual, love-in-a-mist is named for ruffs of filamentous bracts that surround the flower, giving rise to two other common names: love-in-a-puzzle and devil-in-the-bush. The threadlike foliage

inspired yet another common name, fennel flower. Solitary flowers at the stem ends resemble bachelor's buttons about 1½ inches wide.

Persian jewels (*N. damascena*) produces flowers in shades of pale to deep blue, rose, pink or white on 18-inch stems. When young, the flowers are white, but when mature, the pinks have a darker flush in the centre. This is the species to choose for fat, decorative seedpods – the plant's jewels. In the garden, it is attractive with grey foliage plants such as dusty miller.

N. hispanica, about 16 inches tall, has deep blue flowers an inch or two wide, with a clawlike pistil and dark red anthers. The five sepals have ribbed green veins on the undersides. This species differs from *N. damascena* in that it has coarser palmate leaves and inconspicuous seedpods.

N. sativa, about 8 inches tall, has fernlike, pale green leaves and half-inch pale blue flowers. The seeds are edible, hence the common names Roman coriander and black cumin.

Sow seeds directly in the garden in well-drained soil in sun, or sow eight weeks early, covering the small, black seeds lightly, three seeds per peat pellet or peat pot. Keep the pots in a warm place. Nigella quickly

Golden ageratum, FACING PAGE, *with its yarrowlike heads of blooms, is a traditional favourite and a self-sower that should be picked at its peak to hold the bright colour best. Love-in-a-mist has delightful flowers,* ABOVE, *but is better known for its decorative seedpods, which, if left unpicked, will sow a crop of flowers the next year.*

159

forms a long taproot, so it resents transplanting. Sprouting takes about two weeks. Thin to the strongest seedling per pot. The plant tends to sit unmoving until the weather warms and only then develops shoots and flowers.

Love-in-a-mist is good for fresh cutting and for dried arrangements – the flowers wilt as they dry, but they retain their blue colour. The best part of the plant for dried arrangements, however, is the decorative green-and-purple seedpod of *N. damascena*, which fades to a straw colour but still retains the purple marks. Pick this when stripes of burgundy appear between the lobes. If the pods are left too long on the stem, they will turn brown, dry out and split. Seeds from the pods can be used for flowers in the next year's garden.

Love-in-a-mist is a member of the buttercup family *Ranunculaceae*. The genus name is a diminutive form of the Latin *niger* (black), in reference to the colour of the seeds. *N. damascena* is a native of the Mediterranean area, hence "of Damascus." *Hispanica* suggests Spanish origins.

Pincushion Flower
(*Scabiosa* spp)

From seedling to flowering, the scabious plants are very attractive. The beautiful leaves are hairy, toothed and green with a soft yellowish tint. The flowers, described well by both common names, starflower and pincushion flower, consist of a cluster of tubular florets with tall, though inconspicuous, pale grey stamens that look much like pins sticking out of a pincushion. The overall shape of the flower is starlike, as are the seedpods of *Scabiosa stellata* 'Paper Moon,' the best type for drying. Its small, rather insignificant white flower clusters on 2-foot stems turn into quite spectacular seed heads the size of Ping-Pong balls. 'Paper Moon' mixes well with globe amaranth in a sunny corner of the garden.

Use scissors or clippers to cut starflowers, as the stems are wiry.

Pick the seed heads of 'Paper Moon' in late summer or early fall when they are still green and brown; later they will shatter too easily. Dry the seed heads by hanging them, setting them upright in jars or baskets or storing them loosely in boxes in a dry, well-ventilated place. Handle the seed heads gently, as they become quite fragile when dry.

Scabiosa atropurpurea, poetically called mourning bride or fading beauty, is not for drying but for cutting. The wiry stems are long, upright and purplish. The flowers, about 3 inches wide, are white, pink, red or violet on plants as tall as 3 feet and about 18 inches wide.

Sow the brown, shuttlecocklike seeds a quarter of an inch deep directly in the garden in spring, where they should sprout in a week or less. Thin to a foot apart. Or start the seeds indoors four weeks early in individual peat pots, keeping the pots warm and moist under plastic. This plant has a taproot and does not transplant easily. Grow starflowers in well-drained, moderately fertile soil in sun. They will tolerate dry spells.

The genus name of this European member of the teasel family *Dipsacaceae* comes from the disease scabies, which the rough leaves of certain species were once thought to cure. *Stellata* means starry.

Rose Everlasting
(*Helipterum* spp)

There are several species of helipterum that make excellent everlasting flowers. *H. roseum*, rose everlasting, or acroclinium, is the best known. It blooms in several shades but is most valued as a pink complement for the yellow or orange strawflower. This daisy, too, has papery bracts surrounding a centre of disc florets, which may be yellow, black or a combination of the two. When touched by the slightest moisture, the bracts close one by one over the disc and build a tight, impenetrable dome for pollen protection. The flowers also close in the evening and unfold with the morning sun. The grey-green leaves, pointed and grasslike, overlap one another and are closely packed in the

manner of spruce needles.

The outstanding feature of this everlasting is its strong and extremely supportive stems, a foot high or more, each bearing a solitary double flower about 2 inches across with a half-inch centre. Dried properly, the bright, papery flowers will not dangle and need no florist's tricks of wire or artificial stem. Cut the stems just before the flowers open, strip off the leaves, and hang them upside down in a dry, shady place. The heads will slowly unfold.

H. manglesii, Swan River everlasting, or rhodanthe, is something of a smaller version of acro-clinium and has similar flowers, again white or pink although more delicate in appearance and shading. They grow on shorter individual stems that make harvesting more difficult. Flowers, which have silvery grey calyxes, diminish in size throughout the season. They are among the best everlastings for holding their colour.

From a distance, Humboldt's sunray (*H. humboldtianum*) re-sembles yarrow, with bright yellow flowers and silvery, fragrant leaves on erect stems about 18 inches high. If you do not want to go through summer without a true yellow, grow this everlasting, whose intensely coloured sunrays can be sown throughout the annual garden. A close-up view reveals grasslike leaves and as many as 100 tiny, buttercup-shaped sunflowers packed together into a golden half-ball 2 or 3 inches wide. Flower heads diminish in size throughout the season.

Humboldt's sunray is a striking and supportive companion for more fragile annuals such as poppies and will hold its steadfast appearance in windy, exposed places. Humboldt's sunray looks best in full sun, where all the little cups will be fully open. They will close at night and when in contact with moisture. Pick Humboldt's sunray when all the flowers in the cluster are open, as, unlike other helipterums, it will not open further when dried.

Rose everlasting is the easiest member of the *Helipterum* genus to

The pincushion flower, named for its unusual globes of seeds, is combined in an arrangement, FACING PAGE, *with other decorative seedpods, including the horned ones of nigella, the flowerlike ones of bupleurum and a single sunflower head. Rose everlasting, here the cultivar 'Double White,'* ABOVE, *closes in the evening and unfolds with the morning sun. Cut stems just before the flowers open for the best everlastings.*

grow; it is both productive and resistant to transplant shock. It can be started indoors six weeks early in a warm place and set out 6 inches apart after frost. Germination takes 3 to 15 days, and flowering begins some 10 weeks later. The other helipterums are more vulnerable to transplant shock, so the safest method is to sow the fuzzy, yellowish white seeds directly in the garden, lightly covered, after frost danger. Choose any well-drained spot in full sun. Plant any of these flowers throughout the annual garden, interlacing them with corn poppies, Queen Anne's lace or bachelor's buttons — lively colours for an intense group effect. They may be attacked by aphids, which can be countered with a strong hose spray or insecticidal soap. The plants will tolerate windy places and can be used as windbreaks for lower plants.

Helipterum is a Western Australian member of the daisy family *Compositae*. It takes its name from the Greek *helios* (sun) and *pteron* (a wing) because of bristles on the seed. *Roseum* means rose-coloured. *Humboldtiana* honours the 19th-century German explorer and naturalist Alexander von Humboldt.

Statice
(*Limonium* spp)

Statice is one of the best of the everlastings. Its unusual tiers of brightly coloured, papery flowers dry to perfection on the peculiarly winged, tough stems and hold both colour and shape well indoors. Most seed houses sell hybrids and mixtures of the yellow-blooming Algerian native *L. bonduellii* as well as the white, rose, salmon, deep blue and purple Mediterranean native *L. sinuatum*. Both types yield ground-hugging rosettes of divided leaves that erupt into stiff flower stems about 2 feet tall. The plant branches into an intricate candelabrum of three-winged, toothed, cactuslike leaves and tightly packed flowers held upright on ascending platforms within dark green, tubular bracts. The ultramarine-blue cultivars are beautiful interplanted with red flax, especially if there is a cloud of baby's breath behind and a stretch of white alyssum in front — true red, white and blue.

Russian statice (*L. suworowii, Psylliostachys suworowii*), sometimes called pink pokers, is quite different, with slender, 10-to-18-inch vertical spikes of densely massed, reddish purple flowers. It blooms in about 12 weeks from seed and continues for only about four weeks, the spikes finally turning brown.

Sow statice directly outdoors in late spring, making successive sowings every month or so for continual blooms, or start the seeds eight weeks early indoors in a warm place. Covered lightly — the seeds need darkness to germinate — they will sprout in about a week. Prick them into individual pots when the second leaves have developed. Around the last frost date, plant in fertile, well-drained soil in full sun. We plant statice not more than 8 inches apart to obtain a dense effect of platforms on different levels, which are set off nicely by the rich green foliage. The plant does best during sunny, dry weather.

Pick both types of statice when about two-thirds of the flowers on the spike have opened. Flowers will open a little more as they dry, and they should not be left too long in the garden, as they will quickly pass their peak. To dry, hang the stems upside down in a cool, dark place.

Limonium is a member of the plumbago or leadwort family *Plumbaginaceae*. *L. suworowii*, from central Asia and Iran, honours Ivan Petrowitch Suworow, a medical inspector in Turkestan a century ago. The genus name comes from the Greek *leimon* (a meadow), alluding to the sea-marsh habitat of the plants.

Strawflower
(*Helichrysum* spp)

The strawflower is the best-known everlasting of all. Its happy little daisies, arrested forever in bud or midbloom, decorate all kinds of arrangements and wreaths, where

they serve as billboards for the entire group of lesser-known everlastings. In the garden, strawflowers seem relatively modest, with rigid, fat stems sometimes as tall as 4 feet that end in groups of two to four small stems, each bearing a single bud. The flowers bloom in succession and, if not picked, will open to about 2 inches wide, revealing a centre of yellow disc florets surrounded by yellow, bronze, reddish or orange bracts that are stiff and resemble petals — the same floral format as rose everlasting and winged everlasting. When misted, the flower closes tightly into a shingled globe. The lance-shaped leaves are dark green and rough to the touch. If the flowers are not cut, the plants are quite beautiful in groups with black-eyed Susans. Strawflower will survive the first light frosts.

H. bracteatum is the best-known species, but there are as many as 500 species native to Asia, Australia and South Africa. Several are offered by large seed houses and are worth growing for drying.

Strawflowers grow easily from a direct sowing in a sunny garden spot around the last frost date. Sprinkle the small, light brown, cigar-shaped seeds onto the soil surface, gently pressing them in — they need light. They should sprout in about 10 days. Strawflowers can endure heat and drought, and they produce the most blooms if given a feed of fish fertilizer or manure tea once a month.

For harvesting, strawflowers are most attractive while the bracts still form a cone in the flower centre that entirely covers the bright yellow disc. The flowers open somewhat after they are cut, so they should be picked when the outer layer of bracts is just beginning to open. Cut entire stems on a warm, sunny day. There will be a central flower and smaller buds underneath. Strawflower stems are hygroscopic, so even after drying, they will absorb moisture from the air, causing the flowers to droop on damp days. For that reason, many gardeners wire the flowers before drying by inserting a slim wire through the centre from below. Press

Although the best types of statice for drying are the yellow-blooming Limonium bonduellii *and the white-through-pink-to-blue* L. sinuatum, *Russian statice,* FACING PAGE, TOP, *is an unusual pink species. Before they are displayed,* FACING PAGE, BOTTOM, *everlastings should be dried in a dark, dry room. The best-known everlasting is the strawflower,* ABOVE, *which will open out flat if left past the prime time to pick for drying.*

163

the top of the wire into a tiny fish-hook before inserting it, and pull it back down inside the flower. On the other hand, picking entire stems and immediately hanging them upside down in loose bunches will produce upright flowers without wiring.

Strawflower is a tender perennial Australian member of the daisy family *Compositae*. Its genus name comes from the Greek words *helios* (sun) and *chrysos* (golden), a description of the flowers.

Unicorn Plant
(*Proboscidea louisiana, P. jussieni, Martynia proboscidea*)

The unicorn plant lets itself be known in the garden. Given hot weather, it sprawls lazily, its re-clining stems spreading about 6 feet wide and 3 feet high, and like some-one sleeping it off after a night of merrymaking, it smells unpleasant, like old wine. The odour, especially noticeable when the plant is rubbed, comes from fine hairs on the stems and the big, roundly triangular leaves

as wide as 8 inches. Each hair holds a gluey drop that traps small insect pests such as aphids (a phenomenon also seen in the catchflies and *Nicotiana sylvestris*). The flowers, ar-ranged in loose racemes that over-look the leaf platforms, are like pale, 1½-inch-wide mimulus or gloxinia, yellow-streaked and purple-spotted within. They emerge from a cup of fused sepals and are visited by bumblebees. Set unicorn plants next to ornamental grasses, or let them have a spot on their own, trailing out over the lawn or patio. The first frost will kill them.

By mid-August, the seedpods that give the plant its common names, devil's claw and unicorn plant, appear. Pick branches of mature pods while they are green, and hang them indoors to dry and open. At first, each looks like a cucumber with a claw, but as it dries, it breaks open, shedding its skin to become an ornate black capsule treasured for dried arrangements. It is also a source of fibres used in basket making by indigenous people of the

southwestern United States.

To sow, peel the big seeds, which are like quarter-inch chunks of charcoal, by piercing the outer coating with a sharp knife and pulling it off, revealing a beige seed that looks like a small pine nut. Cover the seeds to their depth eight weeks before the last spring frost. They should sprout in a week when the weather is warm. Transplant into individual containers three weeks later, and plant outdoors, 18 inches apart, after the last spring frost. The plants grow very slowly in spring and early summer, but they will quickly make up for any tardiness in the hot weather of midsummer.

The unicorn plant is a member of the martynia family *Martyniaceae*, which includes five sticky-haired genera that are all native to the western hemisphere. The genus name *Proboscidea* derives from the Greek word for an elephant's trunk, in reference to the long, curved beak of the fruit. The species name suggests the plant's origin in the state of Louisiana, although its range actually covers much of the southern United States.

Seedpods

The unicorn plant is not the only ornamental annual with beautiful seedpods valued for dried flower arrangements. In an arrangement, seedpods alone can be as attractive as any of the flowers. Watch for them in late summer and fall, and bring them indoors before they begin to lose their colour and disintegrate. Leave the stems long. These seedpods can be used in bouquets with other everlastings, added to fresh flower designs, tied into wreaths or grouped in baskets, jars or vases on their own.

Since many pods hold their seeds well, the gardener who saves the pods also has a supply of seeds for the next year. Plants with attractive pods or seed heads include all of the ornamental grasses, as well as:
• poppy, with half-to-one-inch grey-blue vases borne singly on stiff stems
• starflower, with inch-wide, beige balls made up of cup-shaped calyxes holding dark brown seeds
• love-in-a-mist, with 1-inch or larger oval, pink-striped shakers borne singly on stiff stems
• bupleurum, with umbels, up to 1½ inches wide, of star-shaped flowers holding dark clusters of seeds
• flowering flax, with many quarter-inch, tightly closed, straw-coloured

pods on each breezy branch
• coneflower, with dark brown domes
• sunflower – the smaller types are best in arrangements – with intricately spiral-patterned seed heads, grey to black
• clarkia, with half-inch, reddish, tulip-shaped pods arranged in a ladderlike fashion up the stems
• coreopsis, with half-inch, cup-shaped crowns, reddish brown inside and lighter brown outside, each on its own short stem on the main branch
• bishop's flower and dill, with pale brown umbels of varying widths holding carawaylike seeds
• jewels of Opar, with the loftiest and smallest seedpods (tiny, red-brown pebbles) in a branching arrangement
• apple of Peru, with large, papery, lanternlike seedpods
• bells of Ireland, with pale green to beige whorls of trumpets cradling small seeds
• corn cockle, with one three-quarter-inch, slate-grey vase on the tip of each branchlet
• *Nicotiana sylvestris*, with a dense cluster of half-inch, parchment-coloured containers, each holding a cloud of dustlike seeds
• balloon vine, with three-sided beige balloons of varying sizes.

A fragile seedpod collection should be displayed in a quiet, sheltered indoor location out of the sun. Such a bouquet is a beautiful way to carry last year's garden into the winter.

After its pale mimuluslike flowers bloom, FACING PAGE, *the unicorn plant produces big, curved seedpods that dry to the unusual shape that suggests the plant's common name. Bupleurum,* LEFT, *has a more open seed arrangement. Its star-shaped green bracts hold tiny yellow flowers that dry to beige nests displaying black seeds. These not only are decorative but also preserve a supply of seeds that can be used in next year's garden.*

Sources

W. Atlee Burpee & Co.
300 Park Avenue
Warminster, Pennsylvania 18974
(215) 674-4900
A good selection of common flowers, including some exclusives. Catalogue free. To U.S. addresses only.

The Butchart Gardens Ltd.
Box 4010, Station A
Victoria, British Columbia V8X 3X4
(250) 652-4422
Old-fashioned flowers, including some mixtures. Catalogue $1, refundable. To the United States, $1 (U.S.).

Chiltern Seeds
Bortree Stile
Ulverston, Cumbria LA12 7PB
England
1-022-958-1137
An excellent source of both common and unusual flowers. Catalogue $2 air mail.

Dominion Seed House
Box 2500
Georgetown, Ontario L7G 5L6
(905) 873-3037
A good selection of common flowers. Catalogue free. To Canadian addresses only.

Gardenimport Inc.
Box 760
Thornhill, Ontario L3T 4A5
(905) 731-1950
Flowers from Suttons Seeds Ltd. of England. Catalogue $5, refundable.

Harris Seeds
60 Saginaw Drive
Rochester, New York 14623
(716) 442-0410
A good selection of common flowers, including some exclusives. Catalogue free. To U.S. addresses only.

J.L. Hudson, Seedsman
Box 1058
Redwood City, California 94064
Seeds from around the world.
Catalogue $1 (U.S.).

Park Seed Co., Inc.
Cokesbury Road
Greenwood, South Carolina 29647-0001
(864) 223-7333
A good selection of flowers, including many that are hard to find. Catalogue free.

W.H. Perron
2914 boulevard Labelle
Ville de Laval, Québec H7P 5R9
(514) 682-9071
French- and English-language listings, including common flowers. Catalogue free. To Canadian addresses only.

Redwood City Seed Company
Box 361
Redwood City, California 94064
(415) 325-SEED
Seeds from around the world.
Catalogue $2.

Select Seeds
180 Stickney Road
Union, Connecticut 06076-4617
(860) 684-9310
Antique flowers. Catalogue $2 (U.S.).

Stokes Seeds Ltd.
39 James Street, Box 10
St. Catharines, Ontario L2R 6R6
(905) 688-4300
or
Box 548
Buffalo, New York 14240-0548
A good list of common flowers.
Catalogue free.

Thompson & Morgan Inc.
Box 1308
Jackson, New Jersey 08527-0308
(908) 363-2225
An excellent flower selection from Britain. Catalogue free.

Glossary

AAS – All-America Selections, a seed-industry-financed organization based in Illinois that organizes annual trials of new flowers and vegetables in designated gardens throughout Canada and the United States and promotes the award-winning species. Plants judged superior to their competitors are designated AAS winners. The European equivalent is Fleuroselect.

Alternate – In botany, a foliage arrangement in which the leaves are not in pairs or whorls but are placed singly at different heights on the stem.

Annual – A plant whose life span, from seed to flowering to seed production, is accomplished in a single growing season.

Anther – The tip of a **stamen**, the male part of a flower, that produces **pollen**. Anthers usually appear as knobs or dots at the end of threadlike **filaments** in the flower centre.

Axil – The place where the leaf or **petiole** (leafstalk) joins the stem.

Biennial – A plant that produces foliage during the first growing season, flowers and seeds the second growing season, then dies.

Bract – A modified leaf that often resembles a stiff, brightly coloured **petal**.

Calyx – The cluster or circle of **sepals** of a flower, which grow outside the **petals**.

Composite – A member of the daisy family *Compositae*, which is the largest family of flowering plants. Composite flower heads are actually composed of a (usually) central **disc** made up of a cluster of tubular florets, or disc flowers, surrounded by **ray** flowers, often called **petals**.

Compost – A soil conditioner and fertilizer made up of partially decomposed plant material, vegetable scraps and other organic material that are moistened and allowed to heat and break down until the mixture resembles soil.

Conditioning – The treatment of cut flowers so that they will last well. For most flowers, conditioning involves plunging the freshly picked flowers up to their necks in hot or very warm water, then placing the container of flowers and water in a cool place overnight. The next day, the flowers may be arranged in vases of cool water.

Corolla – All of the **petals** of a flower.

Cotyledon – The cotyledons are the first leaves that appear after a seed germinates. Sometimes called seedling leaves, they do not usually resemble the later true leaves.

Cultivar – A *culti*vated plant *vari*ety, as opposed to one that appeared naturally (and which is simply called a **variety**). Cultivar names are generally capitalized and enclosed within single quotation marks; for example, *Polygonum capitatum* 'Magic Carpet.'

Cutting – A piece of a stem, leaf or root that is coaxed to root in water or soil and eventually forms a new plant.

Dead-Heading – The removal of faded flowers to enhance attractiveness and arrest seed production, thereby encouraging further flowering.

Disc – The centre of a **composite** flower, made up of tubular florets. The "eye" of a black-eyed Susan is a disc.

Dormancy – Literally, sleep. In botany, it is a period of inactivity when seeds, buds, **rhizomes** and other plant organs are still alive but require more time or a change in exterior conditions in order to grow.

Double – A flower with more petals than usual. A true double entirely covers the flower centre, and the flower may be sterile, while a semidouble has more than the usual number of petals but still allows the centre to be seen. In **composites**, doubling is caused by replacement of the **disc** florets with **ray** florets.

Everlasting – A flower that after air-drying and without pressing retains its shape and often its colour for use in arrangements without water.

Family – Botanically, a group of similar plants. Family names are generally capitalized, italicized and end in the suffix *-aceae*. Families are divided into genera (the plural of **genus**).

Filament – The threadlike stem of a **stamen**, which supports the **anther**.

Flat – In gardening, a large, low-sided container of soil used for starting seeds. Flats are commonly made of wood or plastic.

Floret – A single small flower that is one of a group in a situation such as the **disc** or rays of a **composite** flower or the flower head of a blade of grass.

Genus – Botanically, a relatively small group of similar plants. Genus names are capitalized and italicized and usually end in the suffix *-a*, *-um* or *-us*; for example, *Gerbera, Delphinium, Dianthus*. Genera (the plural of **genus**) are divided into **species**.

Ground Cover – Any plant, whether or not it actually blankets the ground, that forms thick enough lateral growth to deter most weeds.

Habitat – The environment in which a plant is usually found in nature.

Half-Hardy – An annual that will not survive frost and so is usually started indoors and **transplanted** outdoors after frost or sown directly outdoors when the weather has settled.

Hardening Off – The process of acclimatizing plants, usually seedlings, to their outdoor situation after being started indoors. Hardening off consists of leaving the plants outdoors for gradually longer periods on successive days until they can be left out around the clock. Letting the soil dry somewhat also helps harden plants off. The process is reversed when plants are brought indoors in fall.

Hardy – A plant that tolerates light frost. Hardy annuals can be sown in the garden as soon as the soil can be worked. Some can be sown the previous fall or winter and may survive until the ground freezes in fall.

Humus – Organic matter in the soil, often **compost** or another decomposed substance. Humus will make any soil better for gardening.

Hybrid – A plant resulting from a cross between two plants belonging to different **species**, **varieties** or genera. Hybrids may exhibit qualities superior to either of their parents. The seeds collected from hybrids seldom produce plants like their parents and may even be sterile.

Inflorescence – The entire flowering part of a plant, which may consist of one or more individual flowers.

Manure – One of the best soil amendments, as it provides soil nutrients as well as **humus**. Livestock manures should, however, be well aged or composted before they are added to the soil.

Mulch – A soil covering that may be organic, like grass clippings or bark chips, or inorganic, like plastic. Mulches can slow weed growth and retain soil moisture, although plastic mulch will also prevent rain from penetrating the soil.

Nectar Guide – In a flower, patterns, blotches or lines of a contrasting colour that lead pollinators to the flower centre.

Ovary – The "female" plant part in the flower centre at the base of the **style**. The ovary contains immature seeds, or ovules. When the seeds are fertilized, the ovary will swell and then dry, becoming a seedpod.

Perennial – A plant that survives more than two growing seasons. Some **tender** perennials that flower the first year from seed are grown as **annuals**.

Petal – A flower part, often brightly coloured. Petals make up the **corolla**, which encloses the **sta-mens** and **pistils** and which in turn is enclosed by the **sepals**.

Petiole – A leafstalk. In some climbing plants such as nasturtiums, the petioles will loop around vertical supports.

pH – Soil acidity and alkalinity are measured by the logarithmic pH scale, wherein the number 7 represents neutral. Increasingly acidic soil is designated by lower numbers, while increasingly alkaline soil receives higher numbers. Most soil falls in the range between pH 5 and 8, and most plants do best at about 6.5. A soil test, conducted by a provincial department of agriculture or state extension service (which you can contact through the county extension office), can tell you your soil's pH and how to alter it.

Photosynthesis – The biochemical process by which green plants convert carbon dioxide and water into carbohydrates and oxygen using sunlight as their energy source.

Picotee – A flower with a rim of contrasting colour at the outer edge of the **petals**.

Pistil – The "female" reproductive plant part at the centre of the flower, comprising an **ovary**, a **style** and a **stigma**.

Pollen – Minute, often brightly coloured grains that carry the male cells from the **anthers** to the **stigma** via the process of pollination, often performed by insects.

Pricking Out – The careful removal of seedlings from a tray or container of several seedlings into a container where they can be given more space. This is often done with the point of a knife or some other slender tool that will take as much soil as possible around the roots. In pricking out, hold the seedling by the **cotyledon**, not the stem.

Raceme – A long flower cluster with a central stalk from which individual flowers bloom on their own small stalks. The youngest flowers are at the tip.

Ray – The outermost "petal" of a composite flower, or daisy, which is actually an individual floret. Not all composites have ray flowers. Cornflowers, for instance, have only **discs**.

Rhizome – A horizontal underground stem, often fleshy, that produces nodes from which plant shoots grow. Rhizomes can be used to propagate plants. If the plants are **tender**, the rhizomes are planted in spring and dug up and brought indoors in fall.

Scarify – To scrape a hard-coated seed, such as that of a sweet pea or morning glory, to encourage germination.

Seedling – The name for a young plant until it has grown its second or third set of true leaves.

Sepal – A plant part, usually green and leaflike, that grows outside the petals. Several sepals together form a ring called the **calyx**.

Single – A flower with the number of petals found on the wild plant, as opposed to **double** or semidouble flowers.

Species – Botanically, a group of plants that consistently breed true. There may be one or more species in a **genus**, the next largest plant group. The species name is written in lowercase italics following the genus name; in *Monarda citriodora*, for example, the species is *citriodora* and the genus is *Monarda*.

Stamen – The male reproductive organ of a flower, consisting of a **filament** tipped by a pollen-covered **anther**.

Stigma – The enlarged tip of the **pistil**, the female part of the flower, on which **pollen** grains are deposited for fertilization.

Stratify – To encourage a seed to germinate by exposing it to a period of dampness and cold.

Style – The slender stem of the female part of the flower which connects the **ovary** below to the **stigma** above.

Tender – Botanically, a plant which can be damaged or killed by light frost or even prolonged cold. In describing annuals, the word often refers only to tropical plants, which must be raised at relatively high temperatures, while **half-hardy** annuals can tolerate cooler conditions.

Transplant – As a verb, describes the process of moving plants from pot to pot, from pot to garden or from one place in the garden to another. As a noun, it refers to the plant being moved.

Umbel – A member of the carrot family *Umbelliferae*, including such plants as bishop's flower and parsley. Also the umbrellalike flower head of an umbel or a similar plant.

Variegation – The spotting, striping, blotching or speckling that occurs on some plant foliage, such as coleus and polka-dot plant.

Variety – A naturally occurring, slightly different plant from the **species**. The variety name is written in lowercase italics. For instance, in *Gypsophila elegans rosea*, the variety is *rosea*. The term is also used in a general way to mean any particular type of plant.

Whorl – A circle of leaves or flowers arranged around the stem at the same level.

Zone – A geographical region defined by climate. Both the Canadian and U.S. governments have their own systems of numbering climatic zones; progressively lower numbers describe areas with colder winters.

Index

Photo Credits

p.4 Turid Forsyth
p.6 Thomas E. Eltzroth
p.8 Jerry Pavia
p.10-11 Adrian Forsyth
p.12 Turid Forsyth
p.14 Turid Forsyth
p.15 Walter Chandoha
p.16 Jerry Pavia
p.17 Turid Forsyth
p.18 Turid Forsyth
p.24 Walter Chandoha
p.26 Jennifer Bennett
p.27 Turid Forsyth
p.28 Jennifer Bennett
p.29 Walter Chandoha
p.30 Turid Forsyth
p.31 Turid Forsyth
p.32 Turid Forsyth
p.33 Turid Forsyth
p.34 Turid Forsyth
p.35 Jennifer Bennett
p.36 Joanne Pavia
p.38 Robert E. Lyons, Photo/Nats
p.39 Turid Forsyth
p.40 Turid Forsyth
p.41 (top) Turid Forsyth;
    (bottom) Turid Forsyth
p.42 (top) Turid Forsyth;
    (bottom) Turid Forsyth
p.43 Paul Fletcher, Focus Stock
    Photo Inc.
p.44 Turid Forsyth
p.45 Irwin Barrett, Valan Photos
p.46 Turid Forsyth
p.47 Turid Forsyth
p.48 Turid Forsyth
p.49 Debbi Adams
p.50 Walter Chandoha
p.52 Turid Forsyth
p.53 Turid Forsyth
p.54 (top) Turid Forsyth;
    (bottom) Turid Forsyth
p.55 Turid Forsyth
p.56 Saxon Holt
p.57 Turid Forsyth
p.58 Turid Forsyth
p.59 (top) Turid Forsyth;
    (bottom) Charles Marden Fitch
p.60 Turid Forsyth
p.61 Turid Forsyth
p.62 (top) Turid Forsyth;
    (bottom) Turid Forsyth
p.63 Turid Forsyth
p.64 Heiko Fenzl
p.65 Turid Forsyth
p.66 Turid Forsyth
p.68 Gera Dillon
p.69 (top) Turid Forsyth;
    (bottom) Derek Fell
p.70 Turid Forsyth
p.71 Turid Forsyth
p.72 Thomas E. Eltzroth
p.73 Turid Forsyth
p.74 Turid Forsyth
p.75 Derek Fell
p.76 Ivan Massar, Photo/Nats
p.77 (top) Thomas E. Eltzroth;

(bottom) Turid Forsyth
p.78 (top) Jennifer Bennett;
    (bottom) Turid Forsyth
p.79 Turid Forsyth
p.80 Turid Forsyth
p.82 Adrian Forsyth
p.83 Turid Forsyth
p.84 (top) Jennifer Bennett; (bottom)
    Robert E. Lyons, Photo/Nats
p.85 Jennifer Bennett
p.86 (top) Jerry Pavia; (bottom)
    Jennifer Bennett
p.87 Tom W. Parkin, Valan Photos
p.88 Turid Forsyth
p.89 Turid Forsyth
p.90 (top) Turid Forsyth;
    (bottom) Turid Forsyth
p.91 Jennifer Bennett
p.92 Turid Forsyth
p.93 Turid Forsyth
p.94 Pamela Harper
p.96 Turid Forsyth
p.97 (top) Turid Forsyth; (bottom)
    David M. Stone, Photo/Nats
p.98 Turid Forsyth
p.99 Jennifer Bennett
p.100 (top) Turid Forsyth;
    (bottom) Turid Forsyth
p.101 Turid Forsyth
p.102 Turid Forsyth
p.103 Charles Marden Fitch
p.104 Jennifer Bennett
p.105 Jennifer Bennett
p.106 Turid Forsyth
p.107 Turid Forsyth
p.108 Jennifer Bennett
p.109 Turid Forsyth
p.110 Turid Forsyth
p.111 Turid Forsyth
p.112 Jerry Pavia
p.114 William D. Adams
p.115 Connie Toops
p.116 (top) Jeff Foott, Valan Photos;
    (bottom) Wouterloot-Gregoire,
    Valan Photos
p.117 Jennifer Bennett
p.118 Joanne Pavia
p.119 Pamela Harper
p.120 Turid Forsyth
p.121 Jennifer Bennett
p.122 Jerry Pavia
p.123 Turid Forsyth
p.124 Turid Forsyth
p.126 (top) Turid Forsyth;
    (bottom) Turid Forsyth
p.127 Turid Forsyth
p.128 Turid Forsyth
p.129 Turid Forsyth
p.130 (top) Turid Forsyth;
    (bottom) Jennifer Bennett
p.131 Turid Forsyth
p.132 William H. Allen Jr.
p.133 Joanne Pavia
p.134 David Cavagnaro
p.135 Turid Forsyth
p.136 Turid Forsyth
p.138 Turid Forsyth